CHILDREN IN "THE NURSERY SCHOOL"

The range in age is from fourteen months to three years.

By the same author

SCHOOL BEGINS AT TWO
Edited by Barbara Biber

Children in
"The Nursery School"

By

HARRIET M. JOHNSON

Introductory Essay by
BARBARA BIBER
Distinguished Research Scholar
Bank Street College of Education

AGATHON PRESS, INC., New York

Distributed by
SCHOCKEN BOOKS, New York

742449

First published, 1928
This edition © 1972 by
Agathon Press, Inc.
150 Fifth Avenue
New York, N. Y. 10011
Distributed by
Schocken Books Inc.
200 Madison Avenue
New York, N. Y. 10016

Library of Congress Catalog Card Number: 79-166548
ISBN 0-87586-025-7

Printed in the United States

CONTENTS

LIST OF ILLUSTRATIONS

INTRODUCTORY ESSAY

by Barbara Biber

A preface to a book published in 1928 to be reprinted some 45 years later poses a challenge—perhaps, more accurately, a defense. What can we learn from it in these fast-changing times? What does it mean that certain basic concepts of how children develop and convictions about how they can best be educated seem to have had as viable an existence half a century ago as they have today? Does their survival value give them added validity? Which of these concepts seem to have been activated in response to the immediacies of the social-cultural environment of the twenties and are no longer relevant, and which have been deepened and gained added status by accumulated experience and advancing theory in the intervening years? Moving closer to the role of the teacher, can the specifics of things, techniques, teacher role and relationships, and social mores that were established as an experiment for the education of children between 18 months and three years of age in the period before the Great Depression and the Second World War be useful to us now at a time when we are moving rapidly into programs of group care for children younger than usual school and preschool ages?

It is because I am convinced of the uniquely valuable contribution of Harriet Johnson's pioneering work to programs that are now being initiated on a wide scale, under public funding and auspices, that I welcome the re-issuing of her book and undertake to place her contribution in the context of our contemporary thinking. I must add, also, my pleasure that readers are being given the opportunity to read a beautifully documented account of an educational philosophy in practice that was built on humanist values as goals for education at all levels and is congruent with—actually, was often the precursor of—the tenets of modern developmental psychology. Her contribution comes into focus as we consider first, the goals and components of the learning environment she created for children under three; second, the principles and methods of teaching that she considered optimal for this stage of development; and finally, the contribution that the style and volume of her records have made to the discipline of child psychology.

Two points are made by Mr. Ellis in introducing the book when published originally. This is a naturalist's account, he pointed out, a solid body of facts on which to build theory, observe action and reaction, and revise theory accordingly. Equally important, however, was the recognition that what the children were given to react to was a selected environment, constructed on a body of prior convictions not only about children and learning but about the quality of human experience, generally. Values were explicitly stated, in contrast to so much of the succeeding literature in which interest in technology became paramount and underlying values were minimized, either not considered or at most implied. In the last few years—no more than a decade—the importance of clearly stated values has been raised once more as an issue in educational philosophy and research. Miss Johnson made clear that what she wanted to stimulate in the children were qualities and response patterns that she considered optimal in human functioning—the capacity to affect one's environment as well as adapt to it, to sustain spontaneous, expressive modes of responding to experience, to build up readiness to attack new situations and take independent action when confronted with the unfamiliar, to be people with varied integrated powers—physical-motor as well as verbal-social—in the early years especially, to attain a satisfactory balance between impulse and control.

Spontaneity and creativity were treasured as qualities of experience; at the same time, the value of work leading to productivity was a central component of the ethical system. Even for the youngest children, there was the goal to build up distinct patterns of response to specific situations: readiness to get to work on material at hand, persistence of interest and tendency to investigate and experiment in constructive ways and to sustain this attitude. This "work" orientation has recently been considerably battered by certain segments of the youth generation. Maybe when the tendency to dichotomize work and pleasure has been moderated, when the "work" orientation is no longer identified with *all* the tenets of the Protestant Ethic and with contributing to the power of an oppressing social structure, it will be possible to reinstate a concept of work and a kind of relation to work that is deeply gratifying and fulfilling to the individual. This was part of the vision that underlay the philosophy of the early progressive educators— among them, Harriet Johnson.

The goal, in the large, was to create a learning environment that provided opportunities for the full use of the powers of the individual and took responsibility also for helping the individual adapt to the environment—what we would call a planned environment and she called an "intentional, consistent" policy—continuously aware of what it wished to foster. The physical care of the children—their health needs, their feeding, dressing and resting—were conscientiously and thoughtfully provided for, but these were only the minimal essentials in her view. The heart of the matter—the ground she tried to break—was the educator's responsibility for the growth potentials to be fulfilled in setting up group care for young children. This is a task still to be accomplished. Even now we find that we need to make extraordinary efforts on the national scene to assure that expanding day care facilities shall be of high quality, shall be designed and supported as "educational, not custodial care." This book, well-studied, can be a partial guarantee against the possibility that that widely used phrase shall not become a relatively meaningless slogan.

Goals don't make an environment. With a degree of conscientiousness that we seldom encounter in educational treatises Miss Johnson not only described in detail the equipment, activities, schedule, style of interaction and mechanisms of control, but she also explained the choices that were made in terms of the developmental principles she considered optimal for healthy growth. She was determined to honor and provide for the basic impulse to be active, not only to respond to stimulation but to search out experience; she aimed for full realization of capacities at each stage and decried pressures for acceleration; she put trust in the power of self-initiated, satisfying activity to generate the motivation to attack new situations; she wished to relegate formation of habits to aspects of life that can safely become automatized and, instead, favored flexible patterning of responses, allowing for elements of reaction to be combined and re-combined in new patterns.

She was convinced that learning was soundest when

the environment encouraged the child in his impulse
to "experiment" with the exercise of his growing powers
in the widening world of experience. What she called
"experiment" has come to be signified as the exploratory
stage in learning. In both terminologies the activities
through which the exploratory approach is enac-
ted—whether the content is word usage, space delinea-
tion, feats of physical coordination, or representation
of reality experience in fantasy form—are recognizable
as play in early childhood. For this early stage of development, Miss Johnson regarded self-initiated, experimental play use of materials as a prime medium for learning.
It is taking many years to undo the perception of profes-
sional educators and scholars, as well as of laymen, that
the play of children is an indulgence to be granted but
always to be distinguished from the serious business of
learning. Happily, in recent years, play has increasingly
claimed the attention of other disciplines—clinicians and
cognitive psychologists, for example, and is likely in the
future, hopefully, to occupy a more recognized and better understood place in educational planning.

It seems obvious that what she wanted and prized
in children and in people could easily be paraphrased
as the components of positive mental health as these
have been formulated in the many succeeding efforts
to create a working allegiance between education and
mental health: spontaneity, autonomy, involvement.
Society was not waiting open-armed to embrace either
these values as a framework for educational goals or
the developmental principles presumed to be their cata-
lysts. She was working and writing in a period when
rebellion against the stultifying effects of middle-class
convention was just in its youth; more particularly, when
education was conceived as training, the earlier accom-

the better. She considered her school as part of a larger social struggle against the pressures from adults, parents among them, to "train" the child to conforming ways as soon after the first months of babyhood as possible, to have the early years prepare him for the later years —particularly to foster the adjustments that "school" proper would require, placing greatest value on a rapid rate of achievement of skills; all in all, inevitably, to have little concern for the values of creativity and autonomy.

In the intervening years powerful social forces have arisen that complicate these issues and keep them at the center of educational controversy. Our society is still divided on the issue of what basic purposes early education should serve, especially on how the particular problems of the disadvantaged group in our society and their wishes for their children shall be taken into account. Some of the difficulties come from opposing theoretical formulations, some from basically differing value priorities. Some problems arise, however, just from lack of information and misperception about the nature of a learning environment that is designed to protect the growth potential of this particular stage of development for the sake of its own yield rather than its preparatory efficiency. This book provides the images, the feeling tone and the reasoning behind it all and, insomuch, should serve important clarifying function.

The word "intentional" was not used casually by Harriet Johnson. She was as clear about what she did not want this learning environment to be as she was about the ideal image she was working toward, emphasizing repeatedly that in this book she was describing work in progress, an in-gathering of data and thinking in search of more refined and differentiated principles. It was easy for her to reject the kind of program that would dictate, or pre-structure, the children's responses: it would fail to foster spontaneity and interest or readiness to initiate and experiment. At the other extreme, a literally "free" environment or, more realistically, a laissez-faire climate headed by a passive teacher was equally unacceptable. Instead her "intentional" environment was built on principles that had already been evolved from her experience as an observer and a teacher and her book is encyclopedic in the wealth of concrete material on the kind of teaching and learning that follows from their observance.

She constructed a curriculum of self-initiated activities, not pre-patterned by adults, in which play was regarded as experimentation and in which the child's experience, not the final product, was of primary importance. About the children's spontaneous musical chanting, for example, she said: ". . . In this process we believe that the children's phrases represent in terms of enjoyment what any method of expression does to the artist . . . it is not the form that gives pleasure, but the process. We have suggested that their early play with language and their early decorative and balanced constructions are what may later be called literature and design." Similarly, in their experience with color it was not the naming of colors that had primary attention; it was rather the sensory experiences, the emerging differentiation of color and shade without naming which was expressed often in the way the children made choices and created balanced color patterns in their constructions. In the use of crayons, the motor experience, the rhythmic action, the patterning of color on the paper were important. Realistic visual representation was primitive, if present, at all. The child who, after making and naming a "drawing which remotely suggested . . . an automobile

... took another sheet and made a vigorous circular scrawl all over it and said, 'This is what I do to make my automobile go' " was using motor activity as an added form of representation.

The description of the children's use of blocks, made unusually understandable through the detail of the illustrations, bears much of the weight of her curriculum thinking. This, in her opinion, was the material richest in possibilities for offering opportunity for manipulative sensory experience, for rhythmic, patterned and designed invention, and finally, for reviewing, rehearsing and playing out past experiences as the manipulative action patterns evolved into forms that suggested representative meanings. At 35 months one boy's boat had a "moke tack up on top"; at 38 months one girl brought an adult to see her "house" and when asked who was going to live in it, answered, "Nobody's not going to live in it." In sum, the primary principle was to build curriculum around full use of constructive, adaptable materials such as blocks, crayons, music and child-initiated dramatic play, a principle that has come to have fairly wide acceptance in education for the preschool child. Too often, unfortunately, the subtle techniques that are needed if these materials are to fulfill their purposes have not been mastered. The detail of what the children do and how the teacher stimulates and responds to their actions makes this book a rare combination of "how-to" and "why." Particularly useful at the present time is this full practical exposition of a curriculum, a program of activities, for the younger-than-three year olds and the partial guarantee it offers against the tendency to transpose too literally for the youngest children what early educators have developed as appropriate for the next stage in development—the preschool child, four and five years of age.

A second major principle (still so much alive in our thinking today), namely, that learning should be made relevant to the child, appears throughout the book but is most highlighted in the discussion of language. Opportunities for the development of language were planned according to what had been learned from assiduous observations of the children's spontaneous use of language. Taking the cue from the children's language, the adults used "rhythmic phrases or words—chanted, or spoken or sung" to accompany the children's activities, accented their experiences with reiterative, enumerative verbal forms, used the actual sounds of experience whenever possible instead of the conventional verbal forms, used gesture and facial expression as well as words in communicating, minimized confusion by being brief and avoiding elaborate verbal explanations, bringing the children's own experiences into the primitive story forms that were created for them. Here, as in the other program activities, language was not "taught"; instead, its usage was stimulated by being activated as an integral part of the other activities of the children; its creative expressive quality was protected by not flooding the child's early experimental approach to language with adult forms.

These were ways Miss Johnson sought to counteract what she felt was detrimental to the children's development—excessive verbal stimulation by adults in which the child could not grasp meaning and tended consequently to use language without reference to meaning, in contrast to the integrative processes involved when awareness of meaning made it possible to use language to serve and embellish play activities. In addition, over-involvement in adult-stimulated verbalization even when the child was in control of meaning went hand-in-hand, according to her observation, with minimal use of the constructive materials for play purposes and less progress toward physical-motor competence, thus constituting a serious loss in the most important developmental possibilities for this period of growth.

On this point, it is important to take into account that Miss Johnson's children came in the main from a particular segment of middle-class society—the artist-writer-intellectuals of the period—and lived at home in atmospheres of highly developed functional and expressive use of language. Her fear was that the children would use language and verbal forms of socializing as a substitute for productive work and play, almost as though a constant fund of energy could only go one way or another. This view can now be questioned on theoretical grounds.

Furthermore, while this may have been a real problem for that particular child population, contemporary experience with other child populations call for a changed perspective. We are now concerned with the education of a much wider population of children, many of whom have a relatively restricted experience with language in their homes. For these children, there needs to be a special responsibility, in the design of educational settings, to stimulate verbal facility, to engage the children in conversation in ways Miss Johnson would have avoided, to develop language competence that is directed as much toward communicative as to expressive usage. Still, the principle and techniques recorded in this book by which adult language was suited to the child's spontaneous mode of expression, which placed priority on meaning in terms of his encounter with his thing and people environment and, in general, brought the adults and children into closer touch with each other by taking a "play" approach to words and word forms remain significant cues for the teachers of very young children from any population.

Some of Miss Johnson's concerns are not equivalently worrisome to us, in our times. She felt it necessary to make a strong case against teaching children correct social manners in their earliest years because of the danger of sacrificing real feeling to formalism. Though not universally accepted, there has been a radical shift in our style of social interchange marked by informality and an ever-widening range of acceptable social codes—accompanied by a growing morality anchored in sincerity in personal interchange. This is what she was arguing for, especially during the formative years.

But other aspects of her views on socialization remain important and represent unresolved differences of viewpoint and practice. She did not leave it to the children to find their "experimental" way into the social mores of group living. Instead, a mode of living together was established for them that was both protective and demanding of adaptation, albeit pleasant in tone and free of any severe sanctions. The time schedule, the prohibitions of hitting and destruction, the rule of possession by use, the expectation that routines of eating, dressing, etc., would be accepted, the techniques of handling resistance by playful persuasion or diversion or alternately the resort to separation or exclusion—all represented a social fabric established by the adults as suitable first, to a stage of development and second, as a foundation for a live-and-let-live society. In Miss Johnson's opinion, these young children were not ready to be inducted into the kind of cooperative interaction that would be suitable and necessary to collective living of older children any more than they should be expected to conform to conventional adult standards of "good behavior." Instead, she preferred to nurture the natural emergence of awareness of each other and pleasure in communality through their encounters in play.

So much of this book records and analyzes thinking processes at this early stage of development that re-reading the Table of Contents is startling. The terms "thinking" and "concept-formation" are absent: language appears associated with rhythm in one chapter, and with music in another. Yet the fact is that observations about how children think and the ways that were considered appropriate for stimulating thinking processes are prominent throughout, appearing as integral parts of the descriptions of physical-motor activities, of use of constructive materials, of dramatic play, of social interactions and other observable aspects of the total learning environment. The educational principle emphasized in all these contexts was the importance of leading the child gradually to perceive relationships among the elements of experience while recognizing that the young children at first see "things and persons as undifferentiated wholes and use them in an objective fashion which takes little account of cause and effect . . . apprehend(s) objects and phenomena with their qualities, their meanings, in relation to the situation in which they are found." It was taken for granted that education had a differentiating function to perform—optimal, in this view, when the thinking processes were closely tied to physical manipulation, to sharpened perceptions, to self-meaningful content. Thus, she preferred that the child learn about similarities and differences, for example, from experiencing the qualities of objects he played with or from listening with the teacher for sounds coming through the window and hearing them translated into a rhythmic form: "Chop-chop . . that's a horse! Rattlety rattle, that's an old cart! Sh-sh-sh-sh honk, honk, that's a taxicab," etc. The children's striving for the salient differentiation—self from others—was observed in many centers but honored indirectly—for example, in the way a disturbance over "my daddy" was smoothed over by a chant about Yvonne's daddy, Georgie's daddy, Caleb's daddy," etc. or colors distinguished by a song about each child's sweater.

The descriptions of block building weave a continuous thread from manipulation, to patterning, to attribution of representative meanings and the accompanying dramatic play by which the children reviewed and rehearsed their own experience. Much of the record material that would now be used to illustrate the emergence of cognitive functions—such as classification according to functions—is presented in the book as evidence of the surprising amount of "knowledge" that the children were able to organize through their constructive and dramatic play. But it is "thinking" that we are reading about. The sensitive appreciation of the developmental value of representing experience in a variety of play media stands out impressively in the detailed accounting of the perceived relationships—the concepts—that were expressed symbolically as they were being acted out in play. The teacher who offered a wheel to the child calling out "All a bore! All a bore!" as he summoned other children to join him on his boat, made of blocks and boards, was responding to the child's thinking, and attempting to stimulate further elaboration of the components of the concept "boat." And it was also thinking the teacher was stimulating when she turned their questions back to them. "What that nail in kiddy car for? 'You tell me.' 'So handle won't come off. Why handle don't come off for?' 'You know, Walter; you tell me.'

So Walter can ride." with a smile and chuckle that mark enjoyment"—and with the serendipitous result of giving the teacher the chance to understand how short is the span of causal thinking before it falls into the logic of egocentricity. Or, again, when she naturally added "It is cold outside." while putting on sweaters, she was introducing causal thinking as a way of extending the meaning of a routine event.

The records are equally rich in material that illustrates how gradually causal and temporal relationships come to be expressed in terms of standard vocabulary. Study of the records and Miss Johnson's comments about them indicate there is an exploratory phase in which converse processes occur. Children play with words and expressions indicating causal and temporal relationships— "because," "today," "yesterday"—before they understand their meanings. Conversely, they find ways of communicating ideas of time and cause without benefit of the appropriate designating terms. For example, when a child suggests he will bring a boat from home to go under the bridge he has built in school and the teacher agrees, he closes the conversation with "Then I bring it now—next now." There were no exercises particularly designed to reinforce cognitive processes of differentiation, classification or causal thinking. There was, however, a systematic effort to create a learning environment in which the conceptual organization of the elements of experience—the schema for perceiving and formulating relationships—would be continuously and naturally stimulated as part of the child's encounters, physical and symbolic, in the course of his own response to his environment.

There are two points, (of differing significance) to be made about the fact that "thinking" was not extrapolated as a distinct category in the record of this educational experiment despite the recorded evidence that there was extraordinary awareness of cognitive development and a conscious "intentional" policy on how best to further it. First, unfortunately, its central importance and the associated techniques were often missed even by many practitioners who thought they were following this educational philosophy and practice, but who by default, contributed, unfortunately, to an image of early childhood education—now called "traditional"—as being concerned exclusively with the social-emotional aspects of development. Second, it is often misunderstood and misinterpreted by those whose theoretical predispositions make it difficult to appreciate how the thinking processes can be fostered unless the cognitive processes are treated as a distinct target for which special teaching techniques must be created.

The place that Miss Johnson gave the thinking processes in an educational program for those very young children has been in fact sustained and refined in certain centers of early childhood education. The technique has recently been analyzed and published in the interest of bringing it to the attention of educators as part of a developed theory and practice. This book's full record of a 45-year-old experiment that was breaking ground for a developmental-interaction approach to promoting cognitive growth is an invaluable contribution to our contemporary thinking about thinking.

Even though methodology for the study of child behavior has made such phenomenal progress in recent years, Miss Johnson's approach to studying children through observations of spontaneous behavior represents one of the tools of the still young discipline of child development that we cannot afford to discard. It is not the method suitable to an "experiment" in its orthodox connotation: there was no matched control group, no hypothesis to be tested and no measures of the reliability of the data. It was, instead, a sustained study of child behavior in response to a defined environment, meticulously recorded in detail, in narrative and summary forms. Every recording system is necessarily selective even when behavior is as relatively uncomplicated as that of an eighteen-month-old child. In this case the basis for selection of the conditions to appear in the records and events is made explicit and the product stands out as a pioneering contribution to the techniques of interaction recording in a "natural" setting. "We are attempting to study the reactions of children to their environment, what they do to the environment, how they adapt the materials and persons in it to their own purposes, and what the environment does to them, how their behavior is modified by conditions which they find or which their own reactions bring about." This kind of record has variously been referred to as "specimen" recording and as documenting the "language of behavior," both indicating that it provides the kind of data that contributes descriptively to understanding and is a major first step toward more systematic analytical research. This was, in fact, Miss Johnson's view as well.

In addition, there is a quality of generosity and relaxation in this book. There is a wealth of recorded material placed in juxtaposition with rich interpretive commentary on the course of development. There is an open willingness to put into print the kind of conjectural thinking about the possibility of the lasting impact of these early beginnings (or what corrections the next round of observational recording may yield) that is often screened out in more formalistic accounts of how children learn and how teachers teach. The reader is in direct contact with a thinking observer, with the process of inferring and generalizing, tentatively, from the vivid, concrete imagery and reportage about children in action. Though it would scarcely be feasible to expect teachers now to actually undertake a similar task of combined recording and teaching, it is not unreasonable to look forward to an image of a competent teacher who has been prepared for a role that embraces the intellectual processes of the thinking observer, even if the substance is not recorded in writing. There is a loss, both to research and education, in the extent to which the recording technique in its various forms has become the specialized tool of researchers not directly involved in the teaching functions. Perhaps as the movement for greater individualization of education progresses the importance of teacher recording will be once more honored and provided for.

Substantively, this book represents a significant contribution to the body of knowledge about early development, particularly of the later phases of the physical-motor period and the transition to the stage at which the child can begin to deal with his experience symbolically, recognized today as a major leap in the course of maturing. Considering the atmosphere of the field of psychology at the time Miss Johnson did her work one is deeply impressed with the extent to which her organization of the factual material she gathered and the implications she drew from it coincide with the contemporary writings of developmental psychologists.

On one level she organized her observational material sequentially, trying to find those successive changes that could be considered common to the children she studied from age 18 months to three years. While her records are annotated with the children's ages this was not a formal normative age study. Her focus was on the developmental characteristics and changes within a period of growth; the ages were markers for noting sequential trends; the two-year-old and three-year-old profiles were only abbreviated summary statements not intended as normative measurement tools. In each content area, the differentiated qualities and progressive changes of the sensory motor responses to the environment were as of much interest to her as was the emergence of the capacity to deal symbolically with experience. She documented progressive stages in use of blocks—-manipulation, formless stacking, balanced design—that precede the imputation of symbolic meaning either through naming or use as representative of reality. Similarly, she delineated progressive stages in use of crayons and paper—crayoning as part of the enjoyment of muscular exercise, producing circular and angular lines, massing of color on the field of the paper, making lines take an intended direction enclosing spaces—that precede post-hoc naming of drawings according to action or visual resemblance or expressions of intention to make a picture of something. In language, she traced a parallel sequence from production of sounds as muscular activity through progressive differentiation of inflection and modulation of pitch leading to rhythmic, repetitive, enumerative chanting before the use of words and phrases as condensed narrative statements and the emergence of incipient forms of genuine conversation. In her role as an educator the study of these sequences (she traced stages in social development and response to music similarly) were as important to her as the analysis of the steps toward physically integrated use of the body. She was eager to nourish the sensory-motor accomplishments of the locomotor stage by providing a variety of experiences consciously matched to the qualities and capacities of the children's response patterns; to protect this stage of growth from premature expectations of adults which would deny the child the special powers to be developed in the presymbolic stage through satisfying, self-initiated activities that differentiate and discriminate as well as pattern and compose. This was a way of providing a firm foundation for the symbolic stage into which the children were moving. In her interest in sequential ordering of observational material, in the importance of process over product of experience, in her conviction that the child should be actively involved in learning, and exposure to new experience be kept relevant in meaning and form to the child's existing repertoire of skills and interests and in her ideas for a learning setting that should support the gradual transition from sensory-motor to representative functioning, she is to be placed clearly as a forerunner of developmental psychology.

For readers who are teachers these developmental principles, drawn as they are from a natural learning setting, are more immediately usable than when similar concepts are framed in the context of experimental situations. This is also true of other developmental insights that appear throughout the book such as the tendency to revert to younger patterns as part of a natural growth process: "It is interesting, and characteristic of any behavior patterns in process of development, that it is not consistently maintained. After beginning a figure with definitely balanced colors the plan will be discarded or forgotten and an entirely haphazard and indiscriminate arrangement made. After the ability to walk upstairs there will be noticed repeated reversions to the infantile pattern of creeping." Or, in another instance, the fact is emphasized that rates of maturing are not

necessarily consistent in all aspects of development:
"Growth is not like a ride in the subway. The aim
is not alone to get there. Growth is a dynamic process
and in its phases builds something into the organism.
We are too prone to look forward to the mature stage
and to attempt to hurry over or omit steps toward it.
We all recognize that there are periods of wave-like
progress—when an accession of power or ability along
one line is matched by a slower rate of progress along
another. The fact of the alternative growth of parts of
the body and that of variations in height and weight
which are possibly seasonal can be paralleled in the field
of motor, language and social abilities."

At another level, she was interested in documenting
differences in individual style, in the emerging
behavioral patterns that distinguished, for example, one
child's tendency to construct with blocks with a "keen
feeling for balance and form" and then to use "her buildings in play after they were finished", from another
child's tendency to make elaborate plans beforehand as
to what she was going to build only to find that she
lacked the ability to carry them through. Taking a
behavioral view, Miss Johnson stressed the importance
of the child's experiencing positive affect associated with
the pleasure of mastery; she attributed lack of interest
or motivation to the combined factors of predisposition
and a fault in the environment in which he was being
reared. Though she acknowledged there might be more
complex problems in cases of extreme negativism or avoidance she was ready, as an educator, to turn the penetra-
tion into such problems over to the psychiatric profession. For this reason, her work does not deal with the
problems, theoretical or practical, that are associated with
conflicts arising from unconscious processes during this

stage of development. In this connection, it is interesting to remember that there was an active, mutually respecting interchange with her contemporary, Susan Isaacs, whose work was so firmly grounded in psychodynamic thinking. There is much to be gained in reading the work of these two investigators together; it has remained for future workers to attempt a synthesis of the developmental and psychodynamic perspectives.

In coming to the close of this effort, I turn back in a spirit of confirmation to Mr. Ellis' closing sentence: "Miss Johnson's experience will be of historical significance as well as of practical value for the rapidly growing number of nursery school experiments" and with hearty agreement with one of Miss Johnson's many succinct statements: "We cannot expect a child to be a clever parrot and a dynamic personality."

Barbara Biber
Spring, 1972

ABOUT THE AUTHOR*

HARRIET M. JOHNSON is the director of The
Nursery School, an experimental school for children of fourteen to thirty-six months, which is
associated with The Bureau of Educational Experiments. At the time of the school's founding,
Miss Johnson was general secretary of the Bureau. After its research staff was selected and at
work in The City and Country School and the
Bureau had concluded that intensive work in one
school would be most valuable, Miss Johnson submitted to the Working Council a plan for a
nursery school, which was accepted with the understanding that it should be undertaken under
her direction. *Children in the Nursery School* is
the record of her eight years' experience in the
school thus founded.

Miss Johnson brought to her work a background of varied experience. She had been a
teacher in a private school, a tutor, and a trained
nurse; for some years she had been on the Henry
Street Settlement staff; later, when the Public
Education Association was beginning that public
school service, she had taken up the work of a
visiting teacher. In the midst of these activities
she had found time for occasional courses at the
New School for Social Research and at Columbia
University, including the course in Nursing and
Health at Teachers College, and had read systematically along the lines of her chief interest:
the education of children.

*From the original edition.

INTRODUCTION

THIS record of eight years' experience in the conduct of a nursery school is significant for three reasons. It was probably the first nursery school in this country in which the children were kept within the narrow age range of the beginning of walking and three years of age, and held to a number so small that the interests of any particular child need never be sacrificed to the necessities of a group situation. Second, from the beginning the experiment was guided less by the past history of educational procedures and routines than by certain fundamental scientific facts and principles out of which methods could be evolved and by which they could be judged.

It is the idea of the director that it is the facts of growth and development which are the best guide to the knowledge of what is significant in behavior, and that when the needs of growth are met not only the questions of personal care are settled but the all-round questions of educational procedure are in process of being solved.

But it is one thing to collect the facts of growth, both the slender body of facts existing in the literature of the subject and the new facts obtained from a current program of research on the children under observation. It is quite another thing to detect the significance of these facts as they present themselves in the given situation and to follow the leads which they give.

It is out of this situation that a third characteristic feature of this particular nursery school project has arisen, which is, that continuous close recording of the activities of the children with a positive emphasis on the relation of growth facts and growth needs to behavior, is the only means of being sure that one is doing what one sets out to do. It took real foresight and not a little courage to set up the principle that all the experimental procedures in the school should be governed by such a far-reaching method. It has taken infinite industry and sagacity to record in any full way what happened in the experience both of the children and the teacher herself. The story the author has put together here is but brief parts of a voluminous history of very human adult and child experiences. Quite naturally such a history displays two characteristic features. In the first place it contains a wealth of details the importance and the charm of which will appear only as they are pondered over reflectively and with continually deepening insight into their significance. Just as naturally the story that comes out of this experience is marked by an absence of finality in the generalizations that are made. The director of the experiment has proceeded without haste and has grown her conclusions rather than forced them into didactic form by some process of generalization, or in the interest of some philosophical theory of society or personality.

The material accumulated in this, after all, brief span of years is not so much a basis for a philosophy of education as a solid body of fact, like that gathered by the naturalist, which must be faced in all his thinking and which regulates it in a way that continually brings it back to reality.

Nevertheless, it is a record of certain firmly established convictions that are worthy of the serious consideration of all those engaged in like experiments. A brief rehearsal of some of these will indicate their value as fundamental interrogations. Children are physical organisms. As such they grow in size and develop in functional efficiency. The main criterion of biologically useful forms of growth is to be found in activity. The most significant features of children's activity come into view when they are regarded as experimenters. The very fact of growth means that children are being continually led from old to new forms of experimentation. The only habits acquired by children which are biologically valid and educationally useful are those which serve the children in the pursuit of their experimental activities. The fact that growth is by stages means that there are fairly long stretches of time in the child's life when the most normal form of activity is that of carrying his experimentations toward the limit of use of his experimental powers possible for that particular stage; only in this way can he carry over the experience gained in one period to the new situation in the succeeding period. The most natural form of children's activities is play. Play is a form of experimentation. Work is a form of turning out a product. But play as experimentation is also productive, not of course of representative forms of production, but of the power to produce situations that are vital to an enlarging experience. No one can foretell the course of a child's experience in the years that follow his stay in the nursery school, but the school has done its legitimate task if it has for the time enabled the child to advance in the direction of independence of attitude and self-initiation of activity.

It may be objected that such a program is in itself a philosophy and a somewhat Utopian one. There are two considerations to be kept in mind before such a judgment is made. First, the actual story in the voluminous records of the nursery school is a story of how the use of a general principle has been kept within the limits of reality. It is a real story of a real experience, both for the teacher and the children, one that is not divorced in any major respect from the general run of life experiences when children are considered as units in the biological order of existences. Second, it has led the author to a set of convictions that are vital to the safeguarding of the whole nursery school movement. In a sense these are critical, but in a deeper sense they are constructive. This new thing in child nurture is not the discovery of new ways of getting children into a prepared state for handling them in masses in the interests of the school programs which they will come in contact with later. It is an attempt to turn the clear light of scientific knowledge onto the way in which children obtain a rich and useful experience when they are enabled to live in terms of their own present and act spontaneously within the limits of their present powers. The appearance in this decade of a number of nursery schools dominated by this principle seems likely to mark a new era in the education of young children.

While this might well be the main purpose of all education no one can be ignorant of the difficulties in the way of obtaining recognition for it in the present educational and social situation. It is all the more to the point that in the nursery schools the existence of a more desirable situation should be jealously guarded. There are two influences of a strongly didactic nature from which the children must be protected if the main purpose is to be accomplished. One of these proceeds from the family, the other arises in connection with the nursery schools themselves.

The attitude of parents toward their children is didactic to a high degree and to some extent this is a matter of necessity. Society, just as it is, in its current raw forms of custom, opinion and standards of judgment, expects certain of its precepts to be conveyed by parents to their children. Most of them find it both convenient and within the limit of their customary thinking to perform this office for society at large. Even so young as the nursery school age one notices the beginnings of a socially sophisticated attitude in children, the direct product of the presentation to them of adult social attitudes. The conveyance of these attitudes is frequently the direct work of the parents. It is equally likely to operate through the influence of older children who in gradually assimilating the standards of the adults and obtaining their consequent social approval feel that they have discovered something of importance to themselves and also something important for younger children and for their own convenience in settling their relations with their youngers. In such an atmosphere and under the operation of such considerations there is very little chance for the experimental activities of children of this age to have anything like their normal scope. The nursery school, therefore, appears as a counter influence against the almost hidden processes by which society through the parents undertakes the premature exploitation of children's interests in behalf of its own conventionalized and not very natural program of life. It thus happens that one of the first considerations in a nursery school program is that after satisfying the expectations of the family with regard to the physical care of children it should keep its further thinking in firm alignment with biological rather than social understandings with regard to the present and future welfare of the child, and this no matter what new problem it sets for parents, and no matter what amount of diversity of opinion may arise between them and the school. In so far as it falls short of this it falls short of being a really new thing in education, consonant in principle with the spirit of an age which is dominated by scientific thinking.

The other influence to be guarded against proceeds from the fact that nursery schools are for the most part just schools. From the point of view of a spontaneous living experience they are apt to be too large. From the point of view of educators they are apt to be used as teacher training centers. From the point of view of research in psychology or education, they are apt to be invaded by students in search of thesis materials. Even the biologist and anthropologist can overdo their efforts to find in the children new sources of information about the details of growth and functional development. From the point of view presented in this book the existence of a research staff in conjunction with a nursery school is an opportunity, not an absolute necessity. For its own immediate uses the nursery school is interested in growth studies of its children which are of value in helping it to apply scientific knowledge to thinking out its own situations. If additions are thus made to a general scientific understanding of children as growing organisms, so much the better. But this is not the main consideration. Undoubtedly both purposes may exist side by side, and wise understanding and singleness of purpose may prevent undue subordination of the interests of the children to those of the adults. But even where success is approximated in this direction the result is a different situation and one that is less clearly in line with what may be forecast as the future development of the nursery school movement.

The Bureau of Educational Experiments, founded in 1916, very early turned its attention from the task of surveying what was distinctly new and experimental in the field of education to that of intensive observation and research in a particular school * in which it seemed to find a major opportunity in line with its own purposes. Its present program of research in that school is concerned with the children from three through six years of age. It became almost at once apparent, however, that while important factors in a study of growth were operating on these lower age levels, we must have access to still younger groups if we were to get at the most significant period of physical and mental and social development. This conviction came with particular force to Miss Johnson in her thinking on the whole situation, and it is largely due to her initiative and fore-

---

* The City and Country School organized by Miss Caroline Pratt in 1913.

sight that in the fall of 1919 the Bureau set up its nursery school experiment.

The Bureau feels that because of her clear conception of her working principle and her consistent adherence to it in spirit and method, this record of Miss Johnson's experience will be of historical significance as well as of practical value for the rapidly growing number of nursery school experiments.

FREDERICK W. ELLIS

PREFACE

IN offering the following report on the Nursery
School of the Bureau of Educational Experiments I am trying to trace back our educational
principles to corresponding growth needs, and to
check our procedure by the extent to which it is
planned to meet such needs. I believe that certain of
our theses can be established in accordance with
known facts of physiological development; others
have been deduced from observation of children and
have to be subjected to further scrutiny and experimental study. In this presentation of the subject of
nursery school education, I have tried to think of
growth as a dynamic process and of the successful
human being as one equipped to grow and to do,
with a maximum of satisfaction to himself and to
society. If we hold this point of view we must feel
ourselves challenged to know more about how
growth proceeds and more about the growth capacity of the individual children whose development
we are trying to foster.

I have of necessity used the Bureau Nursery
School in my illustrations of environment and
method. I realize that during the time which has been
spent in the accumulation of my material the status
of the nursery school has changed materially. Not
only has the number of schools increased greatly
but also the preschool movement has won for itself
a more important place in education and in research.
Such research centers as those at Teachers College

and at the University of Minnesota are added to those in Iowa City and Detroit.* The training of students in problems of child health, psychology and education is a serious endeavor in such centers as these, and their influence upon the development of early childhood education will be widely and favorably felt.

We organized our group in September, 1919. Our research staff was already at work on its investigations in the City and Country School where it had access to children from three years on through all the age groups. We have limited our registry to one group of eight children ranging in age from fourteen or eighteen months to three years. Our first plan provided for ten children, but a trial proved to us that with our program and resources the number must be cut to eight. Very young children must have more attention from the teachers than older ones in order that their activities and impulses toward an investigation of the environment may not be thwarted—either by the inadequacy of their own efforts or by the interference of other children. This sort of supervision is one of the teaching problems of the nursery school.

Our children are chosen from the applicants as they come, if they seem to be normal babies, but there are so many questions to be considered that in

---

* Institute for Child Welfare Research, Teachers College, Columbia University, New York City.

Institute of Child Welfare, University of Minnesota, Minneapolis, Minn.

Iowa Child Welfare Research Station, State University of Iowa, Iowa City, Iowa.

Merrill-Palmer School, Detroit, Mich.

Institute of Psychology—Arnold Gesell, Yale University, New Haven, Conn.

the final analysis we can be said to have a selected group.

In the first place we give the youngest children preference, regardless of the order of application. We return to their homes at the end of the day the children who live within a specified radius about the school. We do not accept those who live at such distances that they have a long journey to make at morning and night. Hence our children are recruited from the lower west side section of the city. Other things being equal, we give preference to children whose brothers or sisters have been pupils in the Nursery School or are now in the City and Country School, and we take only those whose parents plan to remain in the neighborhood and to send them through the City and Country School. The parents are called upon for a good deal of coöperation, and we try to avoid those who are manifestly using us as a parking place and whose real interest we are unlikely to enlist.

All these criteria affect the status of our group. The children come from a limited area and from a district where the arts and professions are especially well represented. Frequently the parents represent the minority which is really questioning old educational standards and is ready to run the risk of accepting a new and unconventional educational program. There is no effort to find children of unusual mental ability, but probably a survey would prove that our groups rank above the average. We do not test the nursery children before they are three, so we have no record of their ranking in standardized tests and under laboratory conditions.

Our tuition charge is fifty dollars a month, but

we do not let that stand in the way of accepting a child whose parents make him a desirable nursery school member.

There are three full time teachers—of whom the director is one—besides a part time teacher in charge of the preparation and service of meals. With this staff we plan to have two teachers responsible for the children on duty at one time. As a matter of fact the teachers are given this leeway in time so that they may study and record the behavior of the children along lines suggested by the research program. They have been students in a new field, for nursery school curricula and teaching techniques are still in the making.

We have never undertaken any other sort of student training. The director and the teachers have been involved in their teaching and recording problems and the research staff have found the double duty of conducting their own studies and meeting the obligation of a coöperative research program sufficient to engage all their resources.

Members of our research staff come to the nursery to give physical examinations, to take measurements or to make records, but a teacher is always present at these times.

The director is also a member of the research staff and is required to be free for various duties outside the nursery. Record keeping has been as much a part of the teachers' responsibility as caring for the children, and gathering the records and preparing them for the typists have been duties shared by the nursery staff. They have also been responsible, with the assistance of the research staff, for the development of the form and content of the weekly summaries and the full-day records, and whatever value and efficiency these may have as objective studies of behavior is due to the critical and constructive attitude of the teachers toward their work. The fact that our teachers have this double consideration—the education of the children and the keeping of records of progress in objective terms— perhaps necessitates more teachers per child than would otherwise be necessary.

Our attempt has been to put into practice convictions and opinions which are for the most part shared by other workers in the field of education. Each educational experiment will make its own very special contribution to the art of teaching and each presentation of a subject from a different angle illuminates a slightly different phase. The nursery school child has enlisted in his behalf many men of many minds, and it is in the hope that some of them may find their questions answered or more fruitful inquiries raised that I offer these pages from our experience in the Bureau of Educational Experiments.

An enumeration of the persons to whom I am especially indebted, and the share each one has had in these pages, tells very little of the story. The Nursery School teachers and the members of the Bureau of Educational Experiments have had much to do with working up the material and with developing the point of view. They have given me the benefit of careful criticism and correction. Lucy Sprague Mitchell and Frederick W. Ellis have helped me in the preparation of the chapters on language in particular, and it is Mr. Ellis's study of our children which has brought to us a keener understanding of growth in dynamic terms and the need of measuring the environment of nursery school children against the growth needs which it should serve.

Bessie H. Coombs and Louise P. Woodcock, teachers in the School, have shared in the record keeping and have helped in its development as additional questions have been raised by Mr. Ellis in his study of motor patterns and by the research staff in conference on individual children. Mrs. Coombs has also been responsible for the musical script throughout the book, and Mrs. Woodcock for the sketches of block constructions. The language study, as is later explained, follows lines suggested and tried out by Mrs. Mitchell. Caroline Pratt's experiments in education preceded ours by some years, and we have followed her general thesis and have had the benefit of close contact with her school.

The book distinctly represents the thinking of more than one person, and my thanks are due not only to those mentioned but to other friends as well upon whose judgment and criticism I have depended.

HARRIET M. JOHNSON

New York City,
June 1, 1928.

PART I

WHY WE DO WHAT WE DO

§ 1. PLANNING FOR GROWTH

IN discussing environment and procedure in work
with the nursery school child I should like to consider children first as physical organisms equipped
and launched in their careers before their nursery
school experience.

In our school the children at entrance are hardly
established in taking and holding the upright position. Some form of quadruped locomotion remains
an alternative to walking erect for some years. The
topheavy appearance due to the large size of head
and trunk in relation to legs noted in the newborn
has not entirely given place to the next stage in proportional development. Teething is still an active
process with its frequent accompaniment of physical
ill-feeling or unlocalized distress. Speech activities
are of course almost as incessant as activities of the
trunk and limbs, but language as a tool for communication is in its incipient stage. Gesture, and
largely full body gesture, takes its place. Awareness
of other persons in the scheme of things is obscure
and fleeting. Adults are recognized but the other
babies seem to fall into the category of things rather
than persons.

Judged by the standards set up by self-respecting
adults the baby's attention too often flits from one
thing or situation to another. His interests, except
for the one absorbing interest in locomotion, are
short lived. He is easily diverted by accident or by

intention from any tentative purpose which his activities seem to reveal.

When he stands he rests on a wide base. His walk is a wabbling stagger with frequent collapses. When he first sees the problem of stairs and lifts a leg, it is swung about in an arc from the hip instead of being raised by a knee-bend straight out from the body. His broad stance and this method of raising his leg make the technique of climbing narrow slide steps very difficult. His spread is so broad that the lifted foot falls outside the stair boundaries.

If we step up to the usually accepted nursery school ages, two to four, we are still in the period of rapid development and constant shifts from lower to higher levels in control and in understanding. Even the high spots of development will show intermittently the trail of the infantile. Progress cannot be plotted as a straight line forward.

However, the outstanding feature of early childhood is the amount and quality of growth progress made in short periods of time, growth in bones and muscles, in height and weight, in capacity for use and control of the body, and for awareness and understanding of situations in the environment.

Since this is true, the chief concern of all who have to do with children must be their growth. A child's capacity for growth depends upon its physical and nervous mechanisms—their original soundness and maintenance in health—but given a good inheritance and a normal equipment, the most important factors in his development will be the amount and kind of activity that he is able to carry on. This does not mean alone exercise of the different muscles of the body, or of the sensory apparatus,

When he stands, he rests on a wide base.

Winter sports

Stages and varieties of attaining balance.

but the sort of trying-out of his powers that every-one who has had children in his family rejoices to see the little baby doing.

"He found his own hand to-day," "He rolled himself over," or "He pulled himself up and sat for a second or so," "He seemed to recognize his father to-day,"—all these announcements are News for young parents. What is the child doing? He is con-tinually experimenting with his body, with things and with persons in his environment, and in the proc-ess he is establishing himself as an active, thinking, well-coördinated member of the human family.

The little baby from birth to its first effort at maintaining an upright posture is so alien to adult methods of thought and action that for the most part he gets his chance to play out the game. His incessant moving, rolling, grasping and kicking are regarded as indications of praiseworthy vigor, and the adults about him intervene only to give him more opportunity to use his body unhampered by cloth-ing. It is when he acquires locomotion and speech and begins to invade the domain of adults that con-scientious determination to do their duty directs their attention to his acquirements. They think ahead to school and its standards and begin the process of fitting the child into its forms. Precocities are welcomed, especially those which indicate a stage of maturity conventionally recognized as ad-vanced, and if actual training is not initiated, special opportunities are given which may hasten progress toward a goal set by adult standards. The need then is for a fuller understanding of the processes of growth and integration and their interaction, to the end that our educational method may serve them.

In this chapter I shall confine my discussion to the physical environment, but it must be remembered that growth needs include social experiences as well as sensori-motor experiences, and here again our cue can be what is actually happening, if we are heroic enough to suppress our pre-conceived notions and objective and clear-eyed enough to see what is before us.

In any group there will probably be children suffering from physical defects that demand immediate medical care. In other cases the difficulties may not be so obviously physical, and their causes may lead one back into early environment, where habits and attitudes were set up which may yield slowly to remedial treatment. Whether or not we find that children need positive corrective procedure, we regard the free and experimental use and control of their bodies as the first desideratum for physical and mental health. Ability to put out energy effectively, to assume and hold any position desired, to poise themselves with a minimum of support, to throw, to jump, to skip, to hang, to swing, to balance, to recover balance when disturbed and then to carry on these activities with materials and in association with children is a fair beginning toward complete physical functioning. As preparation for our complex social life I believe it carries with it an asset which may be difficult to demonstrate positively but the importance of which will be recognized when it is lacking. The child who stumbles when he runs; who can run alone but who cannot manage a wagon as he runs; who has to make climbing over obstacles a deliberate, not an automatic process; who has not elaborated such simple playground activities as sliding, swinging and using a seesaw, finds himself at a disadvantage in a group. His constant effort is to compensate for his deficiencies. I need not use the psychoanalytic term. The human organism which we call the child is characterized by its tendency to seek activity. It not only reacts to stimuli which are presented but it tends to seek avenues through which it can carry on activities with a maximum of accruing satisfaction.* In other words the tendency of the human being is not only to respond to situations which are presented to it, but also to seek situations to which it may respond. It goes out in search of experience.

As we watch a group of children we see them with few exceptions carrying on experimental activities of one sort or another. This may mean trying out their own powers, as when Joan at two years persisted in returning to the springboard again and again though she was repeatedly thrown off balance, and the physical effort left her dripping with perspiration; it may mean absorption in a process, like Donald's repeated attempt to balance a broad superstructure upon an inadequate base; or it may be shown in persistent social advances such as Ansel's attacks upon Matthew, which took the form of puppy-like wrestlings, not at first well received by the victim.

Though the human organism tends to investigate and control its environment, it will usually build up its lines of control in accordance with its own development. It continues to do what it can do best, especially if it finds itself in a situation where it enters

* Herrick, C. Judson. *Neurological Foundations of Animal Behavior*, p. 17. (Henry Holt & Co., 1924.)

into competition with others of its kind.* It is equally true of course that a child who has gained unusual control of certain sets of muscles so that, for instance, he can maintain his balance standing on his head, will use this ability to call attention to himself or to divert attention from other children and from other activities in which he cannot compete with signal success, but it is only another argument for the importance of the development of general motor ability.

Our choice of equipment and our procedure are largely based upon the belief that the early use and control of the large musculature are of paramount importance, that there should be offered children a wide range of experimental possibilities and that the interests and activities of different age levels should be recognized and given scope.

If we are to develop an educational method which shall be consistent with the needs of growth, we must undertake further researches into the nature of growth processes and their relation to activities, especially spontaneous activities carried on by children. This field of educational research, allied to that of psychology and physiology, should yield us factual material against which we may measure our pedagogical procedure. Such study means, however, that interest must be sustained over a long period during which judgment must be held in abeyance till scientific data are accumulated and a longitudinal section of growth is charted.

Unfortunately the demand of the public is for a recipe—a slogan or a formula—and they are impatient of a study that does not in short order give

* See Part III, § 2, B, Other Children and Adults.

them a scale against which they may measure progress. It was the didactic material as a short cut to learning that won America to Montessori, not the scientific anthropological studies that were as vital a part of her own background and procedure.

Growth is progress toward maturity. It is, however, a continual and a gradual process, complete at each stage, or perhaps I should say capable of functioning at each stage. The duty of the educator is to see that the capacities of each stage are fully realized, not that the stages succeed each other as rapidly as possible. In dealing with the fabricated product we must wait for use till the final stage is reached. In dealing with the living, growing, human product, use—which is function—proceeds throughout growth. What we have to learn is the value to the individual in the total maturation process of a full realization of all that each stage in development holds.

For instance, to go back again to the very little baby, his stage of general body stirring is recognized as important enough so that we are very critical of the races that bind babies' legs or in any way impede their free, spontaneous movements. The runabout, however, develops tendencies which seriously interrupt the serene and orderly routine of an adult setup. His experimental use of his environment seems to adults to net him little in terms of mature accomplishment and they tend to resort to didactic treatment in order to make his contacts with materials and persons worthwhile, and only incidentally, we may charitably say, to protect adult possessions and to make the world safe for grownups. Real mischievousness is the child's escape from this program.

Docility and dependence upon other persons are its fruit.

That the child's experimental activities do net him something very positive in a surer use of muscles and a more ready sensory discrimination, and ultimately in advantageous habits of play and work, seems almost obvious if one has studied growth processes honestly. To preserve this impulse of his is one of the main duties of the nursery school.

The older education quite distinctly assumed that the function of the school was to prepare children for a future in which the activities made possible for them should have value in adult terms.* That is, it was looking for a product that would be valuable, not primarily to the child in the process, but to society in its final stage. In other words it applied the manufacturer's attitude to human beings and to growth. Unfortunately education has not thoroughly outgrown this point of view. For this reason growth as a dynamic process, and the evaluation of growth in terms of what it brings of satisfaction and fulfillment to the individual growing must be repeatedly emphasized.

We are trying to see that the situations which are to be found in the nursery school are such that the children can deal with them profitably in a play way. Therefore our task is that of making sure that the children have access to suitable materials, of protecting them from encroachments and of assuring them safety in their early adventuring. The details of the program that we have to set up, what we call the daily routine, the measures that we take to

* Forest, Ilse. *Preschool Education: A Historical and Critical Study.* (The Macmillan Co., 1927.)

safeguard their health and to assure them proper nutrition, are not the reasons for our being as a nursery school. They are on the one hand responsibilities which must be assumed by anyone who brings children into a group, and on the other provisions which assure to the children a larger opportunity for carrying on their own experimental concerns.

There are procedures which we expect our children to learn; there are skills in dealing with the materials which we hope they will acquire; but most of all we are concerned with their developing an attitude of readiness to act, which is characteristic of the creative, dynamic personality. This may sound like an exaggerated pedantry or undiluted metaphysics, but the principle is so fundamental a part of our philosophy that I must attempt a formulation of it, however inadequate.

In our discussion we are brought up sharply to a consideration of the standards of life and conduct which the educator must have in mind. I do not here refer to ethical and moral development but to the growth and control of the affective life which makes for the harmonious functioning and integration of the personality. Here, as truly as in the physical care of the child, one needs to understand the significance and relevancy in educational procedure of the laws of growth.

We must remember that back of all the activities which we note lies the driving force that directs them, that in every action pattern whose growth we trace, there is an affective component which is just as much a part of the physiological picture as the working of a muscle, though not so obviously. At the present time we have fairly accurate methods of measuring skeletal growth. We can describe the reaction of the organism to its environment in terms of performance and thus trace its progress toward maturity, but we cannot measure increase in affective integration in units now available. The relationship between behavior and the functioning of glands, muscles and nerves we realize, but we are as yet able to do little more than state what we observe and raise queries concerning the effect of one set of phenomena upon the other.

The external manifestations of affectivity are the attitudes and interests which modify or govern behavior. They will be the driving force of the organism throughout life and are roused, developed and modified by the interaction of organism and environment.

One recognizes in the creative, dynamic individual an impelling force, a "drive" which carries him along in the line of his "interests." * The experiences that life has brought him are for the most part responsible for the kind of interests he develops and, probably more completely than we realize, for their quality as well,—their intensity and freshness, and his method of developing and using them. We do not believe that it is only the gifted individual who has creative possibilities, and furthermore we judge the activities of our children not by what they produce in the literal sense, but by the satisfaction and power that accrue to them from their work and by the sort of affective patterns that develop. It is not conceivable to us that spontaneity and interest, a readiness to experiment and to initiate can be fos-

* Woodworth, Robert Sessions. *Dynamic Psychology.* (Columbia University Press, 1918.)

tered by a dictated program even though useful techniques may be acquired and specific abilities may be developed.

It is essential to the task we have set ourselves to find out as far as may be all the limitations set for each individual by his total physical equipment and to recognize them in our treatment. It is the part of education to give opportunity to the individual for as full a use as possible of the powers he possesses and to help him in his adaptation to the environment, whether that means a modification and control of his own behavior patterns or of the environment itself, and of course it will be both.

We must also remember that whatever our theoretical ambitions for our children, whatever opinions we may hold about the relative values of occupations or interests, the children will get what we express overtly by our attitudes and our emphasis.* If we give much of our attention to correcting their speech or giving them some special techniques, they will tend to the feeling that these things are weighty. If we give a child blocks and then put our emphasis upon his making no noise when he builds, upon his putting them away in an orderly fashion in his chest, or upon his sharing with his younger sister and permitting her to demolish his buildings, he may have little interest in real constructions. Parents often say that they do not want their children to be vain or self-conscious but if they spend a good deal of thought over their small daughter's clothing and adornment, if they call upon their son and heir to show how nicely he can

* Gruenberg, Sidonie Matsner. "Twigs of Prejudice." *Survey Graphic,* September, 1926.

say a nursery rime or how he can do his daily dozen, self-consciousness and a desire to appear before the public eye will be fostered.

The examples are extreme and are given only in the effort to emphasize again this point: education demands an intentional and consistent policy. We must know what traits, what habits or tendencies, what powers and what interests we honestly wish to foster, and our attitude and our behavior in regard to those traits, habits, powers and interests must be,—will be if we are sincere,—consistently maintained; we must also provide an environment suitable for the kind of growth which we wish to serve. Our rôle cannot remain a passive one. Our honest inner convictions will take possession of the field.

Here, we place our chief reliance upon preserving a consistent policy within a uniform environment, in which we, as teachers, are able to be less conspicuous and less personal than parents are in the home. In this environment the children's reactions tend to be directed toward the situation as a whole instead of toward the teachers as persons. In so far as this is true and our policy is maintained, the teachers will remain educators instead of caretakers and trainers; the nursery school will be a part of the educational process, not merely a place where babies can be left and trained in habits of social convenience.

There are certain modes of behavior which we desire to develop. We may if we like use the term habits in referring to them just as we do when we speak of the routine responses which we tend for the sake of economy to reduce to the automatic as rapidly as possible. As far as I know the general definition of habits as involving almost all the reactions of the individual to his environment seems to be accepted by all the writers who speak of learning with the exception of the physiologists and neurologists.* The child is said to acquire the habit of thumb sucking or of feeding himself, the habit of consideration for others, or of sincerity in social relationships, the habit of facing a difficult situation or the habit of being ambitious or industrious or judicial.

I believe that our discussion of educational aims would be furthered if we could use terms that were not so inclusive, but perhaps our "habit" in this regard is too firmly fixed to change without too much adjustment. It seems to me that except for the stable sort of reactions to special situations we are attempting to establish tendencies rather than habits. Our justification is found in the attitude of the scientists who are studying the biological foundations of behavior, that continual adjusting and readjusting are characteristic of the individual organism, and that in its history plasticity is more important than a more stabilized form of behavior.

There is obviously quite a distinction between habits which are of importance in the physical development of the individual, habituations gained in other routine physical techniques and the habits which have to do with his attitudes towards specific situations and his tendency to make a given sort of

* Dewey, John. *Democracy and Education.* (The Macmillan Co., 1916.)

Dewey, John. *Human Nature and Conduct.* (Henry Holt & Co., 1922.)

Kantor, J. L. *Principles of Psychology.* (Alfred A. Knopf, 1924.)
Herrick, C. Judson. *Opus cit.* Chap. XXI.

Herrick, C. Judson. *Brains of Rats and Men.* Chap. XIII. (University of Chicago Press, 1926.)

response to them. The first are those concerned with such matters as food intake, elimination, rest, sleep and exercise; the second have to do with definite techniques such as walking, climbing, jumping and other uses of the musculature which eventually are reduced to automatisms—dressing and undressing, speech and later skills in this or that pursuit; the last refer to characteristic responses to situations of a less stable and circumscribed variety. For example, given a strange or new environment, one individual will tend to advance, another will withdraw. Faced with physical materials, one child will seek the familiar, another will tend to experiment with the novel. In the course of his life he may for one reason or another have built up other automatic responses to various situations which hamper his development. He may have a well-established sort of reaction to situations in which certain sorts of animals are found, so that he shows fear as a conditioned response, not as a reasoned or reasonable reaction to a fearful or inexplicable situation. He may have taken on certain other habits like a resort to temper or to tears to gain an end, all of which are serious in so far as they are permanent and so in control of spontaneous behavior that they are preventing the orderly organization of individual resources and hence the beneficent development of personality.

Education must consider and deal with these various kinds of responses. Those which are of biological importance in growth, whether they have to do with health or with techniques and skills, must be cultivated. Those which hamper development must be broken down. But to my way of thinking this must be done in order to relegate them to their proper place and to leave the field clear for more dynamic educational processes. We cannot build up an entire educational system upon the cultivation of habits, important as they are. It is true that we cannot build up an educational system without a consideration of habit formation and the part it plays in character building. If habits hold the man and restrict him, he is to that extent uncivilized,—uneducated. But it is equally true that the habits which a person acquires are of less significance than the use he makes of them.

It is important that a child should have a liberal equipment of acquired responses, that he should learn to carry on many processes with automatic precision and that, faced with certain situations, he should tend to make one given choice rather than another which adult experience has found to be less conducive to the general good. It is equally if not more important, is it not, that a child should learn to orient himself in new situations that present themselves, that he should have the impulse to attack them and the drive to carry him along to a constructive method of dealing with them. These qualities are not mechanisms that can be learned and relegated to the automatic. They grow out of the individual's body of experience and his growth in this regard does not lie in the lap of the gods but to a great extent in the control of parents and teachers. If he is encouraged to make an experimental approach to the unelaborate situations of a simple environment, he is more likely to gain in the power to take independent action when more intricate and unfamiliar conditions confront him.

All the traits cited are habits in that they are habitual modes of responding but they can also be called patterns of action. When we say that this or that behavior is characteristic of a person, whether it is his gait, his method of using blocks or his reaction to a social situation, we mean that it follows his customary pattern of response. The study of these patterned responses, of their affective source and of the interests which develop with them as a fundamental part of the individual's equipment and drive is an essential part of our program.

Every child in a group may learn to coast in a wagon so that he is past master in the technique. He has acquired the habit. The process by which he acquired it differs as his physical, nervous and affective organization differs from that of each one of the other children. In tracing his progress we find that we are tracing a pattern. Certain features of the behavior pattern will occur whenever the same individual is studied. In Part III a record is given of Philip's use of the slide. If I had given his behavior reaction to another piece of equipment many of the same factors would have been noted: for instance, his eagerness at making an initial attack and his tendency to use the pattern once acquired in a variety of ways as well as the high level of affective tone shown in his evident elation and satisfaction.

In the study of behavior patterns, as has been said, I make a distinction between the more or less routine performances which the human being must learn and make automatic as early as is appropriate and the more fluid, plastic behavior that makes up the individual's character and personality.

Freed from the need of attention to the details

Learning to coast in a wagon.

Kiddy Kar and Trailer.

of his usual contacts with his environment because of the mechanization of his routine performance, he can turn his powers to the more dynamic use of establishing himself as an individual in the world about him. He is not isolated so his behavior is not an independent product. It is affected by the opportunities and the physical materials about him and most of all by the use that other individuals are making of the environment, the "meanings" and the relationships that come to form parts of his understanding, his comprehension, his perception of all he is experiencing. It is further conditioned by the behavior of the adults toward his responses.

With all these modifying influences he has, within such a program of self-initiated activities and experiences as the nursery school offers, an opportunity to explore his environment and to build up original ways of attacking it. In the process he is forming characteristic patterns of behavior, some of them as uncomplicated as his individual method of using a wagon or a swing, others as fundamental as his readiness and capability when faced with a new situation.

Habits in the narrower sense, as techniques, we are inclined to treat in a different way from habits in this wider meaning. We are chary of introducing too many techniques during nursery school age for several reasons. In the first place since the object of cultivating techniques such as washing or dressing, for example, is to develop them to mechanical perfection, it is fruitless to attempt them before this result is possible. The dressing process in its entirety is too complicated for a child under three to make automatic. If the complete performance is exacted of him fatigue is likely to follow and the net result is often irritability and eventual distaste. If while demanding a complete performance, the adult is forced to concede help, the child is likely to get the sense that he has not lived up to requirements though at the same time he relishes the fact that he is commanding adult attention. The aim of helping a child to this dressing technique is instead to give him a feeling of power and independence. We think it best to work very tentatively on such processes, seizing the moment of interest but not extending our demands on the child beyond it. In an older group after habits of independent work are established and the span of interest is lengthened, proficiency and self-help can be profitably cultivated and will have a distinct bearing on the ability of a child to organize and carry on his own program of activities.

Another reason for deferring the training period on these techniques is that we consider an emphasis upon them a waste of time. Children have more important concerns. They are becoming oriented in a new environment, that of the nursery school, which is rich in things-to-do. They are stepping out of the shelter and supervision of the home and into a social group of another kind where their own choice and initiative can be operative to an unusual extent. I believe that these opportunities further the cultivation of dynamic interests and the drive to carry them to fruition which should be the aim of education.

We must also take into consideration that there are many habitual attitudes which are in their essence nothing but prejudices, so our effort should be to encourage the "habit" of recombining reaction elements into new patterns rather than of making stable, responses which ought to be the result of intellectual concern. It may be the part of wisdom to flee from a mad bull but to regard all animals with horns as threatening is not to be desired. Some foreigners are undoubtedly inferior to some native sons, but we deplore the habit which we sometimes meet of regarding the American *per se* as a superior product. We are glad if a child is cautious enough to care for himself in a precarious situation, but if caution becomes a kill-joy it is to be deplored. Economy in mechanisms is efficiency but economy in thinking is stagnation.

Some individuals are restless till they reduce most of their rules of conduct to such precision. Most of us prefer not to live too closely to an interrogatory state of mind. But there are situations which we meet in our work, in our play and in our social relationships in which if we are to think in any sort of original way we must stand ready to re-sort our judgments and re-arrange our customary patterns of action and develop new ones or new combinations. In miniature the nursery presents the world to children, and the value of self-initiated work must be kept in mind in developing a program and a curriculum for the nursery school.

The following chapters will further explain our point of view and our practical policy. They will also repeat much of what I have tried to state here, my excuse being the need I have felt for relating our principles to our practice.

§ 2. HABITS AND CONVENTIONS

IN the foregoing chapter, I have tried to state our general educational point of view in regard to two growth impulses shown by children, the impulse to be active and the impulse to experiment.

A very important part of the nursery school's responsibility is its provision for the health of its charges. In choosing the school as the place where most of his working hours are spent the baby has a right to demand that his health shall be protected, that he shall be fed in accordance with the most approved nutritional standards, that his sleeping arrangements shall assure him restful naps and that a maximum of sunlight and open air shall be provided. These provisions imply a degree of scientific knowledge on the part of schools beyond what has been asked of education before.

Babies from favored homes are fairly well established in their daily routine by the time they come to school. That is, they are fed at regular intervals, they are put on the toilet at the same time each day, their naps and bedtime are invariable and these things, with dressing and changing, they accept with varying degrees of good grace if not with enthusiastic coöperation.

They have been observers, not participators, in these processes, and during the next year or two they will be expected not only to become further habituated to them but to acquire the requisite skill and control to perform certain of them with fairly automatic precision,—first to coöperate in them and as a next step to take the initiative in their performance.

When we come to consider the details of our program that have to do with these routine habits, I find that we hold a very special attitude and point of view concerning them and our method of establishing them. Is it consistent to let a child explore all the possibilities of the kiddy kars and nip in the bud his plan to deal experimentally with his food or with our designs to put him to bed?

The distinction I have made between the two is that while getting washed, being taken to the toilet, put to bed and being conducted through the ceremony of a meal, have an importance in growth which can hardly be over-estimated, they have no intrinsic interest for the young child. Moreover his experimenting can accomplish little without interfering with processes which are generally conceded to be biologically essential. Therefore, from the child's point of view, we are high-handed in our treatment of these performances, merely trying to be as pleasant and as casual in our manner as is possible, and depending upon the usual good nature of the young to gain from them a ready acceptance of what must be.

We make it a part of our procedure that each child shall accept what has to be done at these times, that he shall remain seated during his meal, shall eat what is on his plate and that he shall lie down and stay in his crib during his nap. This is usually accomplished just by carrying in our manner the expectation that it will be done. Gradually to build up enough interest so that children will follow it to efficient accomplishment, justifies us in a method which we do not adopt in regard to other details of our program.

There is a tendency on the part of many young parents determined to treat their children like rational beings, to make elaborate explanations regarding matters of getting dressed or washed. The intent is admirable, but the effect is sometimes deplorable because lengthy discussions arise over events which are and must remain in the hands of the adult. We do not attempt to explain to the children our demands and why we are making them. We believe that in routine matters which must be accomplished anyway, in which there is really no element of choice, the fiction of discussion and explanation puts upon the child a responsibility which makes for confusion, so we waste no words over such things.

Undressing the children and preparing them for their naps again gives adults an opportunity for direct contact with them, which we avoid when they are carrying on their play activities. There is conversation with them; they are encouraged to undress themselves as much as they are able; various little games like "peek-a-boo" or "creep-mouse" are carried on, and there is likely to be much gayety if not hilarity. To restore quiet and inclination to sleep a "good-night" chant or the "Sleepy-time" song is sung. As in all the routine performances which mean nothing to the child the effort here is, while expecting and if necessary exacting acquiescence, to make sure that pleasure as an accessory accrues to him.

We do not try to train our very little children to dress and undress themselves. Their attention is called to the process so that they will not stop at the meal-sack stage when they are passively stuffed into their clothing. As soon as interest in unlacing shoes, slipping clothing off arms and any other sort of helping develops, we follow that—not, however, with insistence. It has been our experience that prematurely developed interest in these processes often does not endure, and we try to keep the experimental quality of interest fresh by not pressing it too far. Also the fine muscles and a very concentrated sort of attention are involved in some of the details of dressing, and for that reason we do not attempt to require persistent effort upon them.

Long before Yvonne was twenty-four months old she had a keen interest in all the details of dressing and undressing. She struggled with buttons and buttonholes, she put on stockings and laced her shoes. She had been encouraged at home and showed a marked preference for small objects and finely coordinated use of her small muscles. We found our feeling that she should not be encouraged quite justified by the fact that after the sustained effort necessary for getting her waist buttoned or her shoes laced, she would often show sudden tenseness over nothing at all and scream and cry shrilly.

There are cases in which the interest has failed to develop, and then a training period has been necessary. Walter reached his third birthday steadfastly refusing to do any sort of efficient work in dressing or even undressing himself. We had made the usual attempts at getting his coöperation with little success. There were many personality difficulties to be overcome and we finally threw the whole process back to him. He had to dress himself after nap in order to have his play opportunities. There was

ability but disinclination to use it, and an entire lack
of the feeling of elation which accompanies self-
dependence. Following a period of storm and stress
a sense of power and tremendous satisfaction developed, and he became more insistent than we had
been that no one should help him. We make our
insistence depend entirely upon the individual and
his needs.

At dinner each child is seated at a separate low
table, and soup is served. After a child has finished
he may take his bowl to the serving table and bring
back his plate. Here again we follow the interest of
the child as we do also in the feeding process. Our
youngest babies are given a spoon, and we supplement their efforts by our own. As their interest and
ability increase our help declines. All the children
are given help on occasion. If a child stalls on his
meal and help on the part of an adult makes it go
well, we do not refuse it. The technique of feeding
is not yet developed into an automatic process. It
holds out while the first edge of appetite is still
keen or till the favored articles of diet are eaten.
Unless there is a marked slowing down or an abnormal disinclination for food, it will serve in time
to carry a child as a matter of course to self-help.
If the adult's presence and help will establish the
habit of eating the disliked or unfamiliar vegetable
and of finishing what has been served, it seems to us
unnecessary to make an issue of self-feeding. The
assumption that if a child does not eat, he must be
ready to go to bed, or the decision that dessert follows only an empty plate is usually all that is needed
as a spur to effort.

Each rule has of course its exception. We have

had children who were inclined to dependence upon adults and whose demand for service was stronger than appetite. There are children who bring no zest for food to their meals, but they constitute a special problem either in assimilation or in behavior. All standards regarding feeding and appetite must be held with the physical condition of the child in mind. Real absence of appetite probably has a physical cause for the metabolic process is actually speeded up in an environment like that of the nursery school where active play is going on in stirring air. Some kind of faulty assimilation has been found to be the cause in most of our persistent cases of poor appetite.*

The difficulties in establishing good feeding habits, the whimsies and caprices in appetite that one hears so much about, figure very little in our experience. Excellent appetites and an increasing ability to use one's implements are the rule. We make little point of neatness as regards the person or the table while the mechanics of using a spoon are still a problem. We encourage the children to hold their spoons in their fists because then the movement is not a fine grasping one but an arm-shoulder swing.

We have the usual reports from parents that the baby does not like spinach, is unwilling to take milk or rice or egg. Our most extreme cases of idiosyncrasy were the baby of fifteen months who would eat eggs only hard boiled with lemon juice on them, would take no desserts and only a limited number of vegetables, and one of twenty-six months whose mother told us that he would eat no vegetables

* Aldrich, C. A., M.D. *The Prevention of Poor Appetite in Children.* (National Committee for Mental Hygiene, N. Y.)

which were not cooked for a long time in a large quantity of water in an open vessel. No one who knows children needs to be told that these difficulties were of home manufacture and were so easily overcome that we should have forgotten they had ever existed had it not been for our record of them. There are dislikes that persist but the refrain of one of our children, "I don't *like* my spinach but I eat it just the same," and an occasional helping hand dispose of the offending dish, except in rare cases.

We cannot over-emphasize the influence of the group upon the ease of training in food habits. Individual difficulties disappear in the group. There is no influence that is more corrective. It works in college and in camp as it does in a group of babies. Various factors enter in to take a child's attention from personal likes and dislikes. First comes the interest in sharing a common activity. One tends to do what everyone is doing. Second, the attention of a child is on the others and the general routine program rather than upon himself and his individual performance. This brings us to the third factor which again is the attitude of adults toward his disinclination to eat. Most normal children are not injured by a reduction of food intake for an occasional meal and, if the reluctance is caused by a real lack of appetite, a fast is indicated. It is very difficult for a mother to regard fasting with composure and I believe that her concern and agitation are communicated to the child. The nursery teachers are made of sterner stuff and can be philosophical over it if it is a step toward the solution of a problem.

Most of our children subscribe to our routine as a matter of course. Nap follows lunch and is ac-

cepted. Many times the mothers tell us of special
habits that the children have developed in regard to
nap time. One child refuses to sleep unless a pet blue
blanket covers him. Another must have a small pil-
low in his bed. The enumeration of the formulæ
that have to be recited or of the magic incantations
and rites that must be observed would fill a volume.
One baby always stood in his crib and rocked or
swayed till he dropped. For a few days we did nothing to restrain him with the result that he slept for
less than an hour sitting up. Thereafter we laid him
down and pinned him so that, though he could roll
he could not rise, and he got his usual two-hour nap.
For the most part we disregard entirely the home
ceremony and for the most part we get no demands
for it. We do, however, have difficulty in inducing
lengthy naps when we put our children to bed in one
room or within sight and hearing of each other. A
variety of sleeping places and as many single rooms
as possible are available, and the children are shifted
till we find the arrangement that gives the longest
possible per capita nap.

Upon the subject of training in bladder control
we hold a point of view which is at variance with
that of the usual parent or physician and perhaps
with many persons who have small children under
their charge. I believe that too much emphasis has
been laid upon the importance of acquiring early
control of urination and other habits of self-help.
Parents begin correctly when they attempt to establish regular habits in urination and the evacuation
of the bowels when a baby is a few months old. They
make no demand upon the baby but assume the
responsibility of placing him in the correct position

at regular intervals. By the time he can creep, however, the method is likely to be changed. The child is exhorted to "tell mother." Often he is reproved or even punished for involuntary voiding of urine, and from that time on till control is physiologically established, the subject is one of exaggerated importance in the minds of the parents, of much discussion when children are being talked about and above all when mother and child come together. Various attacks are made upon it, a usual one being the effort to create in the child an aversion for soiled clothing and an association of disgust with the sight of urine and feces.

We have raised the question whether much of the storm and stress experienced in the adolescent and adult years over the problem of sex relationships and an adjustment to sex life are not tied up with an early misunderstanding regarding the processes of elimination and those of sex. However that may be, it is one thing which we have in mind in putting a minimum of emphasis upon the habits concerned with elimination, at the same time endeavoring to get each child's "rhythm," *i.e.,* the periods between voiding, so that he can be taken to the toilet and thus remain dry. We are still raising interrogations as to the importance of even this amount of supervision, that is, if being kept dry has any effect upon the establishment of bladder control.

Another factor enters in here, which is the desire for attention and for personal contact with adults. Nothing wins so direct a response from adults as wet clothing. We attempt to take responsibility for attention to bodily needs from our children until physiological control is established. We believe that it will be established as soon and as successfully if we do not call the need of it to the child's attention as it will if we do, and that the reduction of the subject from its usual place of paramount importance in the lives of adults and children gives room for interests which are distinctly of greater educational value. There is surely in the relationship between adult and child, something of higher spiritual import. Children ought to seek their grownup associates for something besides drab duties that concern themselves with the care of their persons. They ought to associate with us more vital and dynamic subjects of conversation, and to tie up parents with reproof or disapproval is disastrous to a spiritual relationship. The reason so little harm is done is because emotional memory in these early years is so short. We can condition children so that they develop patterns of response to our behavior, but till real emotional awareness enters in, the response is an external manner which does not become a part of organic life. It may none the less surely hold possession of the field so that self-initiation of beneficent activities is delayed.

There is an aspect of the program which I have not discussed and which launches us at once upon certain attitudes which are held about moral and ethical standards. It has to do most of all with method but since the preceding description of our program can hardly be stated without an accompanying explanation of the way it is carried out, this may be as good a place as any to introduce a discussion of table manners in particular and conventions in general.

What do the conventions which play such a part

in the social life of adults mean to little children? How shall they be made a part of the equipment of children and when? From the adult point of view the acquisition of social graces is important because, though they mean little in the observance, the lack of them makes the road of social communication uneven and jolting. It is rare that a greeting or a farewell has in it a personal flavor or originality but because it is commonly given its lack leaves the sense of a hiatus, a gap which makes for awkwardness, and emphasizes mannerlessness instead of allowing the attention to glide smoothly into the midst of the real business of friendly give and take. When is the appropriate time to give children instruction regarding conventional modes of response is a question that we are not yet able to answer. I can only say that we do not believe it to be at the nursery school age. We do believe that the social conventions which hold us mean nothing at all to these children and that if they can be induced to accept the form it means only a mechanical repetition of words. "Please," "thank you," "excuse me," whatever the expression may be, are automatic responses, made however not to the social situation but because only if they are used is the desired toy or privilege forthcoming. They are responses to a situation set up by adults and at this age they must be if a definite attempt at establishing them is made. As has been said, these social amenities have come to be worth while to us through our experience in living together and finding the need of a lubricating medium. We cannot expect awareness of this need to appear before the social experience.

If greetings, expressions of regret or appreciation

and the more formal details of good manners are merely mechanisms, why should we not teach them early and make them automatic so that they will be out of the way as other routine habits are? That might be an admirable plan except for two considerations. First, the routine habits which we have been discussing are of vital importance in the growth of the organism. The social conventions are not. The routine matters with which the reaction of the child is concerned are whether or no a part of each day's essential program. A patterned response to food, to rest, to elimination, will be developed in the course of experience, and we are attempting to establish beneficent or profitable responses. The physical habits which are being formed center about certain fairly fixed items of the child's program. They absorb attention, drain off the energies and interrupt his own interests to a limited degree and for a very limited time. If one is to be consistent about training in good manners it must be a continuous process, for opportunities for conventional social responses appear throughout the day. Since manners are not of intrinsic interest their cultivation must be an interruption to procedures which do hold the child in and of themselves. If we insisted upon a prescribed response to stimuli which are presented so often during the day, we should thwart the very impulse we are trying to cultivate and should tend to build up inhibitions or over-attention to adult reactions on the part of our children.

Second, when we attempt to inculcate in young children the adult forms of social usage, we are asking for a response without a stimulus till we have created a stimulus by our attitude of approval or of

disfavor. Why is not gaining adult approval legitimate as a stimulus to conduct if by this means
courtesy can be set up as a permanent pattern? Before answering such a question in the affirmative I
should add another conditional clause, namely, if
the pattern were gained at no sacrifice of the development of other equally desirable behavior responses
and with no evidence of emotional stress. We are
trying to create an environment in which children
shall find and share growing opportunities for the
exercise and development of their play interests.
Insistence upon techniques which do not present
such opportunities seem to us irrelevant. Concretely,
if a child sees another whom he knows and with
whom he has pleasant associations, he is not naturally moved to greet him verbally on sight. His
response would vary with his age, but it might be to
run laughing away or to go to him and show him a
toy or—if he was much older—to begin talking
about something that had interested them both before. If a child is confronted with a full dinner plate
his response is to begin to eat, not to wait till his
fellows are served, and he must be taught to inhibit
a spontaneous response before he can acquire the
conventionally approved one. Of course I realize
the apparent inconsistency in this reasoning. We
might say that to try to keep all the toys in his possession, to push and repulse his fellows if they interfere are equally natural responses and ask why
inhibition is any more justified in one instance than
in the other. In the one case the inhibition and the
acquired response make for adult satisfaction but
do not add to the child's power and control in his
own social situation. In the other the child may feel

dissatisfaction temporarily, but as the pattern becomes his own there is a gain in power and control because he is able in a freer fashion to deal with his environment.

Feeling usually runs high over this question of the cultivation of manners in the young, and I am ready to admit the charm of the child who is gracious, ready with his thanks or with the right word of appreciation or apology, but at the same time that I am charmed I am wondering at what cost the conventional response has been induced.

Probably there would be ready admission that the young child—we will say the preschool child—does not feel remorse, gratitude, shame, reverence or revenge. He responds to situations in which these qualities are involved as he has been taught, that is conditioned, to respond. In time, it is true, his responses become automatic, and the argument for teaching manners is that these patterns can be set at an early age and they will make for ease and lack of self-consciousness in the child's social life. In so far as it is true that conventional modes of behaving at table, of greeting guests, of thanks and of apology or consideration can be cultivated by an automatic process *in which there are few affective elements,* so far there can be no objection to doing so. It is probably true in some cases. It would be interesting to make a study of differences in children in their reception of training in manners. What are the other characteristics of children who develop these patterns early and easily? What are their main interests? What problems do they present in development? Do they hold consistently their habits of courtesy?

We all have in mind examples of parents who place too great emphasis upon the acquisition of adult forms which result, on the part of the children, in tenseness and strain and extremes of anti-social behavior. One of our mothers was much disturbed because we did not insist upon the formality of an exchange of greetings between the children. She had always been scrupulous in that respect herself, and said that since her child had been with us she was showing traits that had not been in evidence before and that were very distressing. She cited as an instance the fact that Clara had violently slapped a little friend in the park the day before. Fortunately the mother of the slapped child, who was also in the nursery, had given us her version of the affair. It seemed that the two children caught sight of each other in the park and, waving their hands, ran toward each other. As they met the first mother restrained her child, saying very gently and sweetly, "Say good morning to Anne." Clara withdrew, looking shy and downcast. Over and over the mother repeated her request with gentleness but increasing firmness and concern until finally Clara darted forward, slapped the unoffending Anne and burst into tears. That is an extreme example, and there may have been other factors responsible for her reaction besides the insistence of the parent on the observance of a form. However that may be, small Clara, after months of sedulous attention on the part of her mother, seemed to us no more spontaneous in her expressions of friendliness than many of our children who had not had special training.

A mother, not one of our group, was expressing herself the other day as very critical of parents who

did not give their children social techniques at an
early age. Another mother agreed with her in the
main but said that she often thought the reiterated
reminder of duty, "You forgot to say 'excuse me' or
'good morning,' or 'good-by,' dear," which is so
often necessary, was like repeated blows on a sensitive surface. The first mother assured us that she
had never to insist with her children, that it had
never seemed to be irritating and that they had acquired very readily the few forms she had suggested.
She went on to say how unlike her children were.
The second child is over-interested in his relation
to people. He always makes the tactful remark
which disarms one; is so generous that he has sometimes to be restrained; seems very easy-going and
unemotional. The oldest child has a serious nail-bit-
ing habit, is extremely sensitive, has very high standards and worries if he does not live up to them. He
is painfully conscientious, making a point always of
remembering and confessing his faults. He got out
of bed at two one morning to tell his mother of
some sin of omission or commission which he had
failed to report the night before. He is not the sort
of child who should have standards put up for him
to follow and, knowing that he was a first child, one
wonders how much insistence upon them may have
been responsible for his strained attitudes.

Of course speculation is often fallacious reasoning
but one can fancy also that the younger boy, perhaps
temperamentally less nervous than his brother and
more placid because he had come into the family
after the parents' first ardor for having a perfect
child had somewhat spent itself, had been conditioned in his action patterns by the fact that he could

always win attention and approval by the social response. I do not for a moment believe that this sort of thing is coincidence, and it seems to me an interrogation worth raising in the interest of education.

I have said that we do not make conventions of any sort a part of our curriculum. Perhaps that is not quite true. We do not put up to children any sort of ethical reason for their behavior. We exact from them no expressions of regret. We do not give good manners as a reason for social behavior. In trying to bring out my aversion to undue insistence upon adult standards of courtesy I have probably given the impression that we are almost training in mannerlessness. On the contrary we are trying to inject into children's contacts with each other an element of pleasure or satisfaction in graciousness or friendliness. We are doing this by a vicarious method, it is true. We try invariably to be as meticulous in our own responses to the children as we are to each other, and we set a pattern of a sort. If Donald presents a toy to Marion, the adult always says, "Thank you, Donald," which Marion often repeats, as does Donald also. If one of us interferes with a child's construction, inadvertently gets in his way or takes his seat, we excuse ourselves as we should to another adult. They thus become familiar with habits of social usage, and inevitably take over many details which they use as they do new words with interest and pleasure. How little the actual expressions mean to them is indicated when Matthew says graciously to Kurt, "Thank you, Kurt. You're welcome, Kurt," in a single breath. There must develop some sort of technique for getting on together, as this impulse to share activities and schemes of play grows. We attempt to scale this technique to the affective understanding of the child. Philip takes the cart which Karl has just left. Karl jumps up and down and screams. We say, "Ask Philip for it. He will give it back." Karl controls his crying and says, "Give me my cart, Philip." The adult adds, "Karl was using it, Philip," and if Philip has really understood he hands over the cart. The "thank you" or "Philip is a friendly boy" which the adult adds generally becomes a part of this procedure.

For the most part we confine ourselves to getting responses in terms of friendliness. To strike another child or take away his toys is not friendly. I admit at once that friendliness is an abstraction as truly as gratitude, but it is a single term and directly related to behavior which they understand. "Be a friendly child, Lucy does not like that," soon has quite a definite meaning, both to Lucy who is resentful at Yvonne's rough treatment, and to Yvonne as well.

Very well-meaning approaches are sometimes misunderstood, and here as well the explanation that Colin is a friendly child will reassure Caroline, who will accept his advances and gain in poise thereby. It seems to me that if, as the early years go by, children can get a sense of friendliness in social relationships, they will have an awareness of the real essence of courtesy. Later when they begin to analyze the structure of the social forms within which they are living, the acquisition of accepted techniques will be easy because they are sought. There seems to be a stage in development when children become inter-

ested in the "how" of a process, when they recognize
standards other than their own and delight in the
acquisition of techniques. The whole problem re-
solves itself again into a question of growth. I
believe that if we knew enough about physiological—
biochemical and neural—mechanisms, we could trace
processes of growth which would relate as definitely
to phases of social behavior as development of the
walking pattern does to interest in locomotion.

Practically I believe that the question of what we
shall and what we shall not teach a child at a given
age must be decided by reference again to the standards which we hold. What does education mean to
us? One must choose. We cannot expect a child to
be a clever parrot and a dynamic personality. The
law of diminishing returns applies here as well as in
the field of economics. By this I mean that we cannot
crowd a child with experiences, with precepts or with
information and expect a process of integrated
growth to go on. Confusion, inability to see the relationship between experiences or precepts, will follow. In one of his experiments with chimpanzees
Köhler explained the persistent failure of one of his
subjects to reach a successful method of solving a
problem, though other apes had done it many times
in her presence, by saying that "the isolated parts
of the performance were perceived but never
related." The importance of that process of perceiving relationships cannot be over-emphasized in
educational procedure.

One of the outstanding problems met in a group
of children is that of what may be called "nurse-
maid care," that is, attention to physical needs. The

day nurseries have met it by providing servants—often young, inexperienced girls—who are given training in changing babies' clothing, putting them to bed and giving them their meals. These maids are distinctly of the upper servant type and relieve the teachers or "matrons" of all personal service to the children. The same practice has often been followed in nursery schools and in kindergartens, and when one is dealing with large numbers of children it is difficult to see how the need can be otherwise met except by students in training, in which case the details of physical care are a valuable part of their experience.

We have tried to conduct our experiment with no maid service. In the early years—from fourteen months on—the proportion of a child's time spent in attention to physical needs is so large that he would be in the hands of a maid much of the time. He has little control of his bodily functions; he does not feed himself and changing, undressing and dressing, preparing for meals, for nap and for going home take a large proportion of time. But still more important is the fact that all these processes are of the utmost educational value and that how he learns and what he learns during them is quite as definite and essential a part of our program as the development of his language or his skill in handling the swings or wagons. Furthermore, if he goes into the hands of a maid for any number of different processes, then back to teachers for others, he is shifting from one set of attitudes and modes to others which are as different as the habits of thought and conduct of the two persons, servants and teachers. We believe that education in these early years proceeds more quickly and more successfully if there is maintained a consistency as far as possible in the general attitude of the persons in the environment. Differences in personality there must be of course, and one would never wish to reduce social relationships to the dead level of automatism. But the teachers dealing directly with the children have, as has been said, an intentional point of view about the use of the environment and the reactions of the children to it and to each other, and in general like behavior brings from all the adults a similar response. Also each teacher has the same sort of responsibility. There is no appeal from one to another, and so less likelihood of confusion in the children's minds about their conduct.

The presence of grownup visitors who are unconcerned with the children seems for the most part to be undisturbing, but as soon as the attention of the teacher is absorbed or whenever the visitors begin dealing directly with the children, tension develops. Consequently to keep the staff at a minimum and to manage without maid service is the requirement we have set ourselves.

It may be objected that we are creating an atmosphere that is apart from life and unlike it. We are a laboratory and we must, in order to study and note the response to our environment, keep our conditions controlled in some measure. We are not willing to establish control by limiting the children's activities or by setting up a fixed program.

§3. THE SCHEDULE AND THE RULES: HOW THEY ARE MADE

IN the first chapter I tried to give a sort of confession of faith—a statement of the policies in accordance with which the nursery school staff is planning the environment and the schedule of activities.

The second chapter indicated a seemingly different attitude toward habit training and discussed the place given to social amenities and forms in the nursery school.

A definite and detailed discussion of the teachers' procedure and the daily program seems now to be due. In the usual sense of the term we can hardly be said to have a program. We have no opening school hour. We are at the nursery at a quarter of nine, and there are always a few parents who appear promptly because they must be in their offices by nine o'clock. We wish to avoid the agitation and hurry that are brought early enough into the lives of city-dwelling children, so we do not insist upon promptness. It is expected that parents will bring the children as early as they can, but we do not recommend a speeding-up process. It is not always possible to get through breakfast and toilet at a specified time especially if the baby does not wake early; the walk or ride to school holds possibilities in experience which are valuable, and for these reasons our group assembles gradually. As children grow older the procedure varies, and from four on it is probably possible to require prompt arrival on the part of the *parents*. I mean parents for a child does not begin to get a real feeling for such an abstract virtue as promptness till past this age. Of course children at any age must be brought early enough so that they get the experience of joining the group in the early as well as the later activities.

As the children enter they spontaneously choose materials and begin their play. There is no period for general assembly, no formal greeting even expected of the individual children. Often those who are old enough to express themselves in language enter so full of an announcement or a piece of news or a request that they can hardly hear the teacher's greeting, and we never insist upon a response. As a matter of fact, greetings become the rule rather than the exception, and the habit of the social response becomes established though its omission does not disturb us.

There are a certain number of fixed things that happen at fixed times, which makes at once the framework of a program. Drinks of water are served almost as soon as the children arrive. The older ones may drink standing, but younger ones who must be watched are seated and often they all gather about the tables. Mid-forenoon feeding and usually a music period * break the out-of-door play time. Washing up and a session at dinner have their stated hour. Toilet duties and preparation for nap take place as individuals finish their meal, and since they wake at different hours the group is more or less broken from dinner on until the cab gathers

* See Language and Music, Part III, § 2, C.

them all together for the homeward jaunt. With all our intention to avoid rigidity, the program gathers to itself something more than a framework, not in the way of an inescapable routine but because the adults do govern the choices of children in so many directions. There are in the minds of the adults general policies, and sometimes with and sometimes without definite intention we influence the children's activities subtly by our attitudes even when not overtly by expressing our attitudes in words or actions.

In evaluating any laboratory or school set-up, and in judging the children within it, it is very necessary to take into consideration the fact that the children's reactions are conditioned by the environment in which they are placed. This includes the adults with their attitudes toward the children and their interest in the pursuits carried on, even when the program is not obviously in their control. In other words, a literally "free" environment and literally "free" activities are impossible and undesirable. In fact, freedom in the sense of lack of direction would not be education. A group of little children assembled in an environment rich in constructive possibilities and left on their own resources would probably develop along the lines of the weaknesses of its members, and would surely not gain group continuity. There are always to be found in any group children who have destructive rather than constructive interests, and these are easily communicated. It is obvious that no social organization could be evolved by such immature individuals. Our aim is to avoid dictation, to let the children learn by self-initiated experience and experimenting as long as it is within their control, and whenever possible to allow conditions within the environment to furnish the corrective or stimulating impulse. Above all, we wish to make sure that whenever the opportunity for a choice is offered a child it shall be genuine.

We aim to spend as much of the day as possible out of doors. A child may choose to vary that feature of the program by remaining indoors or leaving the group for indoor pursuits during the morning, but the decision as to whether the occasion is propitious remains with us.

The children choose their own activities. We govern their choice by the fact that we have assembled the materials and also because rearranging apparatus or bringing out new or unfamiliar pieces of play material constitute a suggestion of the most obvious sort. We have also made the rule that certain toys shall remain indoors, and certain others belong on the roof, so that there again we limit choice.

Most of the play material is accessible to the children but there are some pieces both indoors and out which are given on demand or when the adult believes that the time or occasion calls for them. Hammers are kept out of reach because their use has to be supervised closely in the initial stage and kept under observation always. The sandbox cannot be opened by the children and the decision in regard to its use remains with the adults. Indoors certain materials are placed in inaccessible cupboards. This is done in part to make a division in the toys so that the children will not be confronted with too great a variety. Also such things as drawing materials are less likely to be put to unprofitable use if presented only when asked for by a child or when the adults judge the time suitable. Special blocks or other accessory building materials are reserved to be presented in case of individual need.

There is, moreover, the fact to be reckoned with that remedial measures are called for in the action patterns of many children. We are not pursuing a policy of *laissez faire*. It requires on the part of the teachers constant attention and awareness of what is doing and of the habits that are being established to discover whether or not they are beneficent and constructive. We see a child's creative impulse thwarted sometimes because he lacks the physical vigor to use the apparatus in the way he desires to do, or because inhibitions that are stronger than his impulse to act have been set up. We see stable rather than labile processes taking precedence with the result that growth is checked.* That is, we see him following early infantile patterns that have become automatic rather than giving full play to his capacity for taking on new patterns in contact with the environment. The part of the teacher should be an active one here, but it should take the form of a re-formulation of details of program rather than a direct attack upon the patterns themselves.†

So much of a program then we certainly have, and however little it intrudes itself upon the awareness of the children the procedure is intentional, and it is only within that intentional form that what we call "free" activities are carried on.

The ages of our children and the range in age from fourteen to thirty-six months too must be kept

---

* Herrick, C. Judson. *Neurological Foundations of Animal Behavior.* (Henry Holt & Co., 1924.)

† Dewey, John. *Democracy and Education,* Chap. II. (The Macmillan Co., 1916.)

in mind in any discussion concerning their activities
and the wisdom of adult control. Of course such
control might consist only in assembling the children
together at certain times and presenting to them certain types of activities like seating them at tables
for work with crayons or small blocks, gathering
them in a group for quiet attention during music or
giving them balls or materials which inaugurate
group play. The difficulty with little children is not
that they do not accept authority, though the suggestion for this type of controlled program would
have to be repeated for some time before they made
an invariable response, but that they are for the
most part very amenable to regimentation. Even
our smallest babies would probably subscribe after
a fashion to an "order of the day," but after these
years of experimenting we still believe that they will
gain more in fundamental integration if their activities are self-initiated. It is too easy to build up by
adult suggestion patterned responses and a corresponding dependence upon adult initiating. Within
the limits here indicated we leave the children to
choose their own materials and to initiate their own
activities.

As adults in a child's environment we find much
of our effort directed toward keeping ourselves in
the background. We are not concerned with training
children. I realize that the word is often used as
synonymous with educating. I believe that too frequently it means narrowing the scope of education
rather than broadening that of training. Training
means, of course, fitting the individual to deal with
situations which he will meet. There is always implied, however, dealing by a specific method with

specific and limited situations. In life the situations which call for a stereotyped and automatic response are comparatively few. Certain acts which have to do with the maintenance of the body in health, taking food at regular intervals, eliminating body wastes and spending an adequate proportion of time in sleep, should be fixed as habits at an early age. Training is a term applicable to the procedure by which these habituated modes of response are set. Before setting up an extensive training program inquiry should be made as to the biological and social importance of the habits to be gained, their intrinsic value to the child as interests and their weighting against activities which the child himself will initiate, and which will build up no less surely patterns of behavior—modes of response, habits if you like —but habits in a wide, less limited sense.*

Aside from those routine habits which are of biological importance we are not attempting to build up distinct patterns of response to specific situations. Our aim, however, is so to plan the environment and our procedure that a dynamic method of acting will become habitual in the lives of our children. By dynamic method I mean a quality which we recognize and approve when we see it in action; a readiness to get to work on material at hand, persistence of interest, the tendency to investigate and experiment in constructive ways and to sustain and develop this general attitude. When this habit of response is laid down the teacher's part becomes that of directing energies into deeper channels, of providing experiences that will furnish content and information for further activities and that will give

* See Part I, § 1, Planning for Growth.

opportunity for the acquisition of skills and techniques. As far as that means education for the formation of correct habits, it can be stated as our
purpose.

Here again the adult, whether teacher or parent,
must hold herself in control, for the temptation is
strong to impose upon plastic materials standards
of conduct and informational matter beyond the age
level of attainment. When planning an environment
and experiences one must constantly challenge oneself with the question, How can the child use the
particular material or experience in relation to
what he already has, either to enrich an activity
in progress or to further related growth? One
will not teach a child to count whose recognition
of number does not extend beyond two. If his
interest in drawing material still takes the form of
joy in the motor rhythm, it is more logical to give
him opportunity to extend his sweep on a larger
surface and with such different material as chalk and
a blackboard or the linoleum floor than to change
the medium and offer him paints. If a restricted domestic play with dolls absorbs him, one will give
him added facilities for carrying it on as the occasion arises rather than introducing unrelated material, such as a stuffed elephant or a set of furniture
which cannot be used with the dolls. One would not
supplement his drive toward boat building and boat
play with a trip to the circus or zoo.

In some of my examples I have strayed beyond the
realms of our age range where schemes of play are
only beginning. The caution is almost more necessary
with little children for the earnest adult with peda-
gogic tendencies is likely to grow restless in the face

of the fitfulness of a baby's interests, the incessant trotting to and fro with no purpose other than to trot, and the placid and persistent disregard of materials believed to be suitable to its age and capacities.

So far I have emphasized what the adults do not do in our environment. It is true that we place much emphasis on inhibitions on the part of teachers, but our duties do not end there. There are quantities of materials—toys and pieces of apparatus—which must not be misused. It is difficult to use the words "misuse" and "abuse" without seeming to imply that we are practicing a didactic method and restraining our children from original or unconventional use of their toys. In general we say that a toy is misused when it is treated in such a way that the toy itself, other toys or apparatus or a child, may be injured by it. The dolls may be taken up the slide but they may not be thrown down to the floor, from the balcony, steps or chute. Blocks may be used to load carts as well as for building but they also are not to be thrown. The crayons are kept pretty strictly to their appropriate use because if they are carried about away from the tables they are sure to be used to mar the woodwork, and then reproofs and further restrictions are made necessary. The hammers are not used for indiscriminate pounding on furniture or toys, but for driving nails and crushing pebbles. When a child reaches the point in development where he can conceive and carry out a plan of his own he is allowed to do so. For instance when Donald wished to drive nails into the shelves so that the shovels could be hung there it was permitted as a matter of course.

There are situations that arise in the social contacts that cannot be allowed to pursue an uninterrupted course, such as physical attacks. There are materials such as the slides, hammers, springboards and packing boxes, the educational value of which lies in the assurance of a child's safety in the initial experimenting. There are, moreover, moods that must be met, days when children's efforts seem to go out in disintegrating channels, or when activity itself seems at low ebb. The last named situation is the most difficult to the inexperienced teacher. It can be met most successfully not by a direct attack upon the offending or unproductive members of the group but by letting one's imagination work upon the environment. A shift of the slide so that it faces north instead of south, or so that the chute may be approached from the top of a packing case, or the presentation of unfamiliar material, will sometimes make an entire change in the day's proceedings. It is here that the teacher's ingenuity is taxed to the utmost. It is here that her study and understanding of the individual equipment and potentialities of her children are most important. It is situations such as these that make the nursery school a genuine teaching problem, not a question of super-nursemaid care.

There seems to be a rhythmic quality in behavior —a swing that carries an individual along and brings about its own repetition. It is most easily observable in crying, and crying is most readily checked by instituting some rhythmic activity such as swinging, running and singing, or hauling in a wagon. Sometimes the whole group is disaffected and persistent misuse of materials, repeated invasions of the adult features of the environment or determined inactivity takes possession of the entire crew, and they swing from one piece of mischievousness to another in an endless chain. Every teacher will recognize these "poor days" which always make her challenge her method and her wisdom. In meeting them I think our success depends upon our recognition of the rhythm which sets them in operation and keeps them going. If it is the joy of rhythm that maintains them, let us recognize it and its potency and meet it by a counter rhythm. Indoors, music will usually be effective, especially if the children are old enough to have developed a response of their own choosing. When our children are well on toward three, they tend spontaneously to run or skip or gallop in a wide circle about the room in response to the piano, and even the younger ones often join such a procession. A vigorous game of throwing soft bags—hurling them into the air and down from the balcony, seems to set the tide in another direction, and tempts nearly every member of the group. Once initiated by the adult she can withdraw and usually by the time the children's interest has died the earlier rhythm is broken and a different equilibrium is established.* Out of doors we are inclined to set the stage for what we call the processional type of play if we wish to interrupt untoward activities. The springboards, laid in a hollow square or in some sort of pattern that gives opportunity for racing or trundling carts up in one direction and down in another, are an example.

* For a discussion of the effort toward a maintenance of equilibrium as the basis of human behavior, see *Complacency*, R. B. Raup. (The Macmillan Co., 1926.) See also Teachers College Record, May, 1927. See also Köhler, Herrick and Child for further material.

Rhythm seems to play an important part in the growth of action patterns. Whatever one can do with control tends to become rhythmic. Whatever one can do rhythmically one does with satisfaction and ease. We observe many examples which bear out these statements in the activities of our children. As control of the muscles is established the body swings into a sure method, whether it is concerned with the problem of racing down a springboard or prancing about the roof with wagons. A tendency to formalize proceedings develops and holds, because of its rhythmic quality. We see even very young children following a form in their recognition of their places at table and their interest in repeating to-day at a given time an activity that took place at the same time yesterday. We need to learn more about its physiological origin and its significance in growth.

In the use of apparatus on which there is hazard, we supervise with great care the child's initial approach. The child's perceptual pattern in regard to objects and phenomena is very immature. Only after he has had experience with them does he analyze them into their parts with their properties and their effect upon him. When he attempts to go up the steps of the slide for the first time, we are usually close beside him. We either follow him to the balcony or stand near the slide chute and, chanting over and over, "Lie down, turn over," we reverse him and let him push off. There must be constant supervision till a child "knows" that he must hold fast by the rails going upstairs and till the habit of lying down for the descent is fixed. As he grows in power he is allowed more freedom to experiment.

As a matter of fact I do not believe as I once did that fears which are lasting are set up by a fall from the slide. As I have seen the willingness of our children to return at once to the scene of an accident and repeat a performance which had just resulted disastrously I feel sure that when strong reluctances develop they are caused by the attitudes of the adults about them, the agitation, the expressed alarm and emotional sympathy. However, we are unwilling of course to risk personal injury.

In any adult community standards governing conduct gradually arise and are accepted by the group as the conditions of living and working together demand them. We try to bring it to pass that in the nursery the rules that shall be made in regard to the set-up and the children shall grow out of the situation, and hence shall seem logical, if not to the younger members of the group, at least to us.

The children as they come to us are frequently entirely unused to sharing their toys. Often their reaction is to collect and hoard as large a store as possible. Sometimes this tendency is so strong that it swamps a child's play interest. He can do nothing but hoard. Sometimes it involves him in disputes and quarrels with other children, for he feels it incumbent upon him to question their right to toys. Sometimes on the other hand he is reluctant, tends to avoid the toys or to give them up at once if another child approaches. It is obvious that there must be some general understanding about nursery materials. In the first place then, there is the general rule that the toys belong to everyone. There follows as a natural corollary that the toy with which a child is actively playing may remain in his possession as long as he is using it. *These two rules are absolute and are consistently enforced: the toys belong to everyone; possession is established by use. With the rules goes the penalty: the toy is taken from the marauding individual and is restored to its rightful owner.* Also we try always to make our procedure constructive rather than repressive. If a child takes another's toy we add to the warning, "That is John's. He is using it," the suggestion that there are more just like it on the shelf, that he may take it after John has finished with it or that some other toy might be used instead.

Some children seem to have developed a very unfortunate attitude toward toys and play material. Hammers are attractive as weapons of offense, blocks are hurled or dropped on the floor, and the general tendency seems to be to break, kick or throw toys instead of to use them in constructive ways. Even if this attitude is not developed there is always occasional abuse of material. In order to make children realize that there is a correct and an incorrect way of using their toys, a refrain of some sort is introduced: blocks are to build with; hammers are to drive nails with; pebbles belong in the pebble pit, for examples. *If a toy is persistently misused, it is taken away*—and the rule and the penalty come to be well understood: "The hammer or the doll or the trains will go away," the children themselves inquire or assert, as the case may be.

Many of the situations that confront the children have in them an element of real hazard. The danger is increased if they interfere with each other. *There must be no pushing on heights.* Each child must keep to his own turn on the slide. In walking up and down the spring boards there is usually one way up and another way down, and the procession must follow the traffic regulations. "We don't push;" "John's turn and then Lucy's;" "Up this way, down that way," come to be recognized and used by the children as reasons and arguments. *The child who refuses to conform is removed,* and if the tendency to interfere with each other persists the apparatus is placed out of reach or the entire group is diverted to other activities.

The same procedure is used in regard to personal attacks. The problem here is more difficult because of the social immaturity of our children. From our recorded observations has come a justification of the hypothesis that before three years the affective life is largely on the sensory level; children are in a sort of twilight zone as far as real emotions are concerned. Memory of injury, sympathy, contrition, emerge and fade out. An awareness of others and a genuine concern for them probably come first but do not hold their places after their first manifestation. What we call sympathy or pity does appear. That is, children begin to seem able to understand the behavior of another child in the light of their own similar experiences. Even when this is true there are many reversions to the earlier response and a child will treat his mates as he treats the blocks and tables. Ansel surprised us one morning by running up with soothing cries and trying to help a fallen baby to his feet. The tones of his voice, the accompanying gestures and the expression on his face indicated genuine concern. It was a short time later on the same morning that Ansel gayly bowled over with a sweep of his arm a small child who was in his path, and went on his way with his characteristic hearty roar of laughter. The two patterns are to be noted almost simultaneously in action. One is almost as truly a motor response as pushing down a tower of blocks to hear the noise. The other might probably be called a more intellectual process, but at this age is as transitory as is grief or objection. There is scarcely any recall. The experience passes, leaving little residue which can modify a subsequent activity. We note how rare it is for a baby to show resentment either toward an adult who has disciplined him or another child who has attacked him. The reason lies in the stage of growth that has been reached, and we try to keep that in mind in establishing the rules of nursery conduct that are necessary to living together.

Up to a certain point we do not interfere with personal encounters. We encourage the puppy-like wrestling that sometimes appears, and we urge a timid child on to resist attacks or to return assaults upon his property. We try, however, to introduce a play attitude toward it. The interjection of humor into our dealings with children will get over difficulties which all our arts and wiles, our philosophy and our authoritative ukases upon them will not affect. Craig seizes Philip's hat. Hats are most precious and inviolate. Philip looks to the adult and wails. If we say, "Catch Craig, Philip. Run, run as fast as you can; he'll give you your hat," both children will laugh, and since running away at this age usually means running into a corner, Philip soon overtakes Craig who, nine times out of ten, hands over the hat with a chuckle.

Certain kinds of attacks are difficult to correct. Charles had a deep-seated habit of biting if he wished to repulse another child or if another threatened him or his possessions. The transitoriness of the affective experience was illustrated by the fact that the baby most frequently bitten did not learn to avoid contacts with Charles. At 18 months nothing seemed effective as a deterrent. At two years a sharp sudden call to him would stop him in the act. We explained to him that the baby was not to be eaten, whereupon Charles with an expression of understanding and a nod of the head inquired, "Eat apple sauce?" The question, "Do you want *him* to bite *you?*" usually brings the response of withdrawal and a shake of the head. We frequently use this method to make a child realize sharply the effect of an unfriendly approach. He pushes another child over. We push against him enough for him to feel it and ask, "Do you like it?" He does not of course, and we assure him that "Max doesn't like it either."

One must bear in mind in dealing with such responses of children to each other as slapping, scratching, pulling hair and pushing that they are not anti-social or unfriendly in their impulse. They are generally inspired by social interest together with lack of social technique. However, they do not carry an impression of friendliness with them to the victim, and we have to make his enjoyment or his resentment of them the test. Personal assault produces a more violent reaction than an equal injury incurred from a fall or bump. There is little resentment shown toward the attacking child and no hangover resulting from repeated attacks except in rare cases. Yvonne, who was inclined to be very disci-

plinary toward adults, would cease her crying to fall
upon us if we attempted to exclude Kurt from the
group as a penalty for his attack upon her. It was
not that Kurt himself was a favorite, for it was her
general principle that it was best to administer cor-
poral punishment upon grownups whenever they
undertook to discipline children. She would accept
an explanation for our actions and retire from her
labors, showing no animus toward anyone. In her
case and in most others a wholly external pattern
had been adopted, having little to do with real affectivity.

The general suggestion of friendliness represents
the positive attitude in the restrictions against personal attacks which we may cite as our fifth rule.
"Lucy is a friendly child. She won't hurt Karl,"
usually has the desired effect upon both—Lucy, bent
upon discipline and Karl who considered himself
threatened with annihilation. *The penalty for any
behavior which is opposed to the social good is exclusion from the group,* and this also comes to be
understood.

An enumeration of laws and penalties for in-
fringement sounds formidable. Our procedure is like
that in a family, informal and as casual as possible.
We try to substitute a desirable for an undesirable
activity whenever possible, and to divert the attention of a child from an idle unproductive pursuit to
a profitable one instead of bringing sharply into
focus the forbidden. We do not call the children
"naughty" or "bad" and, unless we find that a child
needs to be confronted in a poignant way with the
reality of a situation, we call his attention rather
to other possibilities than to the illicit activity that

he has chosen. We follow our remark, "We don't do so and so," by "You may take this or do that." If a child has strong interests and has been given an outlet for them, mischief *per se* will not hold him long in a world so suited to his needs.

It must be remembered that the physical, social and economic environment which surrounds children is administered by beings whose background, interests and standards of conduct are totally foreign to those of children. They succumb to adult demands and take on adult standards because they are plastic material, but, also because of this plasticity, they escape from control and grieve or shock their guardians by "going native" when it is least expected. The nursery school is an attempt to scale civilization down to the child level in its behavior demands and to open up wider opportunities for active exploration than an adult world can afford.

PART II

OUR PLANNING OF THE ENVIRONMENT

§ 1. The Physical Environment—Activities and Materials

§ 2. The Social Environment—Other Children and Adults

§ 3. Language and Rhythm

    A. OUR OBSERVATION OF LANGUAGE FORMS

    B. OUR PROCEDURE

§ 1. THE PHYSICAL ENVIRONMENT— ACTIVITIES AND MATERIALS

I SPOKE in the Introduction of the task of providing a "suitable" environment for nursery school children. In this chapter I shall try to define what I mean by the word and how we have tried to meet its requirements.

In the terms of our experiment suitable must mean favorable for growth. An environment might be planned with specific phases of growth in mind. It would then vary as the aims of the group responsible for it varied. It might, of course, mean favorable for training in certain special abilities, favorable for gaining facility in language, favorable for developing readiness in rhythmic response, favorable for overcoming malnutrition or untoward tendencies which might lead to serious disfunctioning. We are however quite specifically not establishing a system of training, though studies in the acquisition of different abilities and in the development of individual differences might well result from our researches. Our environment must be one in which the processes of growth go on fully and at an adequate rate. By growth I do not mean increase in bulk alone but increase in power and control and in maturation. Development means to us all the progress toward maturity. The moment we begin to look at it from this point of view, we see the importance of giving each phase of development an opportunity to mature. We can trace in many adults immaturities in gait, in attitude toward this or that situation, in taste or what not. The infantile crops up in even the normal adult sometimes and he shows that some experience or lack of it has interfered with the growth process.

Our environment then, as far as concerns the material equipment and the physical arrangements, is based upon what we know of growing children. Practically we make our decisions regarding equipment upon the observation of the behavior of small children. We see them putting forth all the energy they can summon. We observe them pushing, rolling, hauling, pulling; we watch them running, climbing, balancing and, given unimpeded space and suitable accessory material, we see them gaining balance and control of their bodies through the exercise of the big muscles of trunk and chest and of the arm-shoulder and the leg-pelvis girdles. We see them touching, handling, manipulating, looking, listening, feeling, tasting or feeling with the mouth. We see them applying this method not only to their external environment but also to their own bodies, in the process of which they learn to use their hands and fingers with nicety. They include in their investigations the bodies and possessions of their associates, at first in a purely objective fashion but from a very early age with interest and, given opportunity, we can see their progress from their first assaults to a realization of a sort of social relationship with other children.

In addition to the needs of growth which can be met in the environment, there is the necessity of forming certain habits which are of biological importance and of making automatic a child's re-

sponse to items of his daily program such as the
elimination of bodily wastes, taking a proper amount
of rest and sleep, and acquiring taste and appetite
for a variety of wholesome foods. The way our program meets these needs has been discussed in the
second chapter of Part I, Habits and Conventions.

Concluding certain physiological needs from the
observation of behavior, nursery schools have tried
to meet these needs in their equipment. This does
not mean that we can find identical apparatus and
play material wherever we find nursery school children. The adults responsible for the set-up interpret
children's needs in varying fashion. The more literal
minded may provide materials that reproduce literally types of activity sought by the children,—
boards on rockers because they roll, beads and peg-
boards because they investigate small objects. The
academically inclined may attempt to seize the experimenting impulse as a training opportunity and,
looking forward to a future when certain performances will be demanded, seek to prepare in advance
and specifically for it. This group will probably
stress self-help and manners, correct technique at
table, counting and the use of numbers, and a pre-
reading program.

Out of doors and in, we have in the first place,
space. We believe that it is more necessary for the
runabout baby than for the older child who is absorbed in more concentrated play with materials.
Have you thought what it would be like suddenly
to acquire levitation: to find that you could propel
yourself through space, not soaring perhaps but
just freely floating without the contact of feet
against pavements and without the slow pace con-

sequent upon that method? You might find that at
first you would not be able to gauge the distance
above an obstacle that you must allow for—or that
you could manage your corners and street crossings
well if you were alone but that you needed to acquire
more skill when you had companions or were meeting vehicles. Would you not wake eager to make
sure that your new-found power was with you?
Would you not try all sorts of tricks to increase
speed and accuracy, and would you not be so filled
with the joy and interest in your skill and the power
it made possible to you that the day would hardly
be long enough for you to practice it? Reading,
study, the movies and social events would lose their
charm till your body was sure of this facility. I believe the acquisition of locomotion brings a comparable experience into the life of a child. He has
not of course a background which enables him to
analyze either his process in acquiring the art of
locomotion or the possibilities which the new power
has opened up to him. However, everyone who has
watched babies from fourteen to eighteen or twenty
months, has noted their absorbed and incessant
practice of the new accomplishment. They have a
wide stance and their balance of control is poorly
developed, so space is a prime requisite—indoors
and out.

To us the play activity of children is a dynamic
process, stimulating growth and the integration of
the entire organism as no system of training however skillfully devised could do. Therefore in our
choice of equipment we have tried to provide materials which would not only develop the bodies of
children, but which would also have genuine play

content and would follow the lines of genuine play interests. That is, in providing wagons and kiddy kars, pails and shovels, springboards, seesaws and swings, slides, steps and packing boxes, blocks, dolls, crayons and clay, we are thinking of their play use as well as of the effect of exercise with them upon muscular development. We mean for the most part to avoid what might be called static material. By static material I mean things that have a simple and limited use. An example would be a set of blocks cut so they could make only one sort of construction. We try on the contrary to choose things that have a variety of uses or the possibility of progressive use. The blocks are the most striking illustrations. The smallest nursery children who play with them at all carry them about,—handling, manipulating, then shifting from one place to another,—stacking them in a mass without form or design or apparent purpose other than that of putting out energy. From this use to the construction of an elaborate design or a building which is named and with which the children play, stretches a period of months at least, during which various action patterns are maturing. Much of the material is actually novel to the children. Its form, or structure,* and its other properties are unknown and must be made a part of their experience. At first it means nothing in terms of the dynamic relationship between "that" and "me." They see things and persons as undifferentiated wholes and use them in an objective fashion which takes little account of cause and effect. They push the swing and are unprepared for the resulting

* *Psychologies of 1925.* Chap. VI, Kurt Koffka; Chaps. VII and VIII, Wolfgang Köhler. (Clark University, 1926.)

blow; they do not place their blocks evenly and are unaware that they cannot stand securely on the tottering pile; they stride the kiddy kars but are very likely to walk, carrying them between their legs instead of sitting upon them. A block conveys one impression when it is a block-on-the-floor and quite another when it is a block-in-a-pile which is the construction of another child. Awareness of differences, discrimination, interest and initiative in choosing and using the material, the feel of the pattern possibilities, whether as design or construction, are stages through which we believe a child passes at his own individual rate. The stage of the true construction—a building designed to serve an end and used after it is completed—comes later, often after he has left our group.

Blocks are, as has been said, unusually simple and clear examples of educational material, but in all the types of playthings and apparatus mentioned there can be traced the growth processes involved in their use. The use of the swing seems more limited. If, however, the growth and development of the pattern is followed it is found that a great elaboration of the first simple method takes place. The completed pattern shows the ability to use the apparatus and to control the body in a variety of ways, to sit and propel oneself, to stand and pump alone or with another child, to twist and spin and to approach near enough to push a child in the swing without allowing it to hit one on the rebound. When the finished product is compared with the performance of a small child to whom none of the qualities is known and who has continually to be protected from disaster, it can be seen that here again is ma-

Varied uses of blocks.

A train going under a bridge.

Wagon loading.

*Placing with exactness and walking upon the
line laid.*

*Experimenting with the swing at twenty-one
and thirty-three months.*

terial which can be used more or less efficiently and elaborately as the child is more or less matured in physical control, and more or less captured by the rhythmic and balancing possibilities of the apparatus. Like most dynamic material there can be traced through an analytic study of its use marked individual differences.

In choosing materials we avoid those that prove to require in their use adult supervision beyond what is needed to safeguard a child's initiation to them. Materials which are too heavy or cumbersome for the children to manage or which must be used with a degree of caution beyond their powers, we discard. An example of such toys is a large box which the children wished to load upon one of their express wagons. It was too bulky and heavy for them to lift or to mount safely. Another example of unsuitable material was a small shovel which was hinged and equipped with a sharp prong so that it could be tipped and become a hoe and pick. The adjustment, with a ring which slipped down over the pick when the shovel was in use, was too difficult for most of our children, the sharp instrument served as a dangerous weapon and we found no especially suitable and legitimate use for it in our environment. Hammers might fall into the same category except that driving nails and crushing small pebbles are profitable occupations and therefore we undertake to carry on a period of supervision till a child can be trusted with the tool.*

Besides the importance of gaining an integrated use of the muscular equipment a return to our study of children's behavior shows us that they need op-

* Part III, § 2, A, Hammers.

portunity for sense experiences. We might devise a graded series of weights, of color cards and of other selected training material which could be presented at intervals to the children, and in that way trace the process of learning under controlled conditions. We use, however, the same criterion here that we did in the choice of the other equipment. We present the children with a situation that holds in it inherent play possibilities and we encourage them to deal with it in their own way. It is our belief that this method leads to the development of a ready initiative and an inquiring experimental attitude toward the environment which are more fruitful than the degree of skill which might be attained by deliberate training. We do not believe that sense experiences should be given by training, but by providing materials the use of which leads to sense discrimination because again we are convinced that with self-initiated use comes power. Our children play with things of different weights and sizes: boxes, blocks, pails empty and pails filled with sand; with things of different colors: crayons, clothing, dolls, covers, blocks; with things of different textures and consistencies, and as they use these materials they are becoming aware of differences and likenesses, of qualities and relationships which will lead to sensory acuity. They then perceive the qualities in their relation to the phenomena in which they are seen, not as isolated sensations.

Language discrimination may not go along at an equal rate. A child will often choose the superior kiddy kar long before he can tell his reasons. Our records show that a child can often match colors before he can name them correctly. Color as an affect is more important in growth than color as a name, and it may be that the insistence upon naming qualities delays rather than hastens on the process of discrimination. In an atmosphere where children are encouraged to experiment with language as well as with other materials, the interest in naming seems to appear spontaneously however, and most nursery children name accurately and with interest the colors they are using before they leave us.*

Another consideration governing our choice of equipment is that of permanent or progressive use. Our age range is wide, though less so than in many nursery groups. Our equipment is unsatisfactory if it fails to meet the needs of our children as they progress in age. Little children come to us with a very limited experience. When the dramatic element enters into their play it represents an attempt at reproducing details of their experience. The block pushed over the floor may be a boat or train. The play is brief and undertaken largely for the motor and sensory enjoyment of the push across the floor, generally to a vocal accompaniment. There is at first no attempt at even an approach to representative form in the construction. A single block will serve the purpose and the "choo choo" sound may be the only train noise that is given. Gradually more qualities emerge and this mass which is a train shows further details which are reproduced. The bell and whistle sounds, the noise of escaping steam, smoke stacks, sand domes and then wheels are added, and after a time—though usually not before five years—a railway system with tracks, station, turn table and signals develops. The same is true of

* See Part III, § 2, A, Color.

the domestic play that so absorbs little children. Dolls are used, at first usually to put to bed but gradually the entire cycle of personal care which the baby has experienced so intimately and for so many months is reproduced in play. Maternal solicitude and discipline are represented with real histrionic skill and all the domestic processes from laundry to dressmaking are carried on.

The child sees additional possibilities in an environment of materials which he can adapt to his purposes, but his constructive attack upon it depends first upon the sort of growth patterns that are developing and second upon whether life is bringing him experiences which stimulate his play purposes. The baby will play out all that he has of content and will elaborate his play as his content becomes organized. The importance of educational principles such as these must be recognized in planning a nursery school environment.

In presenting a list of the play materials used in our school it must not be understood that it is done with the recommendation that identical equipment should be used in all schools. The school in the large city has to invent opportunities which the country or small town school can find present in its environment. Experience with turf and growing things brings something to a child that can not be imitated in a brick and mortar environment. An urban situation must be faced as an urban situation and attacked and developed for what it is worth, not as a poor substitute for the country. The country environment must be treated in the same way. City life offers vital experiences to a child which he cannot get in the country, and our task is to provide an environment in which the child's developing needs are met, whether it be under green trees or in a city back yard.

We have come to believe that the city roof playground is preferable to the park or yard. It can usually be placed so that it receives sun for most of the day and consequently the snow and wet clear from it rapidly. The expanse of sky, the clouds, the smoke, the occasional sparrows and the building and repair operations carried on nearby are of vital interest to the children. The noise and confusion that continually assault us may well dull city-bred ears to fine auditory discrimination and especially to the enjoyment of listening and identifying what we hear. The sounds that come from the streets and in some neighborhoods from the river or harbor are clearer and more easily recognizable from the roof than they are from a lower level, and bring to children the opportunity for auditory experience.

Pictures of the indoor play room and the roof space will show better than a description the general set-up of the nursery school.

PLAY EQUIPMENT *

Roof:

Slide, 5 feet high, chute 10 feet long—set in pebble pit.
Four low swings, all four corners of seats pierced for ropes
    which are bound together about two feet above seats.
    This is more secure than the ordinary single rope swing
    with a narrow seat.

* See Bulletin VIII, Catalogue of Play Equipment. (Bureau of Educational Experiments.)
  See Bulletin XI, A Nursery School Experiment. (Bureau of Educational Experiments.)

Two double planks, about 12 feet long, 17 inches wide, of fitted tongue and groove boards. These are set up as inclines of varying steepness, up and down which the children may walk, ride kiddy kars, haul wagons or leap as on a springboard. Bridging two packing cases, they afford opportunity for developing confidence and balance on heights. See photographs.

Seesaw planks, 12 feet long, 1 foot wide, which can be set at different heights according to the age and skill of the children.

Two sawhorses, 20 inches high, used as supports for planks or seesaw or to raise the end of slide chute or occasionally in construction and dramatic play.

Two large packing cases, 23½″ x 42½″ x 29½″, and 48″ x 38″ x 30″, the latter being slatted at each end which facilitates climbing and converts the box into a "cage" when turned upside down.

Set of three steps, 18 inches high, top step 9 inches wide, others 7 inches wide, which are moved about to facilitate climbing on packing cases, walls, etc.

Two sandboxes—one of cement, 5¾′ x 4′, with sloping wooden top, waterproof canvassed, which hooks back against a wall; one of wood, also with canvas covered top, 7⅔′ x 3⅔′ x 9½″, cover fitted with castors and with three sides only, so that it may be rolled off forming in this position a convenient surface for sand play.

Skylight peak, 27 inches high, enclosed by a seat 15 inches high which can be lifted off skylight and used by itself when desired.

Work bench—for adult use.

Four dozen hollow yard blocks (closed boxes) 4″ x 10″ x 10″, weight three pounds.

These blocks were devised by Caroline Pratt and in larger sizes are used in the City and Country School. They are described in the *Catalogue of Play Equipment,* Bulletin VIII, published by the Bureau of Educational Experiments. We have them in only one size.

"There must be no pushing on heights."

On the springboard.

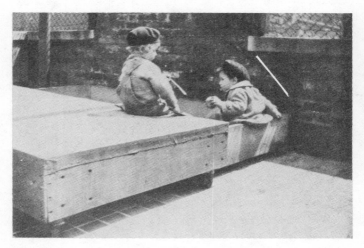

Illustration of the two kinds of sand boxes.

scaled down for the nursery children. They can usually be obtained from a packing box factory, which will furnish boxes of any size desired.

Four dozen spruce blocks, $8\frac{1}{2}'' \times 5\frac{1}{4}'' \times 3\frac{3}{8}''$ (exact size depending on obtainable ready-cut lumber) called "paving blocks" because of their resemblance to those used in street paving—weight about $2\frac{1}{2}$ pounds each.

Boards, $4' \times 7\frac{1}{2}'' \times \frac{3}{4}''$, light enough for the children to load into wagons and to use for construction purposes.

Pails with bails, made of heavy tin.

Perforated sink shovels, used in the sand chiefly; small shovels; wooden spoons.

Small tin pans for sand play.

Kiddy kars of two sizes, largest 10 inches high, lowest 9 inches.

Large and small express wagons, one rubber tired, the others with metal-rimmed wheels.

Two "trailer" carts with hooks on the handle so they may be easily attached to kiddy kars or other wagons.

Toy wheelbarrows.

Brooms.

Coal shovels and snow shovels, both used in the snow.

Rubber balls, various sizes.

Basketball.

Hammers, full size, light weight.

Nails—one-inch wire with large head.

When the children begin to use hammers and nails, we set the nails for them with points just piercing the top of our yard blocks which are closed boxes, thus making it possible for even the younger children really to drive them in. Later we set the points just into the wood. Still later the children learn to set their own nails.

Indoors:

Indoor slide, reached by a flight of eight rather steep open steps with handrails, a balcony of two levels providing extra room and height at top, and chute 12 feet long, end resting on a gym mat. The lower balcony is roughly square, 6½' x 6½', and is 5 feet 5 inches from the floor. The upper is about 6' 3" x 2' 3", and is raised about 11 inches above the other, making a high step to climb from one to the other. The stairway measures 6 feet 7 inches, and has a light pipe railing which goes through wooden slots at the top so that the steps can be hooked up out of the way when supervision is impossible.* The treads are 9½ inches apart.

Small folding tables with linoleum covered tops to provide a durable and easily cleaned surface. These tables are particularly durable and stable.

Small chairs.

We have not considered it necessary to be especially exact in fitting our tables and chairs to the height of our children, which sounds like rank heresy and neglect. When we equipped the nursery for our first group we did so, giving each child a chair in which he could sit with his feet flat upon the floor, with his buttocks well back. His table was just high enough so that as he sat in this position his forearm with elbow flexed rested easily upon it. As the groups have varied since then we have tried to give the appropriate chair and table to each child but we have not followed our early standards. Our children spend a minimum of time at their tables— only while they are eating and the short periods when they are using crayons and paper. The group varies from year to year so much that if we fitted chairs and tables to the fourteen months old children they might the next year be quite unsuitable for any child in the group since we keep the children till they are three years old.

Kegs—painted nail kegs, 14½ inches high, heads 1 foot in

---

* See Bulletin VIII. Catalogue of Play Equipment. (Bureau of Educational Experiments.)

The photo was taken before the present arrangement was made.

diameter, both heads set in; used to roll about on floor, or to roll on and over, astride or head first, and to stand, climb and walk upon.

Rubber balls, various sizes.

Three two-wheeled carts, 15" x 8", converted from gayly painted boxes of which there are eight, used for bedding dolls, to hold cubes or to drag about.

Painted wooden covers for boxes and carts.

Blocks—City and Country School unpainted wooden bricks, half bricks and multiples of that size up to three feet in length, triangles of two sizes and turned pillars.

Nine dozen paving blocks, described above.

Montessori Pink Tower and Brown Stair Blocks.

Milton Bradley 1-inch cubes in primary colors, pierced for stringing.

Interlocking blocks, 5" x 2" x 1½", head at one end, notch at the other so that they may be linked together into "trains" and pushed or pulled about.

Nested boxes, largest about 11½" x 9½" x 6½".

Montessori Cylinders—two sets, No. 1 and No. 2.

Wooden jointed dolls, 11½ inches, Schoenhut.

Covers about 16" x 14" of various colors and textiles, used with dolls or flatirons—more easily manipulated by small children than dolls' clothes.

There have been many attempts to devise dolls' clothing which could be used by very young children. An admirable garment is made kimono style with a wide neck into which an elastic is fastened. This can be stretched over the doll's head and is so simple that the arms can easily be thrust into the wide sleeves. Children below three seem to be more satisfied with such covers as we provide and get such a variety of uses from them that we no longer offer clothing. A favorite play is spreading the covers out on the floor and putting the dolls into them. The technique of holding a cover by the corners and flipping it out so that it will lie smoothly on the floor is acquired only after quite a practice period.

Children keep at it till they have acquired proficiency in it—and longer because that particular arrangement is used in their play with dolls and with irons. The older children ask for safety pins and make "suits" or sleeping bags for the dolls.

Doll's bedstead with mattress and pillows.

Flatirons—sad iron variety.

Plastilene.

Manila drawing paper and large size octagonal crayons—Milton Bradley.

Four Swiss tuned bells, key of E flat.

These can be ordered from R. H. Mayland, 54 Willoughby Avenue, Brooklyn. The price is five dollars for each bell.

Musical bells, set at either end of a handle, dumb-bell fashion.

Scuffers—unit blocks with handles, covered with sandpaper.

Bags 10" x 14", made of stout cloth, filled with paper. These may be thrown about or at one another by the children without fear of injury, and are used as a substitute for the block-throwing impulse which breaks out from time to time.

There are also in the play room a piano and a table and chairs for adult use.

§ 2. THE SOCIAL ENVIRONMENT— OTHER CHILDREN AND ADULTS

THE social environment is as important as the physical and, whether we will or not, we are faced with the necessity for dealing with it when we put children in a group for a large part of their waking hours. Before discussing the social aspect of the environment some classification of terms seems necessary. "Social" as applied to adult human beings and their relationships to each other means something fairly definite. Does it carry with it the same connotations when used about children and their group associations?

The Century dictionary gives gregarious and sociable—delighting in association with one's fellows —as synonymous with social. I think in our use of the word "social" there is usually implied a more positive sharing in common activities than in either of the other words. The responsiveness of very young children to the presence and to the advances of their kind has seemed to me more truly gregarious than social. To pursue the dictionary a little further—the word is used in zoölogy to refer to such insects as ants, bees and wasps and to certain birds. As we know, these creatures are characterized by their formal association in the construction of their dwelling places and the details of their communal life. I believe that most persons are thinking of the association of children in coöperative undertakings when they speak of "social" play. We should have in mind the distinction between "social" as indicating a normal outgoing tendency to respond to the presence of one's fellows, and "social" in its evolved form—the capacity of children to join together in working out a common problem.* In the first instance there is no *form*. There is a general diffuse awareness of others, influencing the affective tone— the tide of energy—the drive without which the organism ceases to function above the lower animal level. If growth progresses normally there emerge gradually from the gregarious stage the beginnings of coöperative play, and a real social technique develops.

Growth is not like a ride in the subway. The aim is not alone to get there. Growth is a dynamic process and in its phases builds something into the organism. We are too prone to look forward to the mature stage and to attempt to hurry over or omit steps toward it. We all recognize that there are periods of wave-like progress—when an accession of power or ability along one line is matched by a slower rate of progress along another. The fact of the alternative growth of parts of the body and that of variations in height and weight which are possibly seasonal can be paralleled in the field of motor, language and "social" abilities.†

It used to be quite generally conceded that a more or less sequestered life was indicated for babies. One of the chief objections to the nursery school

---

* Pratt, Caroline. "Collective Formulations in Curricula." *Progressive Education,* 1925. Vol. II, No. 4.

† Pratt, Caroline and Stanton, Jessie. *Before Books.* (Adelphi Co., 1926.)

Godin, Paul. *Growth During School Age.* (The Gorham Press, 1920.)

and one most frequently voiced was based on the belief that the young child is and should remain an individualist. It was suggested also that the school situation would prove too stimulating and that children could not, at nursery age, make the concessions and adaptations necessary in group play and the common use of material.

All those convictions were undoubtedly based on actual growth stages, and in introducing very little children into a group, especially one in which there is a wide age range, we run a real danger unless we safeguard them against close contacts.

Children are too adaptable. They conform so readily to almost any condition that is presented to them that its effect upon development is not easily observable. This is especially true when the affective impulse is as strongly engaged as it is in the social situation. Children respond to advances from their kind. They often accept attention and dictation from older children as they do not, without protest, from adults. It is easy to swing the weight of their interest, their activity and their investigations into channels in which contact with each other takes precedence of any other sort of play. The attitude of guardian or mentor is as devastating as that of infant and inferior, so older children as well as babies must be protected from a program that makes social demands upon them beyond their capacity for making that experience an integrated part of their maturing powers.

The mechanisms for dealing profitably with the intricacies of social intercourse mature later than those which make possible profitable handling of the physical environment. Practically this demands from the teacher that she make provision in space and staff so that individual play and very loosely organized group play can be carried on without the application of obvious pressure or coercion. With this provision and with an environment that opens up to children rich opportunities for adventure and experiment, their individual needs can be served.

In many nursery schools there is a wide age range, and the family is the model. Older and younger children are brought into contact with the expressed intention of reproducing the relationship found among older and younger brothers and sisters.*

If one has any intimate conversation with adults about the conflicts and difficulties in adjustment that have beset them in their growing years, one is almost sure to hear some of the blocks to progress ascribed to the place in the family which the individual held. "I was an only child and missed out entirely in the discipline which I should have gained in contact with other children" is of course one explanation. Others are given with equal conviction and fervor. "I was the youngest of ten—and never knew what a self-initiated activity was till I grew up and left home." "I was the oldest and always had to give up all my schemes and toys and later my free time because the younger children interfered or I had to take care of them." "The middle child has never had the sympathy she deserves. She walks in no man's land. She wears made-over clothes as much as the baby. She has all the difficulties and none of the advantages of the oldest and no one realizes

* Flügel, J. C. *The Psycho-Analytic Study of the Family.* (International Psycho-Analytic Press, 1921.)

it"—and so it goes. If it were our intention that the nursery school should replace the family we should probably follow its age distribution, but since we are offering to the children a situation which supplements rather than supplants the family we have decided to reproduce as little as possible of that particular complicating element of family life.

We have assumed that the individual tendencies of young children mark a level appropriate to their development, and we have put the emphasis upon protecting them from interference with each other rather than upon encouraging social contacts. We are faced with a communal life of a sort, however, and with a social situation which is further complicated by the fact that children seem to be strongly attracted to their kind. The first response given by a baby to the presence of children is a general elation manifested by shouts and laughter at the sight of the group. There is often no effort on the part of our youngest babies to approach the others or to join in their play activities. We attempt to make possible the prolongation of this period as long as it will naturally last. This is another reason why we have insisted upon providing ample play space indoors and out, so that it is possible to segregate a child or several children from the others.

Group life in the nursery school is as much a part of our intentional procedure as is the strictly physical equipment. Our plan takes cognizance of the fact that the children's responses will be stimulated by each other, that the *things* which form the material environment will have meaning as they are seen in use, and that a group, even as flexibly organized as the nursery and as readily separable into independent units yet has a coherence that affects each member to some extent.

Herrick * says in a discussion of the sense organs that ". . . all stimuli in order to be effective must . . . bear some relation to the mode of life of the species." I believe that this is true all along the educational process and that it should be borne in mind especially in the responses we expect from very young children to the social situation.

It is essential to our plan that the social organization should be so fluid that escape may be easy for any individual at any time. There should be a group but no insistence upon organized or consistent response to it from its members. It must be recognized that children have an affective impulse for all sorts of social activities long before they are mature enough really to take a share in them. It is the meretricious imitation of adult social relationships that we are trying to avoid.

We think of the social situation and the social experiences that the environment opens up to children much as we think of the physical situation and experiences. There are many pieces of material that are not suitable for the use of the child of eighteen months, for instance, if one means by use the matured, appropriate use for which it was intended. Let us take for example two such different things as hammers and swings. The child of fourteen months will seek hammers if he sees them in use, and whatever he does with them is adding to his quota of sensori-motor experiences, though he cannot raise

* Herrick, C. Judson. *Neurological Foundations of Animal Behavior.* (Henry Holt & Co., 1924.)

a hammer in the approved position for pounding. On the other hand, his physical and his perceptual powers are so immature that his own unsupervised investigation of the swing is not profitable for him. He will, therefore, not be allowed freely to pursue the disastrous line of his own impulses, but will be introduced to the swing by the adult until he has at least enough control of his own body to manage himself alone on a level. Even then he will be protected from injury as far as possible.

The social situation is more complicated than the physical. Our effort is to follow the growth stages in the demands made on the child for participation in social activities, to give opportunity for group play in which he can take his part, to protect him from the sort of supervisory attention that older children attempt with their juniors, and furthermore to make sure that the ability to control and modify the physical environment takes precedence of the attempt to control and modify the social environment. Our aim is that each child shall bring a constructive contribution to the social situation, not merely persuasiveness or the ability to dominate by conversation.

An appreciation of differences in human beings, differences not in external appearance but in their modes of behavior response to given situations, which involve subtle temperamental variations, is more difficult than the appreciation of responses to be expected from such materials as blocks, wagons and swings. I have said on a preceding page that the child's ability at analyzing the objects or situations which he perceives as wholes is immature. He apprehends objects and phenomena with their qualities, their meanings, *in relation to the situation in which they are found.** He sees his blocks, for example, as forms, structures, that have a certain relationship to each other and to the floor but he does not at first see them as things on which he can climb to get something out of reach. He may use a stool or chair for this purpose and still fail to see the block as a stool. A child is regarded as "too young" to use crayons but that does not mean that he has not physical strength enough to mark with them. He perceives them as things which may be sucked or bitten, fingered, dropped and picked up, but does not perceive them and what they can do in relation to the sheet of paper that accompanies them. The fact that he does not hold the paper down when he makes his earliest effort to mark but moves crayon and paper together further illustrates the immaturity of his approach. If this is true in regard to his material environment, how much more is it so in regard to the human and social environment the structure of which is so much more complex.

In discussing the fitness of a child for a share in social life with its complexities, the question of his language must enter in. The details of language development, its acquisition, its use and its relation to other phases of growth will be discussed in the following chapter. In speaking here of language in connection with the social demands made upon children, I am referring to language as a tool for social

* Koffka, Kurt. *Growth of the Mind.* (Harcourt, Brace & Co., 1925.)
  Köhler, Wolfgang. *Mentality of Apes.* (Harcourt, Brace & Co., 1925.)
  Psychologies of 1925. Chap. VI, Kurt Koffka; Chaps. VII and VIII, Wolfgang Köhler. (Clark University, 1926.)

communication.* If one is interested in the speech of little children, one recognizes at once that very little of it in the early stages is directed toward another person. There are individual differences here and occasional marked exceptions, but even the most precocious child does not usually practice his art of conversation with his peers, and attempts at a real interchange of thought are feeble. This means that another tool necessary for a social technique is lacking.

We assume that the most significant activities for our children are those which have to do with motor and sensory growth and maturation. Therefore the general tendency of the nursery school environment should be to open up avenues for physical investigation, to make possible experimentation in the use of limbs and body and to turn children to a free attack upon play materials. Because, however, we are dealing with children in a group and because we value group association as an essential factor in the educational process, we must plan to introduce them gradually to the social life, the privileges and restrictions of which they share.

It is quite evident that there are individual differences in children's reactions to persons and to materials. At fourteen months, as our records show, one child will seem to get the impulse to activity from his contacts with persons, and another largely from the things about him. We are convinced that this is derived as much from influences in early environment as from a native quality, although we have always of course to reckon with an inherited nervous

---

* Piaget, Jean. *The Language and Thought of the Child.* (Harcourt, Brace & Co., 1926.)

and physical structure. That this is true only means that the problem of education is to that extent more complicated. It does not affect the fact that growth is an orderly and an integrative process, nor prove that taking its stages as hurdles will be of service.

The whole subject of the removal of children from the home at the tender age of two years or earlier is one that cannot be discussed in a general group without deep feeling. In an urban situation like ours there are enough obvious reasons why the parents come to us to place children in the nursery environment. In fact their applications are based on such reasons: the baby does not get out of doors enough because either the mother or one maid does both housework and baby tending; the apartment is small, the baby has no separate playroom and there is no park near; the child is eager in his interest in other children and has no opportunity for companionship, and last is one less commonly given which shows a realization of a serious problem,—the baby is growing so dependent upon mother or nurse that there must be an effort to wean him from the close home companionship. If claims are to be made for and against the nursery school, it is only fair to contrast the two environments and see what the child gets in one that is lacking in the other—what opportunities, habits, attitudes are present to condition him, what action patterns tend to develop in each.

The baby in the home is of course as truly a member of a social group as he would be in a nursery school. At his advent he finds a household of adults already equipped and in operation. Provision, more or less ample, has been made for him, but because so much more of life, even of his life, is spent as a grownup than as a baby, and because the care of children as well as of adults requires a set-up which is essentially adult planned and adult managed, he finds his quarters and his share even of the equipment which serves him limited.

Before he is able to extend the sphere of his activities by his own efforts that fact affects him very little. He is the center of interest in the household and though he lives in a world of Olympians, he rules there. Whatever alien concerns may occupy them his schedule is maintained and his requirements—chiefly for food, sleep and exercise—are fulfilled. The habits set by this precision are of biological importance, but among the other patterns that it helps to lay down may be a dependent attitude which makes later adjustments more difficult. This is by no means an argument for less meticulous care of babies, but for a recognition of one of the educational problems of infant care. The satisfaction that suckling gives to a baby sometimes tends to be prolonged beyond the appropriate period and to give rise to thumb sucking or even, so one author maintains,* to maturer habits of smoking, gum chewing or candy eating, but no one has suggested that breast and bottle feeding should therefore be discontinued.

The aspects of the infant's world change with his acquisition of locomotion. As a runabout he is a factor to be reckoned with, and as he begins extending the limits of his environment he meets new situations which again have their share in conditioning

* Mursell, James L. "The Sucking Reaction as a Determiner of Food and Drug Habits." *Psychological Review,* September, 1925.

his responses. He finds new and alluring materials and possibilities for experiment and encounters as well the incessant prohibitions that lie inherent in the situation. Questions of danger to his life and limb and of destruction to property put restraints upon his adventuring spirit.

There is within the child, however, an impelling force directing him to activity unless his growth processes are being slackened by inadequacy of physical and nervous equipment. Consequently he is apt to turn from the investigation of the inanimate materials which are forbidden to the human material which is constantly at hand. It is less well adapted to his use because it is not stable in its reactions. He learns with certitude the response that a wagon, a doll, a springboard will make, given a specific sort of treatment. This sort of material also lends itself to control. It can be made to do the will of the person manipulating it. It is not swayed in its responses by unforeseen and unmeasurable factors such as mood, fatigue and weather which affect the reactions of human beings. A child attempts to experiment with whatever material lies at his hand and he is usually persistent if he gets a response, whether or not it is agreeable.

There are many points of difference between the home environment and that of the school as far as its influence upon the child's activity is concerned. As most of the home furnishings are inappropriate for his use, either because he will injure them or because his use of them is dangerous to himself, those of the nursery school are planned so that he will find experimental possibilities in them, avenues of exploration, exercises of his skill and suggestions for further use. Adult possessions are reduced to the minimum required for record keeping and for getting meals. This means that prohibitions are few and that when they are necessary the argument that certain things belong to grownups is logically convincing because the share of the children is so large. The stress is placed upon the *opportunity for activity* with as few restrictions and reproofs as possible.

Another essential difference between the school and the home is in their emotional appeal. At the risk of getting involved in a definition of emotion I shall use the word here in reference to the phase of affectivity which has to do with personal relationships. The affective life, the directing force, maintaining motor activities, seeks to find an opportunity to expend its energy and to preserve an equilibrium in the fluctuating environmental conditions surrounding it. The environment, and I use the word in the larger comprehensive sense as including physical and social features, controls in large measure the affective components of the motor patterns, as much as it does for instance the physical behavior in patterns of speech and of movement.

Though the advent of a child into a home makes only a limited difference in the physical arrangements, in the lives of the parents it marks an epoch. It means a readjustment of their scheme of living and, on the part of the mother, the development of a new set of behavior patterns. This is especially true of the coming of the first child, and this is probably one of the reasons why a first or an only child is often less sturdy and more nervously tense than others in his family. In extreme cases the young mother finds in the experience of child bearing and rearing a keener emotional satisfaction than she had expected and sometimes, when her married life has not brought her a continuous return in affection or companionship, her attitude toward the baby is a compensating one and as such affects his dependence upon her. The father is less likely to be affected by his paternity while the child is an infant. Later he too may be surprised by the depth of interest and emotion aroused by the developing personality of his offspring. The future of the family relationship depends upon the wisdom and mental balance of the parents.

The mental hygiene of the normal family situation has to do with these problems. There are probably few persons in the world whose affective life is so freely flowing and truly functioning that there are no conflicts. For some women bearing children and caring for a home is a rich and satisfying life. For others it has no charms or soon loses them. Even if a wife and mother does enjoy it she must keep up activities and interests outside its walls or home will lose its attractiveness. If she has had a career which marriage has temporarily interrupted she will have the same impatience to get back to it that a man would have in a like situation.

All this has its effect upon the reactions of the parents to the baby and to each other, and it is all conditioning the child's responses, overlaying the "inherited tendencies to growth" by acquired tendencies to this or that behavior pattern. Because of the intimacy and the interdependence of the family organization the threshold of affectivity is low, that is, the emotional balance is easily disturbed, and the patterns acquired become so deeply set that their origin is submerged though they often control to a large extent the development of personality.*

I do not think that in order to vary the home influence the nursery school needs to be institutional in its atmosphere or even impersonal. It is my belief that an informal homeliness is important in the environment that the baby meets when he takes his first step out of the family. There should be intimacy and warmth and an avoidance of the traditional "teacher" attitude. As far as possible there should be opportunity for the children to establish real relationships with the adult members of the group, as well as with each other, and that is not possible if adults are not making a genuine response to the children and to the nursery situation. A part of a child's experience comes to him through contact with varying personalities.

It is important, however, that a consistent policy be maintained. In life outside the school the individuals with whom a child comes into more or less intimate contact are widely different in their points of view. He has to meet the adoring grandparents with their long past experience for a background, the modern parents trying to work out newly acquired theories, and the maid or nurse who, left with much responsibility and no authority, tries to steer a safe course and keep the peace. Do we know anything about the confusion in a child's mind result-

* Cameron, Hector Charles. *The Nervous Child.* (Oxford University Press, 1919.)

White, William A. *Mental Hygiene of Childhood.* (Little, Brown & Co., 1919.)

Lay, Wilfred. *The Child's Unconscious Mind.* (Dodd, Mead & Co.)

ing from the varying attitudes he sees taken by the adults about him toward similar phenomena?

In the nursery there are different personalities but we try to maintain consistency if not uniformity in our treatment of situations. As our set-up is intentional so is our attitude toward nursery life and its problems, and we try to indicate our policy and bring about in the course of living the responses that seem to us beneficent. We do not, however, try to disguise our personalities behind a veil of bland neutrality.

Furthermore, without definite plan the nursery school differs from the home in its emotional quality. Persons whose chief interest is in an objective study of children are unlikely to have an emotional attitude toward them. The sort of responsibility is different. It is not colored by the personal and the intimate nor marked by the self-accusations that parents often feel when their children's habits or tendencies are called in question. As parents, we feel personally involved and responsible for our children, and it is impossible to become less involved or to shift responsibility. To feel detached and philosophical is difficult. As teachers, regarding a group of children, not one or two, we learn to weigh the varying phases of development against each other and to recognize them as phases. Our responsibility is of short duration and is shared by other members of the staff. Our problem is to understand, to apply remedial measures as we know what is needed and to enlist in this educational undertaking the parents' coöperation, without which most of our efforts are unavailing. There are many minor variations from the normal which can be corrected entirely in an environment where the child's attitudes and behavior are matters, not of less interest, but of objective rather than personal concern.

It is true that attendance at the nursery school means an earlier breaking of the close family tie. The psychiatrist tells the mother that weaning the child from his dependence upon her physical presence is as important as weaning him from her breast. Though fiction has given us many pictures of the mother choking back her tears as she sees her first-born trudging off for his first day at school, I believe that the feeling of the nursery school mother is quite different and much more wholesome and understanding. It is normal for her as for the father to have interests which absorb her. She leaves the baby in surroundings that ensure for him better physical care than she can procure for him in most cases, under the direction of persons who are usually better equipped for the task than she is or than she is able to add to her menage. She goes back to her work or her home, free for the day to pursue the lines of her own interests, as the world expects the father to do. This is true whether she chooses to remain at home, take her place as a wage earner or seek a more creative type of productive life. Mother and child meet each other at the close of the day fresh from other activities and relationships. Mother and father are more nearly on the same level in the time they spend with the children and the quality of their relationship. When the family is reunited they come together as individuals each from his own group and with his own interests, and the child comes to realize that the life of the mother as well as that of the father includes concerns beyond the circle of which he is the center.

My comparison of home and school opportunities may seem an unjustified criticism of the home environment and a lack of recognition of what it holds for children and the efforts parents make within it to provide play space and suitable play materials. Family relationships, acquaintance with domestic processes, which is more possible in the majority of homes than in the nursery school, and the sense of special belonging are all desirable experiences which belong essentially to the family and with which life in the nursery school does not interfere. We are not proposing to substitute the nursery school for the home but to supplement the home environment by one in which the baby is not the center of attention, where he has the companionship of his peers in age and where his opportunities for play are as seriously considered as work opportunities for the adult in office or home. I believe, in fact, that the home environment and the hours spent there are richer and more precious because of the nursery school, more precious because they are less a matter of routine.

In a section which proposes to discuss the social opportunities offered children by the nursery school, too much time has perhaps been given to a weighing of differences between the home and the school environments. I have done this in the effort to emphasize the point that an early attack upon the social situation is a less profitable play activity than an attack upon the physical, the material situation, and that stages in growth should be considered in planning social experiences just as surely as in planning other play experiences.

All this emphasis upon social immaturity of children does not alter the fact that the opportunity offered the nursery school child for experience in playing and living with other children, is one of the most valuable that we can give him.

The impulses to be active and to be experimental are assets for the school in its method of dealing with the social environment no less than with the physical. The difference is not one of importance but of its dating in the life of a baby. Any parent who has lived with his child for some eight or ten years realizes that he has many times offered an experience which has been an entire failure only to see an interest in a similar sort of activity spring up some years later. No one would say that a knife and a chisel were appropriate toys for a very small child, not because they would never be valuable to him but because at three—let us say—certain powers of control, of discrimination and of strength have not matured.

Perhaps I am not quite ready to call social intercourse an edged tool for the young, but to impose upon them a social situation which demands a sustained sort of coöperative effort in advance of an equal maturity in their dealing with their physical environment seems to me equally disastrous. We do impose the social situation upon them if we do not temper it at all, and if we allow it to be presented with as much emphasis as are the opportunities for full body activities. Children differ in their sensitiveness to differing stimuli, and the child who has perhaps been strongly conditioned to make a social response and who consequently needs to develop his interest in dealing with materials, will not be caught by them unless he is helped. On the other hand, the

child who has for one reason or another social
reluctances can escape from the group and establish
himself in isolation or in the position of a watcher
unless help is given him to join the group.

The social environment must be one which is
favorable for growth. The teacher's part is not to
take refuge in a didactic method to safeguard the
children from the over-stimulation of too close contacts, but first to give the right of way to a general
sort of group play which any individual may enter
or leave at will. Next, to let each child follow his
own experimental interest in his fellows, as he proves
himself able to keep himself in hand, and as long as
his social activities are of a sort that do not unduly
interfere with the other child's similar tendencies.
That is, if experiments toward gaining social technique take the form of bullying or domination, they
are not to be encouraged, but the teacher must
endeavor to show the children the alternative possibility of a common interest in a coöperative problem.
If the experiments seem to be leading to excitement
or to general physical inactivity or a form of
unprofitable or interfering mischief, again they are
to be checked, whenever possible by draining them
off into other channels.

In other words the teacher attempts to safeguard
the social environment for each child until he arrives
at a stage in which he can pursue his investigations
with profit to himself and without detriment to
his fellows. We believe that at that point of
development he can build up his social technique
experimentally.

As we weave the fabric of nursery school experience, the thread of social activity runs through it

all. In the beginning it is an accompaniment only to the pattern of physical activity. After that design is firmly woven the two patterns are more and more closely united till they become practically one since the human individual is essentially a social being.

§ 3. LANGUAGE * AND RHYTHM

A. OUR OBSERVATION OF LANGUAGE FORMS

WE have tried to think of the speech activities of children as we have their other motor activities. They are responses to the stimuli offered by the environment. They are roused and they are elaborated in the process of growth. We are interested in studying the situations in response to which language seems to arise, and the way the individual develops his patterned language responses along with the growth of his other motor activities and in relationship to it.

In this section I have tried to work back from our observations to what the observed behavior implies in terms of teaching method.

It is beyond dispute that the acquisition of actual language marks a stage in social growth and awareness, but it is preceded by many steps in the use of the vocal apparatus which should be included in any study of speech, even though they seem chiefly to serve the impulse for motor exercise. Vocalization takes its impulse from the desire for muscular activity before communication enters into awareness. Inflections, modulations, pitch and placement

---

* The thesis which the Nursery School staff has held in the language work is so largely inspired by Lucy Sprague Mitchell that it would have been appropriate for her to write a section upon the subject. Because the practical application of her thesis and the observations of the children's responses have been made by the Nursery staff, I have taken the responsibility for this chapter.

In the introduction to *The Here and Now Story Book* will be found Mrs. Mitchell's statement of her approach to language.

of the voice show marked individual and age differences. Too commonly language is regarded only as a tool for the communication of thought and the language of children is studied as vocabulary. Increase in the kind and number of words is an indication of growth, and the ability to use language for getting our thoughts to our fellows is important as an aim in education, for clarity and definiteness are rare in this age of slovenly and tabloid speech. To be able clearly to say what one means is also a part of the process of integration, that is a part of the ability of the organism to function fully in its environment. The more wholeheartedly an individual enters into the life about him, if he does it harmoniously, with profit to himself and to his fellows, the more satisfactorily is he growing.

We attempted in our early studies of vocabulary to note how a child adds to his store of words and what kinds of words are preferred. There has been some indication that action words lead if a baby acquires language in an environment which is rich in things to do. The use of a word to stand for a sentence, the gradual growth of sentence structure and of the full verb form, the appearance of words which make possible qualifications and shadings in meaning,—while these have been the subjects of tentative explorations on our part, we have not pursued them because there is a considerable body of literature dealing with an analytic study of language.

We regard the speech of children as an activity of the speech mechanisms, just as we regard their other activities as the product of their motor equipment plus their interest drive. I have spoken of the normal individual as characterized by a strong impulse to activity. This impulse causes him to use his body in various ways even before he can control it enough to raise his head. It shows him going through alternate flexion and extension of his legs before he can walk. The impulse to use his muscles extends to those of his throat and pharynx and from that impulse all language,—social communication, poetry and literature, argument and logic,—is developed. In tracing the development of the language of little children we have chosen to study the situations which seem to arouse the impulse to use the speech mechanisms, and to inquire how the inflections and syllables used vary with the occasion, whether there is any relationship between pitch and general motor control, to what extent and how syllables continue to be used after real words are formed. We include not only actual words, phrases and sentences but also the earliest syllables and shouts and vocalizations.

We did not raise these interrogations until we had amassed considerable data. We worked over our records in the attempt to classify the vocabularies and the indications they gave of growth,—an increase in maturity. We found ourselves constantly drawn back to the records by the need we felt of making our judgments on the basis of the total behavior situation. It seemed to us that the events in progress when speech was noted and the effect upon a child's language impulses of activities of one sort and another were as important and as revealing as the actual language used.

As the activities of the trunk and its appendages are responses to situations met in the environment or in the individual's own bio-chemical processes, so we must regard the vocal activities no less as reactions to stimuli. In our study of the speech impulses we have tried to trace the features that would throw light upon needs which we could meet in the environment.

We have tried to approach our environment with the physiological needs of children in mind. We are trying to give children an opportunity for free activity and for experimentation with their environment. We are trying to plan that environment so that they will find in it a variety of sense and motor experiences. It is essential to the educational process that as children gain an acquaintance with the world about them they shall come to see the various processes in their relationships, that they shall not have isolated experiences and bits of information but that as far as possible, experience shall have continuity. In studying language development and planning language opportunities, we are holding ourselves to the same standards. Our program ought to apply to language as well as to other experiences involving motor and sensory activities. An outstanding and inevitable factor, to be sure, is the fact that in language adults are featured strongly, which indicates that there must be an intentional and controlled policy in regard to it if we are to make our attack on it consistent with our general program. On the other hand, whatever is done must be carried on along with the ordinary living together.

Sensory experiences bear an intimate relationship to language, especially those concerned with the auditory interest. The impulse to make sounds would probably go little beyond the bellowing stage if the ears were not attuned to fine gradations of pitch and inflection. We try to keep ourselves as aware of sounds as of sights in the environment, to use them to enlarge the children's experience and to preserve their sensitiveness to auditory as well as to visual impressions.

I think we do not realize how clouded and confused are the sounds that reach our ears in a city environment. City dwellers try not to hear since the sounds are so largely brute noise. The city hums and murmurs continually, and it is the siren of the fire engine, the clang of the hospital ambulance or the sharp whistle of the tug boats in the river that breaks through to consciousness. We find that from our roof, however, there are a good many sounds that can be picked out and identified and the auditory experience is just as pleasing as the visual experience that adults seem always eager to bring to a child. We emphasize it not because the power of seeing clearly and of noticing relevant details is not a precious and a rare gift but because auditory activity has a special relationship to language and because it tends to be forgotten. The steamer whistles, the drone of an airplane overhead, the heavy trucks passing, the clank of milk cans, often the sounds incident to building,—the sawing, the mason's trowels, the rattle of ropes and wheels as building materials are sent up on elevators, or the snorting of a steam shovel when building operations are beginning, these and many more recognizable sounds and accompanying sights come to us sharply on our roof. The children listen, imitate the sounds they hear, speculate upon their source and use them in their play.

Watching and listening from the roof.

Illustrating types of social contact.

Playing with the same toys at the same time.

A social impasse—22 months versus 30 months.

Passengers on the boat.

What is a child's reaction to his sound experiences? Is it not usually a response with muscles and voice? One of our babies, whose attention to sounds seemed especially easily roused, always looked up if another child dropped a block or other hard object. His head turned in the direction of the sound, usually he said "Bum!" and often brought his hands down violently on the surface of a table or chair if he were near one or sometimes flung himself down bodily in response. One day he was standing on a height overlooking the nearby roofs. The street was not visible but sounds from it came to us very distinctly, especially from the raised portion of the wall where he stood. We heard a heavy truck turn into the street from the avenue east of us. His ears caught the sound, he turned his head in that direction and so definitely followed the progress of the truck as it came nearer and nearer the house that the adult with him had to look twice to be sure there was not a point at which he could really see it.

Under what conditions does a child use his vocal equipment? As we observe him it is most frequently when he is using his other motor mechanisms. As he runs about the roof or playroom, as he slides or pulls a cart or propels a kiddy kar, as he climbs or jumps he carries on with his speech apparatus activities of one sort or another. If he is very young the sounds he uses will be shouts and bellows, grunts, squeals and roars. At the next stage of development definite syllables will be used, with a wide range of consonant and vowel sounds and a marked differentiation in pitch and inflection and in the movement of facial and throat muscles. Still later, words, phrases and sentences will also accompany the postural activities. They will bear a more or less close relationship to the materials he is using and to the persons with whom he is associated.

If he has not yet achieved words the child will use such syllables as the following, while he is carrying on active play: "Dee-dah," "Oo-woo," "Wuh-wuh"; when naming interests him he will murmur, "Kah-kah," as he takes one, "Bok-bok" when he sees blocks and so on; "I cover dollie," "I sit here," "I slide down," "Dollie go sleep" are statements of activities in progress. Repeated interminably they are characteristic language responses to the situation in hand and do not usually occur unassociated with full-body activities.

What characteristic features do these speech reactions show? What relation do they bear to the activities of the larger musculature? We find marked individual differences but in so many instances do we discover a tendency to markedly rhythmic forms that we are convinced that it is a significant feature. By rhythmic form I mean an arrangement of syllables or words that has a beat, regular emphasis or cadence.

> "*Munna, munna, mo,*
> *Munna, munna, mo,*"

spoken over and over as Jane trotted about the playroom is an example. *Dee* bee-a *we* we *wo*, chanted on the notes indicated, further illustrates a rhythmic

use of syllables, this time with the addition of a patterned variation in voice pitch. "Up go, Down go" repeated again and again as the seesaw board was tipped up and down swings into a monotonous beat.

> "Go s'eep, *dollie, dollie, dollie,*
> Go s'eep, *dollie, dollie, dollie,*"

though spoken has the measured beat of a lullaby.
Dan, pretending to mend his car, chanted,

> "Mend the wheel and make it go!
> Mend the wheel and make it go!"

till his work was satisfactorily finished.

Lucy was laying the last blocks in a big construction and as she ran back and forth for them she chanted over and over,

> "Now it's *done,* un *un*
> *Done* un *un* un *un.*"

Another time she wove the statement that she needed another block into a singsong, *"One* more, *one* more, *one* more," and repeated it over and over as she trotted from the block stack to her construction.

There are other characteristics which we note if we study the spontaneous language reactions of little children. The brevity of the phrases and the interminable repetition are indicated in the records cited. Enumeration of the names of persons or objects occurs repeatedly and when used by adults gains attention and response almost invariably. In the nursery group almost before the impulse to play together appears there is the tendency to name all the children, usually in connection with their activities or their possessions.

Lucy stood on the table being dressed. She pointed to the towels and face cloths hanging nearby. She asked, "Is that my towel?" pointing to the wrong one. She was answered, as she expected, "Oh, no, that's Geordie's!" She went on pointing to each one and waiting for the answer, leaving her own until the last. When the reply came, "Oh, yes, that's Lucy's," she hugged herself, gave a joyous little squeal and repeated the whole performance. Sometimes she varied her question and used the names of all the other children, "Is that Kurt's towel?"

This type of play in which there is a sort of antiphonal element occurs again and again between two or more children or between child and adult. Reiteration and enumeration characterize it.

In one of the earlier sections I spoke of our interest in the affective element in all motor activities, and our effort to take cognizance of the interest drive and of what are commonly called emotional manifestations, as components of the action patterns which we are attempting to trace. If we confine ourselves to the study of language as the activity of a set of specialized muscles we are leaving out of our reckoning a factor of enormous significance in the spontaneous speech reactions of children and one of equal importance in the development of educational method. This is equally true of any reaction of course.

Every individual tends to seek and to maintain as continuously as possible a condition in which a feeling of active satisfaction accompanies his performance. Doubtless this state of "dynamic equilibrium" is largely a physiological matter and will

eventually be reduced to neuro-muscular and bio-
chemical components. Its external manifestations
will always be observable in conduct which shows a
feeling element. When speech in a more elaborated
form than the earliest crows and shouts begins to
take its place with other activities, the extension of
experience which the use of another mechanism
brings about adds to the vividness and satisfaction
felt by the reacting individual to his activity. But
beyond this there seems to be a definite elation,
pleasure, joy or satisfaction felt by children in the
sort of language forms that have been described.
They seem to seek occasions to use these forms and
with wide individual variations, to play with them,
to elaborate them and to show immediate responsiveness if adults employ this language method with
them.

Under what other conditions do we find speech
reactions taking place? Confronted with a difficulty
which he cannot readily master or overcome, the
child resorts to speech. Before the remarks are addressed to an individual, who is at first invariably
the adult, the "Uh, uh," or "Wuh-oo" of effort, the
"Ee, ee," "No, no" of remonstrance, or even real
remarks are directed to the materials or to the
world at large. "Come out," to a ball that has rolled
out of reach, "Don't run away," to a wagon rolling
down grade, are sometimes spoken without apparent
reference to the human audience. From "Uh!"
(Give me that), "Want up," "See horsie" (I wish
to see the horse), "Want kiddy kar," to such a
well-developed, well-elaborated sentence as, "Will
you push dose bibs over so I can see,—so show me
which kind I shoose?" desires and needs are indi-

cated by language. Answers to adult questions are as often as not answered by acquiescent action instead of the negative or affirmative word. Comments on other children's activities are made. "There's Billy!" "What's Donald doing?" "See little Joan!"

These various language reactions are social only as there is implied some sort of relationship to other persons. They are not communication in the sense of the interchange of thought, except of the most perfunctory sort. Materials, situations and adults are stimuli which seem to cause the earliest speech reactions. The stimulus of other children acts only indirectly for a long time. That is, the social stimulus is the last that is operative. Children are for a long time a part of the material environment and as they are a very active part their reactions affect each other. Their language, however, is not directed at each other till late in their nursery life and then not consistently. As with all behavior patterns and as with all acquired techniques there is a long period during which there is repeated reversion to earlier methods. A baby "learns to walk" but will resort to the creeping pattern repeatedly under stress or as a "normal" variation. A child may have a fairly rich vocabulary and may be able to express himself clearly but he will return to a baby term or method from time to time. So with language as a tool for making social contacts and for the communication of thought: conversation between children,—the social give and take that is implied by the term, is as fleeting as are manifestations of a genuine social interest.

May I repeat what has already been said in the section on social growth? There seem to be various levels of social behavior. The pattern goes through many stages. A readiness to enter into some sort of social relationship differs with different individuals. At first there may be an almost complete inattention to other children and their activities. Gradually awareness of them and elation in their presence is shown. From this stage the pattern shows various stages of elaboration, from playful approaches without actual contact through the period of violent attack and into the form of joyous and amicable play together which is characteristic of most of our older children's relationships. At first this is merely play with similar toys at the same time,—sliding in procession, trailing each other with kiddy kars and carts, building with blocks or constructing trains in a room together. The adaptation and modification in impulse and conduct required by such a situation indicate a good degree of maturity and control, and when this stage is reached we consider that a satisfactory nursery school pattern has been developed. Up to this time language as conversation plays little part in the social reactions. Language is used continually and as has been said, it takes the forms of calls and cries and shouts, commands, requests and answers to questions, but for the most part the pattern shows little that can be considered true social intercourse.

The conversations that I can report sound like parodies or like the skit in a popular revue which responded to applause by doing itself backward,— situations, sentences and all. Piaget says that real social conversation is rare at six or seven years. With our younger children it is little more than a prolonged antiphonal chant, in which certain statements or words are pronounced and the answering choir member incorporates them or something similar into his refrain, often just failing to make a connection, as in a mirror when one fails to adjust enough to the image to touch an indicated spot or to trace a line. As has been said an audience is demanded only in the most general way, and whether or not one is understood is quite beside the point. It is satisfactory to direct one's words to a group just as it is to play in a group.

In conversation with adults a child shows a much more sophisticated sort of speech whether in his answers to questions or his attempts to convey information. Probably one reason for this is that the adult lends him a ready, understanding ear and the fragmentary, disjunctive manner of his communication does not debar him from getting a response in terms which are satisfactory to him.

Children make other language reactions which seem to be responses to language itself. They experiment with words which they hear used, with their uses and meanings, with time relations,—to-day, yesterday, to-morrow, last year, with words indicating causal relationships, with number, with sentence structure and with verb forms. These experiments, I am convinced, are not really concerned with meaning, value and use but with rhythm, with sound and with form. They are much more than is realized, sensory and motor responses at the ages represented in our nursery school.

"No, sweaters can't get washed because the buttons break," is not a proof of an astute understanding of laundry processes on the part of the three-year-old child, but is no less a step forward in language growth. She had doubtless heard the remark or a similar one in a relevant situation and was rehearsing it though she could not have explained it. The child who called out over and over, "What about the reason," and when asked, "Reason for what?" answered, "Strawberries," was also practicing words that he had heard but he was not by that means increasing his vocabulary or his language facility. The use of more elaborate language does not necessarily indicate the degree of awareness of meaning that is commonly implied.

Children also ask questions incessantly. They ask the names of persons and things, beginning very early. "Eh da ?" is one of the earliest social remarks, social in that it does establish contact, that it is addressed to a person or persons, that an answer is expected and that answers are stimulating to action or to further questioning.

There are questions of another sort that are equally incessant. "What is that for?" "Why does Jerry do that?" "Why do you turn the box over?"— these are examples. Again we are convinced that they are not so much due to a thirst for information, which would imply maturity in thought processes, as to an impulse toward social contact with adults, together with a keen interest in language practice. They are less often than is believed indications of an inquiring spirit, though they have meaning. They are rarely demands for an explanation but mean, "I know and I should like to tell." "Why" and "What for" are sometimes treated too seriously by adults. Elaborate and technical explanations are not understood, though the words may be repeated and memorized. For the most part the child's purpose is better served if the question is turned back to him.

"What that nail in kiddy kar for?"

"You tell me."

"So handle won't come off. Why handle don't come off for?"

"You know, Walter; you tell me."

"So Walter can ride," with a smile and chuckle that mark enjoyment.

Craig hears a sound in the street. "What that noise?" he asks. "Listen," answers the adult. "What is it?" We are high on the roof, out of sight of the street, and though the adult recognizes the jangle of bells on the strap of a push-cart she knows that the sound is the dominant factor and a familiar one to the child. The details,—junk man, cart with two wheels and so on, are irrelevant and confusing. Craig listens and answers in a moment. "A dingle dongle bell in the street."

If it had been a question of a visual experience the adult's attitude would have been the same, to throw back to the child the details of his observation in order to preserve the capacity, natively possessed, for acquiring visual impressions and registering them with photographic distinctness and detail.

The power of logical thinking and of the use of an instrument for expressing his thought is new and brings the child a sense of adequacy as well as the opportunity for social contacts which he seeks. Even when he is older and does wish to know, his thinking will be more stimulated by the suggestion that he try to answer his own question than by giving him information. Adults often do not realize how many of the phenomena of everyday life can be ex-

plained by a thoughtful child and, full of the tradi-
tion that education is served if a child's questions
are answered with respect, with attention and with
patient accuracy, make of themselves a "Book of
Knowledge," to the child's disadvantage. After all,
the power to think comes in response to situations
in which doubt, uncertainty or conflict arises.*

There are actual questions at this age and those
we attempt to answer, but as simply as possible.
"How did this bridge get built?" does not indicate
that the three-year-old is ready to be introduced to
engineering as a profession, or to the techniques
involved in sinking piles into the river bed. "Many,
many men, with many big machines brought the big
stones and stretched the long steel ropes," probably
gives him what he wants at the time. "Why does the
sand box smoke?" is an actual question frequently
propounded and concerns a phenomenon which we
cannot hope adequately to explain. "The sun makes
it warm and then the water on the box makes steam"
is an over-elaborate reply but one which we offer
our oldest questioners. "The sun makes it steam" is
probably equally satisfactory.

What then have we noted as outstanding features
in the early speech patterns of children? First,
speech responses are found closely associated with
postural activities and accompanying them. Second,
they often follow a rhythmic form. This is evidenced
in the beat and balance of their language and in the
tendency children show to toss their words and
phrases back and forth in antiphonal fashion. Third,
enumeration, repetition and reiteration are commonly, almost universally observed. Fourth, ques-

* Dewey, John. *How We Think.* (D. C. Heath & Co., 1910.)

tions are frequent but are often asked for the sake of social contact.

As we look at later language development we find similar characteristics persisting. We also find children adopting with readiness and often inventing terms which recall the sensory and motor elements in an experience. "This plate is wavy on the edge," was the comment about a dish that had a series of depressions as a border. "Do you want to make your finger go bumpety on the ball?" said by a child who was rubbing her hand over the ball's rough surface. Adults are so responsive to this type of language that it is easy to accept it as of universal interest. It has always been one of the methods of literature.

Furthermore the language of children concerns itself with well known, self-experienced incidents, and usually features themselves as actors. Robin, down stairs after the others had gone out of doors, was playing a naming game with an adult, a popular sport. He would ask, "Where John?" "John is on the roof." "Where Dorothy?" "Dorothy is on the roof," and so on through the list. From time to time he would pause, smite himself on the chest and say with great effort and emphasis, "Me—Wobin—not —on woof. Here—here!" It was almost as if he were at pains to identify himself or to make sure that he was represented in the group.

The statements children make, whether spontaneously or in answer to questions, consist of brief phrases and of discrete episodes. In answer to the question, "What did you do in the country?" Leo answered, "I did have a wagon in the country. Daddy did pull me. We did get milk in my wagon."

For the moment that episode represented the country experience.

We find also that when children attempt to reproduce our songs or phrases or remarks we get an abbreviated version. A child's span is unusually short.

Choo, choo, choo, says the big engine. As it pulls the train a-long Too! choo, choo, choo, choo, choo, choo, choo.

was cut down to,

Choo, choo, choo, says the big engine Choo, choo, choo, says the Train!

"Tell Millie that you are all ready for dinner," was given back as "All ready, Millie."

There is a marked alternating rhythm in language and full body activities, as there probably is in the growth of language and the growth of facility with other parts of the musculature. Again and again our records show absolute silence during a period when the group or individuals in it are absorbed in an activity. Driving nails, making block constructions, digging in sand or pebbles are group activities which are conducted for long periods in entire silence. Whenever an individual is intent upon a process or construction, that is, experimenting with a piece of play material,—wagon, kiddy kar or slide, or carrying out some scheme with blocks, trains or dolls, or working with crayons or with musical bells, his vocalization usually subsides entirely until there is a break in the activity. In other words when a new adjustment is demanded, the activity involved gets the right of way. The break may come because success or failure has brought activity to a natural close, the adjustment has been made, or because the child feels satisfaction or because interest has spent itself. When this happens, language begins again. It may be of the rhythmic type, a crow, a lilting onomatopœic series of syllables or a mere matter of fact statement of what he is doing or an announcement of future plans. Examples are: "Oo-ee, doh-ee!" (dollie) crooned by a child who had just succeeded in spreading a cover over a doll. "Ding, ding, go, Ding, ding, go, My boat go," when the notched blocks were interlocked and pushed over the floor. "Go upee steps. S'ide down?" after a child had made a few successful descents. "I fru wi' hammer," when nail driving palled.

If the group activity is one which involves the entire musculature and demands a tremendous output of energy, there seems to be no tendency toward silence. Sliding together, racing over the roof with kiddy kars or wagons, bouncing or coasting down planks are usually accompanied by calls or shouts on the part of those children whose technique is well developed. That is, the language impulse seems to be released when the performance becomes automatic or nearly so.

We may then add to our classification: Fifth, children tend to use words or syllables that recall sensory and motor experiences and to attend and respond to such language. Sixth, the language of a child deals largely with his own activities and experiences. Seventh, his statements are brief and in the form of episodes rather than of narratives. Eighth, there seems to be a definite interest in being represented,—included, in any account of happenings. Ninth, there seems to be a rhythm observable between language reactions and full body activities.

It is obvious that with an age range of about two years the characteristics noted may not be equally applicable to all ages. Except for the more elaborate form of questions, however, maturity seems to enter in very little. Young and old are different in degree, not in kind. The sort of language a child uses to accompany his play on the slide or seesaw depends upon his age, as does the elaborateness of his other verbal responses. Whether or not he shows rhythm in his language forms, whether or not he is readily responsive to auditory stimuli is a matter of individual variation at whatever age.

B. OUR PROCEDURE

If, as I have said, we are to adopt a consistent point of view about our educational procedure we must include language in it. Speech interest and facility come along as a process of growth. How can the environment and the reaction of adults to it serve growth needs? This can be answered only in the presence of children and through observation and study of their language responses.

We have attempted to develop our procedure in line with what we think we have discovered about the growth stages of speech. We have however never tried to "teach" children to speak. We do not call their attention to things about them and name them. It is obvious that we do not use baby talk. We do not often use the children's terms for objects or activities because it is not wise to perpetuate baby expressions.

Children come to us before they have a formulated language but there is usually little need to stimulate them in a direct way. They are already carrying on elaborate experimentation with their speech mechanisms, though within a very wide range of individual variation. Their readiness to adapt their early syllables to the words they hear differs as much as their facial appearance differs. To one child of twenty months a combination of linguals with the G sound repeated many times and represented inadequately by the syllables "gug-gle," will be applied as a generic term for clothing. To another of the same age "ha," "coh," "shuh," mean "hat," "coat," "shoe," and are always differentiated.

Why these differences are found I do not know. I believe that the attitudes and interests of adults affect to a marked degree the developmnt of a child's language interests. That is, it is just as possible to condition a child in his speech activities as it is to give him any other conditioned response. There are very apparent differences between individuals in their tendencies to make verbal responses, in their attentiveness to auditory stimuli, in their impulse to a rhythmic use of the body or of the vocal apparatus. I suspect relationships between some of these factors and the course which language development pursues, but the data are not yet complete enough for us to do more than hazard a conjecture that they are all significant.

As we have built up our environment in accordance with what we have observed in spontaneous activities of the general musculature, so we have tried to develop our language practice by watching behavior. Language and music are so closely allied that a discussion of what we do in language answers the question of what we do in music aside from the regular music period.

We believe that we have discovered certain general trends and tendencies in the language patterns of children. We believe that they carry certain educational implications which we must consider in our language dealings. In accordance with these beliefs we accompany many of the children's activities, usually those in which a degree of adult supervision is necessary, with rhythmic phrases or words,— chanted, spoken or sung. This is directly derived from the children's habit of announcing their activities as they carry them on. "I on kiddy kar," "I bump," "Build house." Our phrase, "Go up the

steps. Slide down," the children wait for and reproduce themselves.

The scale or other ascending or descending intervals we use as we all go up and down stairs. The
children reproduce our phrases or improvise their
own songs. For instance, Phœbe sang a charming
variation which we adopted,

A month after Phœbe left school Don remarked on
hearing it, "That's Phœbe's song."

Another example carries with it a direction which
we find it necessary to emphasize.

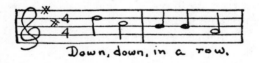

The seesaw has its chant:

up. Don-ald goes down, down, down.

Another variation is as follows:

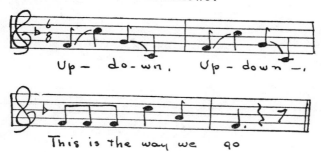

Up — do-wn. Up — down —,

This is the way we go

Falling down causes less consternation if it is greeted with a song:

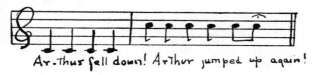

Ar-thur fell down! Arthur jumped up again!

or

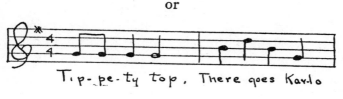

Tip-pe-ty top, There goes Karlo

Tip pa-ty top. There goes Karlo Tip-pe-ty top

There goes Karl-o - Up he jumps a-gain

Roll the ball a-long. With a song

Roll the ball a-long With a merry song

This refrain keeps the game going and with keener enjoyment than if it is unaccompanied. We have to proceed with caution, however, for if the adult joins a child in his effort to give back a phrase he usually subsides at once.

There is almost unlimited joy in a reiterative phrase. Mere enumeration sounds commonplace but it is so universally the child's method that there can be no question as to its satisfying quality. Parents have told us that they administer dinner or induce quiet at night by the repetition of the names of their child's mates and the reminder that each one is going through the same program.

> "Susan's eating dinner,
> Matthew's eating dinner,
> Mary's eating dinner,
> Don is eating dinner,"

and so on through the entire list.

The time-honored "Mulberry Bush" gives us the tune for our taxi song:

> "Here we go to Lucy's house,
>   Bumpety, bumpety, bumpty, bump!"

"Now my house," or "My house next" are part of the game.

The poets have recognized the charm of enumeration, and when the list enumerated is intimate, familiar and personal it never fails to win a baby's attention and delight. The example given on a preceding page of Lucy and the towels could be duplicated over and over. The antiphonal element in it manifestly adds to the charm since it introduces a social feature. It seems to us to hold a kernel of language appreciation worth encouraging whenever it appears. We try to meet the evident humor in the child's question, to make our response identical each time and to swing it into a rhythm.

Babies begin this sort of humorous question before they can form real sentences. "Mah tow'?" (My towel) or "Mah bax-it?" (My basket) may introduce the game, and it is always played with real appreciation. Enjoyment of the antiphonal chant is responsible for much of what appears like contrariness. As undressing for nap goes on Charles will say, "*I* not going bed!" whereupon the adult will answer, "Not going to bed? *Oh, no,* of course not!" "*I* not going bed!" "*Oh, no,* of course not!" is repeated while more clothing is taken off. After several repetitions Charles changes his remark: "Yeth—am," and the duet is over. Sometimes the names of all the other children are introduced by the adult as a variation.

The children play much the same sort of game with each other. "My daddy brought me," one child will remark. *"No, my* daddy," another will say and thereupon the entire group may join in, asseverating, "No, my daddy," with more and more emphasis, with bangs upon the table and sometimes with personal violence, unless the adult is wary enough to anticipate it. The storm can be calmed and calamity averted if a chant is introduced which takes in the names of all the children. "Yvonne's daddy, Geordie's daddy, Caleb's daddy, Ansel's daddy, etc.," sung up scale and if necessary down again usually gets attention and the children suggest additional names and forget the antagonism of contradiction.

When the children use the indoor slide they are very likely to shout from the balcony. If their tones are full and unstrained we do not interfere, but the excitement of noise is likely to affect them, and if their voices become shrill and raucous we attempt to change the generalized shouting into controlled calls. We are likely to call, "Hoo, hoo," and the child's name, to which they reply, imitating our intervals with more or less accuracy unless they are possessed by the rhythm of opening their mouths and forcing through a volume of shrill sound. There is no necessity for interfering with their shouting out of doors, but in the house it has to remain under control, and a chord on the piano will break the boisterous rhythm so that the adult's chant will reach their ears.

Our efforts are very crude and are instanced here only to illustrate the method so that more inspired teachers or parents may develop chants and jingles that have musical or literary value.

The foregoing statements may seem to indicate that we use rhythm and pattern in the language we employ with the children as a means of imposing upon them our standards and of correcting tendencies that seem to us unfavorable. Our real aim in the language patterns that we use is to encourage in the children an interest in dealing with language experimentally and as a play instrument. We have tried to choose a form that seems native to children and upon which they can embroider their own themes if they like. It is true that we have found the method particularly effective in diverting children from activities which from the adult viewpoint are undesirable and we have used it rather than repressive means.

In watching a child's growth of power over his body one does not find that he merely learns to walk steadily and to increase his speed if he has need of reaching a given spot quickly. One sees him besides come to a keen enjoyment in his facility. He plays with his new ability, getting pleasure and satisfaction from capering, stretching, stamping and swinging from one gait to another. The use of muscles for the joy in it is paralleled by the use of words for the play element. It is the art aspect of language and means intensification of the enjoyment of a situation. It makes more emphatic an experience as it is in progress or recalls it with its accompanying sensations. It represents the elements of which poetry and literature are composed. I believe that children can all share in the joys of creation in all sorts of arts if they are given a play approach to the world about them. Adult standards are entirely out of place in judging children's output. Satisfaction to the child and growth in power or initiative or independence are our tests of worth. As regards our babies the implication is that we cultivate with them a play attitude on language; that we try to use with them a speech that is vivid and specific, not drab and generalized.

I have spoken of our habit of calling the attention of the children to sounds that reach us from the city streets and the river. In referring to them we try to give each the appropriate sound instead of the sober utility word which has come to mean something to us because of its connotation. Even with us, sober-sided and unimaginative adults, the description which reproduces for us a sensory or motor experience makes its invariable appeal. The fact that it also makes its appeal to children would be reason enough for developing the habit of giving things names suggested by the feeling they arouse, but I am convinced that the children themselves in many cases take over the method, in fact that it is an elaboration of their own pattern and appeals to a native impulse of their own. "I make my feet go thump thump up the stairs," "Here goes my auto, buzzing along," "I don't want the so-wiggly kiddy kar," referring to one which was loose in its joints, show picturesque elements in language which for the very young are effective though very simple. The vivid and the rhythmic come to be modes of expression if they are employed in the hearing of children whose ears are attuned to respond to them and they lead, I believe, directly into a creative use of language.

All adults assume this attitude with children about certain things. The time-honored custom of bow-wowing with the dog and baa-baaing with the lamb has its origin in a real understanding of the child's impulses, but has never been developed. The water at the tap, the distant door bell or telephone, the street car, the whistle of the wind, the rain, the child's feet on the stairs or floor,—all these things have characteristic sensory elements which we use with their names.

On one occasion a house going up nearby roused so much interest that the adults perpetrated a chant, bringing in a personal though fictitious refrain at the end, a device which increases enjoyment and follows the child's impulse to feature himself as a participant in the events narrated.

> Tap, tap with their shovels,
> The masons lay the bricks.
> Zu, zu with their saws,
> The workmen saw the wood.
> Whang, bang with their hammers,
> The carpenters pound the nails,
> And build a house for Lucy!

Brevity is a characteristic of the speech of our children. Keeping it in mind, the requests we make of them are put in simple short sentences. When we give them reasons for action which we are requiring we try to avoid elaboration but not repetition, for that seems to be a method native to a child and helps the thought. We do not hesitate to use gesture and changes in facial expression to make ourselves understood. Our aim is to avoid confusion. We do not know what a child's span is, that is, we do not know how much he hears accurately and at a time.

We do not know the emotional effect upon him of elaborate discussions of whys and wherefores, or even of a great deal of conversation with adults, so we try to follow the scriptural injunction to keep the door of our lips.

It must again be asserted that the stages in growth themselves and the amount of functioning that goes on in terms of the possibilities of each stage are important items in the total maturation process. Language is used in order to establish social contacts, but in the history of individual speech development much occurs before its chief use as a tool in the communication of thought is perfected. Furthermore we have noted the episodic character of early communications, the fact that they deal largely with the experiences and activities in which the child speaking has had an important share, and that they tend to emphasize the child's place in the situations recalled. We have regarded these features as characteristic of a growth stage and have scaled our language to them.

Another suggestion that we gather from the language characteristics cited has to do with the stories we tell children.

The stories given at this age would best be in episode form, brief, reiterative and featuring the child or a familiar as chief actors, and they should deal with well-known and well-understood experiences. It is only to the oldest of our children that we tell stories even of this embryonic type. We do not feel that this is the time for cultivating literary appreciation. It is the time for extending the child's experience with language activity, for encouraging him to use his vocal apparatus in a variety of ways.

We wish our children to be able to play with language, to make it serve their ends as clay and paint serve them later.

We have no story telling hour but there are occasions when we rehearse an experience in progress by a patterned arrangement of words describing it or recall a past event in the same way.

Looking from a window sometimes fills in a waiting space or diverts a new child from woe. We listen and describe the sounds we hear and the events observed:

> Clop-clop, clop-clop, clop-clop,
> That's a horse!
> Rattlety rattle, rattlety rattle,
> That's an old cart!
> Sh-sh-sh-sh, honk, honk,
> That's a taxicab!
> Thumpety-sh, bumpety-sh,
> That's a bumpy truck!
> Bing-bong, kling-klong,
> That's the fire engine!

As we return a child to his home we sometimes do the same thing and later repeat the story, rehearsing thus an event which has happened and which is to occur again:

> Bump we go to Philip's house,
> Buzz buzz buzz, ring Philip's bell!
> Click click click, push Philip's door,
> And mother's there for Philip!

The Mulberry Bush song mentioned on page 127 is another "story" of the same sort. As our cab is halted by an officer we explain traffic rules:

> Big policeman says, "Can't go,
> Got to stop. Can't go!"

The whistle is blown, the cab starts off and our story goes on:

> Big policeman says, "Can go!
> Hurry along. Can go!"

This explains why the taxi stops and the procedure is later taken over in the children's play. Maisie and Donald were playing traffic officer. "I turn my sign around," they shouted. Then they called, "Go," loudly. Each one seemed to be directing his own traffic chiefly. Donald would hold up his own hand, say "Stop," and hold up his own cart. Maisie did the same. Later when red and green lights were put down Seventh Avenue and the attention of the older children was called to them, there was added to the refrain, "Red lights—can't go! Green lights—can go!"

I have cited instances of our using rhythmic or melodic phrases as accompaniments to certain established activities like going up and down stairs, sliding, using the seesaw. It must not be assumed that we have reduced our intercourse to such a mechanical routine that a child's fall elicits invariably from adults the chorus of "Tippety-top" or that we all burst into an arpeggio when one of the children comes hurtling down the slide chute. If one has a genuine relationship with children spontaneity in response is implied. As a matter of fact our refrains and chants are gathered together here for the first time and are never used as routine.

However there is something to be said for routine. The "satiable curiosity" of the elephant's child was a part of his personality and we enjoy the anticipation of the repetition. We listen to be reminded that Epaminondas "ain't got the sense he was born with." There are certain situations or events in nursery life that children associate so closely with the language accompaniment that it is demanded invariably. The swing and the taxicab, both rhythmic, suggest at once the refrains that we use with them. The children sing, "Swing, swing" themselves and as the cab jolts off one child or another often says, "Bump to *my* house" to give the adult her cue.

In consequence of our conviction that these findings are significant we do not attempt to stimulate the conversational powers of our children. That is adequately taken care of by all the other adults whom they meet, among the groups from which our children are chosen. The development of language is a fascinating subject. Parents, teachers and friends are sure to do all that is necessary to encourage children to talk with them, to enlarge their vocabularies, to answer questions and to give them information. If we felt the pressing urgency of giving little children a social experience during the nursery school years, we should probably emphasize conversation. As has been repeatedly said, we regard this as an inappropriate time to stress social relationships. The experience of living with a group of their peers and of making the adjustments which such a situation calls for is an invaluable preparation for real social playing together. The closer details of coöperation or organized group play belong to a later period and moreover should be allowed to grow out of the early impulses toward brief social contact.

Occasionally we find that language has not shown a development coördinate with the social interest, and the child is unable to make himself understood readily enough to serve his purpose. There often results from this cause irritability and quarrelsomeness which subside with increased language facility. This condition is frequently met in cases of speech defect and is a development that must be taken into consideration in a group or in the home. Even here a didactic method is not called for but more intentionally directed conversation with the child and a supervision of his social contacts to make sure that his efforts at communication are understood. When a child has reached this stage of social development the urge to speech will carry him over the ground with little delay.

In citing the fact that we do not try to stimulate the conversational powers of our children I do not mean to imply that we do not respond to their social advances or that we maintain a stony silence when they talk to us. We reply to their remarks but I think that we are less inclined than many parents and teachers to take an informing and corrective attitude toward their speech. We try out their ability to answer our questions and to take directions and we listen to their attempts to give us accounts of their experiences and give them the stimulation of interest and enthusiasm.

The older children so often come to school with some announcement to make that they seem soon to get a feeling for this sort of social intercourse and wish to have a part in it. As we climbed the stairs one morning Lucy, who was just past three, and very able in the use of language, said, "There's a bridge across the street. We go under it." We happened to know that she had to pass a place where the sidewalk had been roofed. Her statement probably conveyed nothing to the other children but Ansel, ten months younger, laboring up beside us, remarked as if eager to make his contribution to the discussion, "Ah see hordie,—park!" (I saw a horse in the park.) His remark was probably equally unintelligible to his mates. I do not feel that it was the teacher's function either to make the one child more fully articulate or to correct the faulty pronunciation of the other. The children were getting a sense of social sharing and the adult's response was in kind. On the other hand, although at this stage there is a strong temptation on the part of the adult to enter into conversation with them, we have stalwartly held off. Without doubt progress in language as a social tool could be greatly stimulated by adult participation and adult-directed practice but we believe that interest which could be turned in this direction could be used more profitably on the material equipment.

In our observations regarding the place of language activity in the reactions of children there is implied, among other things, the warning to adults not to break into silences by remarks and directions. Whether or not there is in progress during silence, implicit speech, which is probable, the organism is sustaining itself in a pattern which is disturbed by conversation. The ability to become absorbed is too precious to risk. I believe moreover that whatever the child is attempting to do, an imperfect or unfinished product achieved by a child's own efforts is more valuable for his growth than the perfected performance which might result from adult direction and explanation.

There are various problems related to the language responses of children which our experience has brought before us, and certain conclusions which they have suggested. I hope that we are still holding these conclusions tentatively and acting upon them experimentally.

One of these problems is the tendency to negativism on the part of children. It seems to be an almost universal manifestation at some period of the life of nearly all children. The course that it follows and the depth of the impression it makes upon personality are largely decided by the treatment given it at the incipient stage. It is commonly a mere phase, arising much as the slapping or pushing stage arises, from an experimental effort on the part of a child to establish himself and his own power as dominant factors in the program and in the group of which he is a part. The one passes or is modified as the other is, if it is treated as a phase and not set more deeply by being met with corresponding negativism on the part of the adult.

In the course of the day there are certain processes for which adults are responsible but for which the coöperation of children is necessary. This often necessitates adult interference with a child's occupations. Our habit is to make our approach with a question, a form assumed because of adult respect for children's work and a desire to let them share in the program as it develops.

"Who wants to get washed for dinner?" "Will you come to the toilet?" "Do you want to go out of doors?" are rhetorical questions requiring only monosyllabic responses and "No," "Yes," "All right," "I do" or silent acceptance is usually forthcoming. Questions which arise in the course of real social intercourse are another matter, as are also those used in rhythmic play which add a distinctly social or rather a personal feature to a situation like naming the baskets or identifying the towels or clothing. The questions under discussion are for the most part attempts to gain the coöperation of the children and to include them in the adult's procedure and the answers given are usually perfunctory. Sometimes the questions carry with them a suggestion which is not welcome and then one meets the negative attitude which seems a very common behavior manifestation. "Do you want to get washed?" may be met by a snarling "No," or the threat of tears. "Shall I walk you on your hands to the bathroom?" puts the emphasis on the idea of wheelbarrow play instead of upon washing which the child may be disposed to resist. "Will you walk in or roll in?" or "Shall dollie go with us to get washed?" gets a child over the necessity of a refusal.

The fact that the affirmative word usually enters a child's vocabulary later than the negative is sometimes responsible for apparent refusal to accede to suggestions. The question, "Shall I give you some honey?" gets the answer "No," with dish extended and a push forward of the entire body. Sometimes "All right" is adopted as an affirmative before "Yes" is made a part of the vocabulary.

The negative attitude is often taken very seriously by adults and so much insistence made upon immediate acquiescence that it sometimes persists and becomes a deep-seated pattern which proves a stumbling block to social behavior. A frequent sequence in negative response runs somewhat as follows: A child decides that he must take his pail of sand into the house; it cannot be done, and the nurse or parent says so gently but firmly. With heightened color and with added emphasis the child reiterates his firm intention to carry out his plan. More gentle firmness on the part of the nurse and a crescendo of objection and determination in the child's response end in what may be termed a "tantrum." A counter suggestion made without a trace of opposition, that the pail could be set under the steps where it could wait for its owner or that it could be taken to the back porch, would carry the idea of holding it safe for the child and of the adult's interest in his plan and approval of it. This method is in most cases at once disarming.

There are children who, for some reason which psychiatry alone can answer, avoid coming to grips with real situations which make real demands upon them. It is important that such children learn to face reality and to conform to it. It is a mistake in such cases to depend on a fanciful and indirect appeal because it is clouding a real issue. The fact that a child would go willingly to the bathroom only as a hop-toad seemed a slight matter till it was realized that he was evading many other situations in which he was called upon to take decisive action in his own person on practical matters.

Usually however, negativism comes as a phase and does not persist if it is given little to feed upon. There should always be avoidance of the dogmatic attitude on the part of the adult that the child must accede on the moment to adult requests. A little leeway in time given the child and a little humor or playfulness in the request will often prevent the development of a negative attitude.

If it constitutes a really serious problem there must be an effort to trace its cause and to remove it if possible. Then often decisive action on the part of the adult, like immediate isolation of the child till he is ready to be a member of a coöperating group, is better than argument, reasoning or tact. The important thing to do is to change the rhythm which is too strong for a child to manage by himself.

Another language problem which has been the source of much thought is the effect on language development of dictating the speech of children. It seems to be a spontaneous impulse of many adults to suggest to a child the words that he shall use whenever the occasion for speech arises. It is not only the frequent reminder to "say" thank you or please or excuse me that is given but the child is told the answer to all questions asked of him and the explanation for all his actions is made by the adult and placed in his mouth. "Say, 'I will come again tomorrow, boys and girls'" is given him as he leaves, or "Say, 'Good morning, teacher,'" as he arrives. The parent or nurse is not regarding the question of growth in her relationship to the child, but is entertaining herself with the sound of more or less sophisticated expressions on the lips of the baby, for this sort of treatment is only effective when it begins in infancy. Under the stimulus of the repeated "Say" the child usually echoes, especially I believe if he is sensitive to sounds. He gets the habit of echoing till he echoes even when he does not hear. He recalls and repeats adult expressions and scraps of adult conversation out of their context. Sometimes it seems to be the situation which reminds him, as when a child looking from a window into a garden said, "See the taxicab coming take you to school." Probably looking from a window into the street his mother had made the remark to him, and his position at the window had recalled the occasion and the words. Sometimes it is a phrase or an emphasis that is recalled, the child's reaction to his own language response being more language, but a fixed and automatic form rather than a fluid and adaptive form. One child who had a tendency to adopt phrases used by adults would put a toy out of sight, then say, "Block *all* gone!" and then usually follow it up by saying, "Block *so* sleepy!" or *"so* dirty."

From time to time we have had children who seemed to acquire their language in this way. It sometimes gives them a facility but we question whether it is facility in language or in mimetics. Their language seems to lack the original flavor which characterizes that of children who acquire speech as they acquire other facilities, through experimental practice.

There is needed more study on individuals in order to determine what relationships there are between types of vocal and verbal expression and types of movement and posturing; between language performance and observed interests, the kinds of stimuli that tend to rouse spontaneous responses, the course followed by the responses and how they eventuate. By this I mean the progressive maturing of the action patterns, the beginnings of which we trace in the early years.

I am inclined to believe that the progressive

acquisition of language through self-initiated use means that a process of integration is going on; that a more satisfactory development is assured by this means than by a method of setting a pattern for a child to follow. I believe it even though he may gain a large vocabulary at an earlier age under the latter condition. Moreover a child may seem precocious in the number of words he uses, and immature in his content. He may be echoing phrases because of an interest in sounds. I have said earlier in this section that enjoyment was a legitimate and potent factor in language development. The child who chanted " 'Way around to Africa and 'way around to Greece" may be getting satisfaction from words, the sound and the rhythmic quality of the syllables and their arrangement. Though enjoyment is a real factor in language, it is one that can be given in ways that enrich meaning instead of impoverishing it. The habit of speaking without thought, of making social contacts as far as language is concerned through the dictation of a third person seems to me distinctly unprofitable even if the vocabulary gained by this means can be drawn upon in a later stage of growth.

In language as in other developmental processes, one's conception of growth governs one's attitude toward children in regard to it. If growth means learning tricks the process can be speeded up, the method of dictation adopted and a large vocabulary acquired early together with a repertory of rimes and songs.

There is another danger, it seems to me, in stimulating a child's interest in language forms before language meanings can be grasped. The degree of attention which he will show in his responses depends upon certain physiological factors, which are at present unevaluated. Beyond the verbal reaction which he makes to the forms he is being conditioned to a failure to respond to the meaning. We all tend to talk to children too much but sometimes adults fall into the habit of continuous conversation with children because of the result. Disturbed mental cases are quieted by the continuous warm bath; over-excitable or over-active children are sometimes kept immersed in a flow of tepid conversation for exactly the same reason. The result is that they become dependent upon adults for support in verbal form. The content is not important to the child and in fact he frequently seems not to hear the language as communication. It is a sedative rather than a stimulus. We question the wisdom of this method because of the danger of cultivating in children the habit of inattention.

It is for the same reason that we do not teach songs or rimes to children of this age. The lilt and swing of "Mother Goose" is inimitable and its place in literature has never been taken. Its content however rarely touches the experience of children below three years in age. It introduces a vicarious element that we are trying to avoid in the program which we intentionally present to children. They usually meet "Mother Goose" and other verses at home, but we do not attempt to develop the acquaintance. "See-saw Marjorie Daw" is a good rhythmic accompaniment to the tip of the spring board, but "Donald goes up, up, up; Donald goes down, down, down!" adds to the rhythm, words that are personal and fitted to the activity in progress. During these years

when a baby is acquiring so many new and significant experiences, it seems important to us to keep
the intentional environment as related and as consistent as is possible.

A child has the capacity for perceiving relationships almost from the time when he first starts out
on his independent existence. Adults remember their
childhood impressions but they usually place the
events which they recall nearer infancy than is probable. For this reason they tend almost universally
to reach beyond a child's stage of growth, perception and interest in the experiences they offer him.
Language figures largely in any relationship between
children and adults but it should always carry meaning within the scope of a child's understanding. One
of the most difficult problems presented by a deaf
child is his acceptance of inadequate hearing. He
learns so thoroughly not to listen that a process of
reëducation is necessary after his defect is remedied.
We note a similar tendency on the part of children
who have been drowned in adult conversation.

Sometimes there is instead a real precocity, adequate understanding of adult remarks and an early
development of mature language patterns. The
trend of a child's development depends upon his own
"inherited growth tendencies" and upon the sort of
interest in language shown by his adult companions.
It depends also upon the stage of growth on which
the language interest is grafted.

I have observed that the age range covered in our
nursery school might be said to represent a locomotor stage. Toward the end of it, when control of
the trunk and limbs is well established, there is
noticeable a gradual maturing of the social technique,

so that there are fairly long periods of play together and associated with this a more mature attitude toward language, whether or not the mechanics of speech show maturity. I mean by this that children listen, even to their mates, and respond, and tend very abortively to keep the ball of conversation rolling in some cases, even while their pronunciation and their sentence structure may still be infantile. It is not to this period that I refer in saying that there is danger in stimulating a child's interest in language prematurely. I think, however, that in general adults need to be cautioned against setting the clock ahead in their dealing with children and especially against absorbing their interest and attention in activities which demand language sophistication.

As we have studied our children, precocious facility in language has seemed to be coincident with dependence upon adults and a lagging interest in what we call full-body activities. That is at the age when we have learned to expect to see a child absorbed in establishing control over his body in a variety of situations and in developing the ability to use various pieces of apparatus which call for various degrees of skill, we find him carrying on fewer energetic activities of the postural sort, and we find language figuring to a greater extent in his program.

The language interest shows itself in various forms. There may be a very mechanical sort of repetition of learned language forms,—songs and verses the content of which the child cannot understand, or words and phrases, irrelevant to the immediate situation but applicable to a similar one; there may be on the other hand a truly admirable understanding of language meanings and an adequate and relevant use of language forms. In both the types cited we find the play activities on a lower level than we should expect and we are forced to conclude that the unsuitable verbal interest has been substituted for the non-verbal activities which we commonly find in operation at this stage.

Education cannot answer the questions that these observed behavior reactions have raised as to their biological source, but education must deal with them. A child to whom speech is mainly sound and rhythm must be introduced to language which carries a message to him; the child who is using language as a tool for social intercourse must be diverted from the adult companionship which he seeks because there only does he find a conversational equal; both children must be turned back to the constructive play situation and their interest enlisted in its possibilities.

There are physical conditions that seem sometimes to be responsible for an unusually early awakening of language interest or an unusually sophisticated use of it. If a child's physical development is retarded so that he is less able in the use of his body than others, he sometimes develops faster in language and compensates for his deficiencies. It is difficult to tell which is cause and which is effect, for similar behavior may result from quite different situations. A child with weak musculature tends often to use language, either to serve himself in lieu of other activity or as a tool to bring him into the social limelight. However, whether language is employed as a drug, a compensating tool or a lure to catch adult attention, the corrective elements reside in the environment, in the materials and experiences available and the group use of them.

It is true that the function of language is to make possible the substitution of the verbal for the postural expression. At first the child can indicate only with his full-body movements the things he desires, and one sign of his maturing is his ability to make a word or an expression stand for a movement or a gesture. This kind of substitution comes gradually with growth but sometimes children who are over-precocious in conversational ability tend to use words when activity of the large muscles is called for. "Let's play" at this age does not precede a scheme worked out and followed but is likely to precede more words. The reason for this is that even when a child has an unusually large vocabulary and a real precocity in the use of language, he has not a true social technique. He is not seeking an interchange of thought. He is seeking contact, attention and a method of making himself felt. The desire for power is probably a fundamental one with most normal human beings. The child who wins interest and gains control over his fellows through the power, initiative and skill which he shows in his dealing with the play materials is on a firmer plane in development than the one who can attract his fellows by his ability to use words.

Lucy, at three, was a child who showed power in both directions but her constructive ability was not operative when her social drive was most in evidence. She would spend long periods at building, at climbing and jumping or at play in the sand and pebbles. Certain types of dramatic play, initiated by her, games of shoe shining and of delivering coal, for example, were popular with the group and were embroidered and elaborated by individual children.

All Lucy's activities stimulated her mates. She was one of those beings whose interests are at once interesting to those who come in contact with her,—a definition, I suppose, of that elusive quality called charm. As long as she carried on such activities as those mentioned the stimulation took the form of constructive motor activity. There was usually a language accompaniment, rhythmic, repetitive or onamatopœic or a running comment, and here again she won response in kind. When she deliberately attempted a more mature type of social play the language component absorbed her and the accompanying play which developed was unimportant and flitting. Even though she seemed to be concentrating on conversation, it was not sustained or especially related to the activity.

Children are so largely sensory and motor beings that they are unlikely to make this sort of substitution complete until they are well along toward adolescence. Tell the ten-year-old a story of a man escaping from a cave by crawling through a narrow opening, and you will see him drawing his arms close to his body and making himself as small as possible. Read him about a famous baseball pitcher's famous curve and his arm is likely to draw back to illustrate the position described.

When a child's interest in language draws him to adults and inactivity instead of to his mates and a sharing in their play we consider that the growth stages have not been well served.

Of course no child is actually inactive in the sense of being without movement of the muscles. One of our children who was especially inclined to seek adults to satisfy his impulse for social conversation was very active but his interest span was short and the occupations chosen were very immature. There was much movement of the facial muscles and of the hands and fingers and there was probably an accompaniment of dramatic play going on implicitly. There was also a tendency to seek illicit pursuits, such as interfering with adult possessions, which would result of course in attention from adults and opportunity for conversation with them.

The results of precocious ability in communication seem to us to indicate that a stage in growth,—the locomotor stage, with the constructive interests which develop with it, suffers in consequence. We make this conclusion from observations of the behavior of the children whose language development progresses at the usual rate and those in whom the language facility is especially stressed. Our judgment is based as well upon the response of children in the nursery school to the withdrawal of adult language stimuli, and the presentation of the stimulation of children and materials. The outstanding differences noted are that the language of the child and his constructive activities show a relationship, that is he becomes more aware of the meaning of language and uses it to serve his own play purposes. He seems, one might say, to grow up to his language.

The question arises whether this increase in maturity is the result of time or environment. We believe that it is the result of an integrative process for which the educational method sets up favorable conditions.

PART III
RECORDS

§ 1. How We Keep Records of the Children's Growth

§ 2. Records of Children's Use of the Environment

    A. ACTIVITIES AND MATERIALS
        SLIDE, HAMMER, BUILDING MATERIALS, COLOR, CRAYONS AND PAPER

    B. OTHER CHILDREN AND ADULTS

    C. LANGUAGE AND MUSIC

§ 1. HOW WE KEEP RECORDS OF THE CHILDREN'S GROWTH

IN the measurement program of the Bureau, records are kept of certain general and proportional details of growth. These are made with the coöperation and aid of the nursery staff and are subjected to statistical treatment. The weight is the only measurement that is regularly taken and charted as a routine nursery procedure. There are also data collected at the time of the physical examination, and X-rays of arm, hand and wrist, X-rays of chests and hearts, and electro-cardiograms are taken at regular intervals, all of which constitute material for our research study.

The records of the nursery staff are for the most part qualitative in character. The attempt is made to observe and record the behavior of the children in such a way that it will be possible to trace the development of patterned responses * and to discover their significance in age-level differences or in individual and personality differences.

The data gathered are used for long term studies, but also currently to keep the teachers oriented in regard to the use of the equipment by individual children, its educational value, the necessity for change or modification, the needs of individuals and the general status of the group.

What does growth demand of education? Can we

* See Part I, § 1.

find out facts about how children gain control of their bodies and the materials in the environment which will throw light upon educational method? Can we discover what part social contacts should play in nursery school experience and how social techniques develop? How different are children at the different ages represented in the nursery school? How ought they to be grouped?

I shall not attempt to give definitive answers to all these questions but I hope to show our method of studying them and of gathering evidence in regard to them.

What is going to keep such questions before us unless we have a record of activities and unless we have some method of current study of them,—for the act of recording does not in itself increase wisdom.

The records are taken in three forms: the daily chart, the weekly summary and the full-day record.

One of the responsibilities which we accept when we take children from their homes is that of keeping the parents informed of the events of the day and of progress as the weeks pass.

The daily chart, shown on page 156, was not originally made up for the parents. We felt the need of keeping a check upon the adjustment of each child to the nursery school and his progress from day to day. We chose outstanding situations which we considered constant and typical, things that would show the child's degree of adjustment at any time.

Naps are liable to be shortened or disturbed before a baby feels at home with us. Control of urination depends upon age but also upon the affective state. Frequency, for example, often increases after a child is adjusted to nursery conditions. The bowel movements are an index to general health and we need to know facts about elimination as well as about food intake. A record of appetite from day to day gives us a check on the general physical condition but the topic is more important as showing how habits of feeding are established. The use of implements, the willingness to eat novel articles of diet, the way whimsies or distastes for certain foods are overcome can be traced and the amounts taken can be reckoned by reference to the charts.

At first a child is likely to seek adults. Later his own brand of sociability develops and is shown by the record. Variations in his technique or in the sort of advances he makes indicate fluctuations in his physical state. The same thing is true of crying attacks. At first the actual parting from parents or nurse causes crying, then any proceeding that revives the memory of home brings tears. Individual differences in a resort to crying and individual progress to serenity and control can be traced by the record.

By jotting down a comment under each heading we keep ourselves reminded of the status of the individuals in the group and as we go over these brief daily records we can check up on the need of establishing remedial measures. At the end of the month a general summary is made and typed on the back of the chart.

We found parents much interested in these daily charts and as we were sending reports home with the children whenever there was need of informing the parents of irregularities in routine, we began making a carbon copy of each day's record. Each family is given a sample chart and the carbon slip

NAME Caroline

INDIVIDUAL DAILY RECORD

DATE May 19..

Date	NAP				URINATION			DEFECATION Time—Quality	APPETITE AND GENERAL BEHAVIOR AT TABLE	SOCIAL CONTACTS CHILDREN—ADULTS	CRYING ATTACKS—CAUSES	NOTES ON PHYSICAL CONDITION
	In Bed	Asleep	Awake	Length	Vol.	Invol.	Nap					
1	12.45	No	Nap		9.30 12.00 12.45			0	Spilled milk. Left half her soup. Took rest of dinner alone.	Group and social play with older children.	0	Weight, 28.75 + (Voided.) Mother reported cough. Physician examined.
2	12.50	No	Nap		10.50 12.45			0	Ate main course (egg included). Did not finish milk or touch junket.	Group and social play with older children.	0	
3									Absent.			
4	1.05	No	Nap		12.00 1.00			0	Refused bacon. Fed self rest of dinner.	Group and social play as usual.	0	
5	1.00	No	Nap		12.00 1.00 3.00				Ate main course promptly alone and assented when offered more. Named liver as her choice—ate it. No soup.	Excluded P. and J. from her boat. Later allowed two others on. Group and social play.	0	
8	1.00	No	Nap		11.00 12.00 1.00				Finished dinner promptly and alone (without help).	Group play. Social play with P. Also showed resentment of P.'s teasing.	Squawked at P. (See Social.)	Weight, 29.25 (Voided.)
9	1.05	No	Nap		12.00 1.00 3.00				Finished. Was helped with last of tomato and bread crumbs.	Group and social play.	0	
10	Went home		after	dinner	11.25				Finished alone.	Group play with older children.	When S. pounded her finger.	
11	1.10	No	Nap		11.35 1.10 1.25 2.50				Was helped. Left soup and part of dessert.	Group play. Independent play. Social with P. and S.	0	
12	1.00	No	Nap		9.35 12.20 2.35				Slow. Finished. Her spoon was filled for her several times but she actually fed herself.	Group and social play	Tears in eyes during chest x-ray but she showed great control.	Chest and hand x-rays.

USE OF DAILY CHART

The record under the first three headings needs no explanation. The actual time of the various occurrences is charted.

"Appetite and General Behavior at Table" may read as follows: "Fed himself. Finished. Second serving. No spilling." In another case there may be variations from day to day, as: "Was fed entire meal. Slow. Refused celery" or "Fed self soup. Asked for help with liver. Ate it when fed. Took remainder of dinner alone."

"Social Contacts" may be recorded as follows: "Independent play with hammer. Joined group on slide. Social play, dramatic, in packing box with J." or "Social play with M. Excluded S. and P. Refused to join group, interfering with their activity."

"Crying Attacks" are checked with the attendant circumstances rather than the causes which often can only be surmised. For instance, of a new arrival, "Very sober when nurse left. No tears. Cried hard at feeding time. Refused orange juice."

In the last column the weekly weight is charted, notes are made on physical condition, such as coughs, fussiness or fatigue, and on any examination or measurements given the child.

can be placed under the printed headings and the record read.

The charts are made up just after dinner each day. Then the length of nap and additional data are charted as each child is taken up and the slip is put with his bag or with his outside clothing to be taken home. The report serves a double purpose. It informs the mother of details which she needs to know about her child and at the same time relieves us of the responsibility of special reports when something out of the ordinary has happened. It makes a much more stable and satisfactory coöperative arrangement for we not only are sure that our report gets to the parents but we receive their comments and are able to regulate our procedure.

For instance, Philip's mother notes that his naps are under two hours in length. She brings back to school her record of the week-end, when his naps were nearly two and a half hours long. We then shift sleeping places, giving Philip a room where we can assure his being undisturbed. The result is a monthly average of two hours and twenty-five minutes which, though only a slight advance over the previous one, is enough to relieve the mother's anxiety and to establish confidence. At home Donald refuses many of the fresh vegetables and will never eat junket. The mother sees a record of uniformly good appetite and prompt self-feeding in the nursery and realizes that there is no basis but caprice for his vagaries.

The daily chart shows the inconsistencies that are often found in a record gathered for a current need. Its data are all factual but are expressed in different terms. Its original purpose was informational. The data under the first four headings can be written numerically, can be reckoned in percentages and can be treated statistically. The last three topics admit only of qualitative statement. On a single day Yvonne joined the group but also played independently. She made both affectionate and belligerent advances to the children. She cried when her mother left, when her activities were balked by her inability to deal with some piece of material and when removed from the group after attacking a child. These facts as part of a consecutive record add to our understanding of Yvonne as a person and of the stage of adjustment that she has reached at any one time. The facts that Craig cried more than usual, was inactive and refused dinner have a relationship. We may not be able to express it in figures but it is recognized by our entry in the last column, "Seems not up to usual form. Watch for cold." That is, the facts show a relationship which it is important to place before parents and teachers. It is also important to maintain a consistent method of checking one's opinion on such subjects as crying and social advances. Whether a record which answers the above purpose can be used as an exact measure of progress in a statistical treatment of data is extremely doubtful. The reduction of such fluid material as behavior to checks or percentages carries with it two different kinds of risks,—first that behavior which can be so treated may not be the most significant and second that in the process the significant features may be sacrificed.

The weekly summary is an attempt to keep a running, current record of the activities of the children. Throughout the day the teachers in the Nursery

School take diary notes of the behavior of the children. These records are as full as the exigencies of the situation permit. They are the result of experiment and study and still need further development and modification. Each set of persons who has worked upon them has helped in method, form and content. In the beginning we made the usual mistake of observers of young children: we tended to record the unusual manifestations; we missed out on the every-day and the consecutive. We were at that time in the most experimental stage of a piece of work which is, we hope, still tentative and experimental, and we had not fully defined the purpose of our recording. We came early to the realization that we did not wish our diary notes to deal with children as single units but as members of a group. As stated early in this chapter we had the evaluation of our environment in mind in developing a method of record keeping. We wished also to trace the development of individuals along various lines,—in their use and control of their bodies, as concerned with the materials, as concerned with the other human beings with whom they were associating and as concerned with their own affective impulses. We finally made a tentative organization of topics under which our notes were taken, and with certain modifications this form seems serviceable and is still followed.

How are the pieces of apparatus used? What do the children do with wagons, blocks, dolls and trains? How much true social contact is there among children of nursery age and how much should it be stimulated? There are affective impulses in all behavior. How do they show themselves in nursery relationships,—with children, with material, with adults?

Our interest in language development has been stated in Part II. We look to our records to answer the questions raised there: What part is language playing in general growth? What urges to speech do we note, how do they differ with different children, and especially how are the affective needs being served?

We recognize the rhythmic element in the growth of the body, in language and in affectivity. Music gives us the opportunity to mark specific rhythmic responses. These responses are noted whether they are made during the daily music period or as reactions to melodic or rhythmic phrases used by adults and accompanying the activities of the children, or as a spontaneous rhythmic use of the vocal apparatus or of the body.

The daily notes are taken on perforated scratch pads. We attempt to keep our entries separated so that no more than one topic is treated on one page. At the end of each week the pages are torn off and assembled in the weekly summary. First comes the Weather for each day, then the Attendance. Thereafter follow in order: Activities—Out-of-Doors and Indoors; Social-Emotional, that is activities which are especially marked by their affective element; Language—not only vocabulary but also understanding of situations met in the nursery life, syllables and phrases, and ability to communicate thought, and Music, the last topic.

After the scratch pad sheets are arranged in this order the recorder makes sure that the necessary interpolations, interpretations or additions are made and then the mass of notes is handed over to a secretary for typing. Before we devised this method we had either to dictate, rewrite or closely cross reference our rough notes and the task was almost beyond possibility in time and effort. We have found the use of the perforated pad very practicable and simple and a great labor-saving device.

The value of this type of record is also its weakness. That is, it is made by persons who best know the child but for that very reason it runs the danger of inadequacy, for significant manifestations may go unrecorded because of lack of time—not to observe them but to find time to describe them adequately. If a close check-up method is devised so that the week's records are read by the staff and discrepancies or omissions are met in the notes of the following week, it is possible to maintain a fair degree of consistency. We are meeting the question of checking by a staff reading of the weekly summaries as they are typed and by the introduction of an index sheet as illustrated. By this device the representation of each child under each topic can be seen at a glance.

In the Index cited, March 14-21, several questions are raised by the actual number of checks to each child, and by their distribution against the materials. The fact that Mary is mentioned under only four heads may be because she does not yet walk. Investigation of the record shows that she is fully recorded under Motor Control, showing that her drive is especially upon the attempt to use and control her own body.

Harriet is the only other child who seems to be inadequately represented. Whatever the reason it is

WEEKLY SUMMARY INDEX *

March 14-21

	Caroline	Gretchen	Harriet	Philip	Joan	Timothy	Saunders	Mary	Peggy
Planks	x	x		x	x	x	x	x	x
Swings		x			x		x		
Knotted Rope		x		x	x				
Sand	x	x	x	x	x	x	x	x	x
Kiddy Kars					x	x			
Wagons	x			x					x
Brooms	x								
Hammers	x								
Balls	x			x	x				x
Blocks				x		x			
Motor Control	x	x	x	x	x	x	x	x	x
Soc. & Emot.	x	x		x		x	x		x
Language	x			x			x		x
Music	x	x	x	x		x	x	x	x
Inc. Music				x					
Special									x

* One child in school for forenoon play-time only.

WEEKLY SUMMARY

March 14-21

WEATHER:

Monday —Warm, humid.
Tuesday —Clear, cool.
Wednesday—Clear, mild.
Thursday —Clear, mild.
Friday —Clear, mild.

ATTENDANCE:

Caroline, Gretchen, Harriet, Philip, Joan, Timothy, Saunders and Mary present all the week. Peggy absent Monday, present rest of week; first day since her long absence.

the task of the staff to account for it in further summaries. If she also is still in Mary's stage, the records must unmistakably reveal it. If she is one of the children who concern themselves unobtrusively with a limited number of materials and make few social advances, that must be stated and a policy toward it adopted.

Why are only two children checked under Blocks? The fact that it is only the older children whose language is recorded calls our attention to the necessity for checking up on that of the younger in following summaries.

Many of the questions which an inspection of the index raises can be answered at once by members of the recording staff, but the fact that they are raised brings into focus discrepancies, omissions or undue weighting of materials or children.

We do not regard our recording procedure as finished, and we are still working on our technique, but some such regular method of scrutinizing the behavior of children in their reaction to their environment seems to us essential in order that teachers may keep themselves aware of necessities for action on their part, whether it may be for change in the equipment, the teaching method or the arrangement of the group. As a research method it seems to us a necessary preliminary at least to more specific and definitive study.

The full-day record, which is as closely as may be a literal account of the behavior of some one child through a nursery day, is taken primarily for purposes of research, so that the information gathered week by week may be supplemented by a detailed and consecutive picture of the behavior of each individual for a whole day. The record includes not only the reactions in conduct and in language of the child under study but also the social situation calling forth the response or observable at the moment even when it seems to concern only the other children in the group. The records are repeated at regular intervals, not further apart than every two months. They constitute a mass of material for intensive study and for further record of individual development. They are illuminating from the teacher's point of view because they force her to concentrate upon each child at definite intervals and because they invariably contribute to her judgment of him. They are now in process of modification in the attempt to study through them more thoroughly the physiological growth patterns that are initiated, develop and come to maturity during these nursery school years. They are used always with the weekly summaries as supplementary material. They are at the disposal of the research staff and with the weekly summaries constitute the behavior material for the studies of personality and of growth patterns. It is from these behavior records, weekly and full-day, that will be drawn material to relate to our more exact measures of growth. The research staff now includes two psychologists who are making records of the development of certain patterns and activities among children in the Nursery School and in the City and Country School.

A description of our method of taking records and the use to which they can be put may seem unconvincing because of our tentative approach to it. We are attempting to study the reactions of children to their environment, what they do to the environment, how they adapt the materials and persons in it to their own purposes, and what the environment does to them, how their behavior is modified by conditions which they find or which their own reactions bring about. These are fundamental problems in education and in psychology, and we are still in the initial stages of attack upon them. In the nature of the case a discussion of our records is not in terms of reaction time to definite stimuli; it does not involve the method of presenting a controlled laboratory situation with its result. We are attempting to study a child's individual and characteristic way of responding to situations set up by the Nursery School environment. We are calling his way of reacting his behavior pattern in regard to this or that situation. We realize that there may be no observable beginning and end to a given response, that there is implicit as well as overt behavior, of which we may remain entirely unaware, or the implications of which we may trace in posture, in random movements or in a speeding up of the learning process. We record what we can observe and we isolate for our purposes the portion of the child's response which seems to have to do with the situation under observation. Such a procedure is demanded by the limits of human powers of analysis. If we did not define our problem we should have only a mass of unrelated observations.*

Children come into the Nursery School with very immature perceptual development in regard to many of the objects and situations which they find there. Before they leave they have set up many different

* Kantor, J. R. *Principles of Psychology.* Chap. II, Vol. I. (Alfred A. Knopf, 1924.)

habitual modes of response, indicating progress in the awareness of meanings in their dealing with such objects and situations. We are trying to record the development of their patterned responses—the earliest tentative attempt to set up a pattern, the degree of persistence after it is initiated and the way it is elaborated and matured.

In succeeding chapters I shall give excerpts from the records in the attempt to illustrate what they contain and how they may be used.

§ 2. RECORDS OF CHILDREN'S USE OF
THE ENVIRONMENT

A. ACTIVITIES AND MATERIALS

I SHALL try to draw from our records material that illustrates how we are studying the growth of children; that shows by what even steps and in how individual a way the action patterns are developed, and also how varied can be the method used by a child in dealing with one piece of material. It must be remembered that the excerpts are taken from a body of material that often totals a thousand pages for each child. What I have given is merely a sampling which I hope may indicate our method of study. It shows also the teachers' attitude and the amount and kind of supervision given a child.

In choosing illustrations from the nursery records I have used those of a limited number of children. They are taken from the files of several years. The number of children in each year's group at any one time is eight. The same children frequently appear in nursery records for two years.

The photographs are chosen for the activities they illustrate and do not necessarily represent the children mentioned in the record.

In illustrating our method from the records I shall attempt to follow roughly each time the early chapter headings, taking longer and more consecutive excerpts than it was possible to insert in the text. In the section about the equipment and how it is used I have said that children learn the various processes called for by the use of the physical equipment without instruction and usually without definite encouragement on the part of the adults. The nursery world is an active and doing one, and the impulse of its inhabitants is to share in that doing as soon as they become thoroughly aware of it. Everything which a child does on an impulse of his own tends to make him depend upon his own initiative for succeeding activities. The more he is encouraged to wait upon adult suggestions, the more a dependent attitude is fostered. There is every evidence, too, for believing that self-initiated activities and accomplishments bring with them a sense of elation, satisfaction and fulfillment that taught processes fail to provide with anything like the same poignancy. This is as true of children as it is of adults.

In speaking of leaving children to take their own initiative I do not mean to imply that adults are withdrawn from the situation. As will be seen, the teacher's rôle is not passive. Until a child has dealt with the material himself even its obvious possibilities may be unknown to him. The teacher must be aware of each step while he is learning to recognize the meaning and the qualities of the piece of apparatus he is using—while his perceptual pattern in regard to it is maturing. She must be sure that his experiments are conducted in safety and that he does not imperil his welfare.

Slide

I will take from the records citations to show the growth of a pattern in dealing with a specific piece of play material. I have chosen the slide because it is a popular piece of apparatus and because the two slides we have are used in rather different ways. The indoor slide (see picture, p. 171) has space at the top where the entire crew can foregather. The chute is steeper than the outdoor slide so that we have to encourage and even to teach the children to make the descent lying on their stomachs feet foremost. Our method is to put the child in the required position as we say, "Lie down, turn over," and to repeat the procedure until the habit is established. With the out-of-door slide, we let the child devise his own method if he can, and he may choose to slide head first, tipping forward from one of the upper steps or to go down sitting. He is of course closely supervised till his technique is assured. Philip's initial attack shows his general attitude of readiness. I have not given dates but instead have separated the citations so that it is evident that they were taken on different days and in chronological order, and have placed the child's age at the left.

Philip was twenty months old when he entered the nursery school. The first note on his appearance and general reactions is as follows: Philip is short, fair with dark brown eyes. He was serene and undisturbed when his mother left. He does not seem dependent upon her and accepted the ministration of the nursery staff without demur. He got in and out of carts with a sort of fumbling but did not fall. He runs with a babylike waddle, tipping from side to side, feet wide apart, so that he has a broad stance. He falls seldom except when he hurls himself ahead so fast that he cannot keep his control and his momentum carries him forward till he falls. Is not disturbed by such accidents. He goes about with a smile as if in anticipation of the next delightful experience. As the

Sliding.

Tipping over from the top.

Sitting backwards.

Walking up the chute.

The indoor slide.

year progressed he continued to carry this atmosphere with him. It was evidenced by his shouts and leaps and chuckles of laughter, by his clapping or clasping his hands when pleased with something he had done and by his eager vocal accompaniment to his many activities. He was an eager and experimental small person and the record of his performance illustrates the impulse of the baby under two to employ himself in full-body activities and in the expenditure of energy for its own sake.

20 months—Philip walked for several steps up the chute out of doors, holding the side—slipped and repeated. Walked up four steps of the indoor slide in company with others of the group.

21 months—1. Walked up the steps of out-of-door slide— smiling. He stepped up a bit over top, but with a little help he got his second leg over without its getting caught. He seated himself beaming and held the side of the chute. He was held back by adult so that the speed would not alarm him, and slid, squealing with joy. He sat at the foot, then scrabbled up the chute, climbed on as far as he could reach from the side. He *did not go back* to the steps and paid no attention to the 3-steps which were placed at the side so that he could get on the chute from them.

There is shown here an example of immaturity in the perceptual pattern. Though he had just had the experience of getting to a slide by climbing the steps, the two parts of the experience were not appreciated as related and his first impulse was to scrabble up the chute to repeat the activity. The interest in walking up the chute persisted however, and one day when he had his rubbers on he succeeded in getting half way up.

21 months—2. With rubbers on he was interested in walking up the chute holding with both hands. He did well,

spreading feet wide apart and bracing against the sides.
He got almost half up and slid. Repeated . . .

This citation shows his readiness in seizing upon
the method which will help him most as does also an
account of further experimentation during the same
week. Children differ very much in the rate at which
they learn to modify their procedure to varying
environmental conditions. These immediate, spontaneous muscular adjustments to unfamiliar situations like the sliding or running on a spring board
or accommodating to the rhythm of the swing must
be due to an especial innate capacity, and as surely
are not concerned with what are called intellectual
processes. There seems to be a sort of muscular
alertness which acts to the same end that later deliberation or reasoning does.* It is observable in
operation in children who show other signs of motor
ability and interest, and must be due to a balance in
nervous and muscular equilibrium.

21 months—3. He ran to the new slide (out of doors). Got
up steps pulling by rails, two feet on a stair, baby-wise.
At top he sat, stretched his right leg over the top of the
chute leaving the left leg. He retrieved it and made
the descent, beaming. He ran with radiant smile to the
steps again. He repeated four or five times. Occasionally
his leg got hopelessly caught. Finally he was encouraged
and shown how to climb to the top step before sitting.
He did this once or twice and then used his original
method. At the top he made a soft "Too, too," which
seemed an echo of an older child's call, "Too, too, I'm
coming." He showed no apprehension when he found
himself on the chute with others. He has a technique

* Head, Henry. *Vigilance:* "A Psychological State of the Nervous
System." *British Jour. of Psychology.* October, 1923.

often noted but quite lacking in Ralph's and Pat's procedure so far. He *spreads* his *legs, bracing* his *feet against the side of the chute and also grasps the sides.* In this way he puts a brake on his speed and can be trusted to go down without adult's hand. As it is, the impetus causes him to bend almost completely double at the foot of the out-of-door slide. He seems now completely to have achieved the sitting method, standing on the top step before sitting. Often he pauses at the top to look about him over the walls bounding the roof, beaming and squealing with joy.

22 months—1. Philip went down the out-of-door slide on his stomach, feet first, after turning himself over on top from the normal sitting position. Indoors he has been given the usual pattern of lying down at the top of the chute, turning over and making the descent feet first on his stomach. One day he evaded control and went down sitting. He could not at first nor always maintain an upright position so he went hurtling down with one leg in the air and almost over the edge. It filled him with intense elation and he showed no signs of reluctance or trepidation such as Karl showed even when facing the chute from a sitting position at top. Rose, laughing loudly and squealing, ran to the steps again. He repeated several times and was able to keep the upright position for part of the time. He sat poised at the top and thumped the chute with his heels once or twice. He has also been practicing going down the slide steps both facing out and backing down.

This citation and the next show Philip's tendency to experiment, and also the way apparatus like the indoor slide lends itself to variations in method without actual danger. Of course it proves the need of very close supervision if children are allowed to devise methods of dealing with the materials. The more they can be given such opportunities the more equal they will become to handling themselves. Philip's pattern is here shown in the process of becoming more elaborated and his actual skill more assured.

22 months—2. Philip spends much time indoors climbing the slide steps and coming down again facing out, holding railings and bumping down two feet at a time. At each jounce he says "Ba," and laughs. He experimented at the top of the slide chute, sitting at the top, feet over the edge, then sliding down on his back. At first he lay on the balcony with his feet just over the edge of the chute and then tried to squirm forward far enough to slide. Gradually he evolved the technique of sitting with his legs in the chute, then lying back on the balcony, arms over his head and hitching with his heels and pushing with his arms until he got himself over the edge and slid down on his back. Often he changed his mind at the top, turned on his stomach and slid in the established fashion. He also slid several times sitting. One day he laid himself down in position to slide head first, on stomach, but did not do so. He had a narrow escape when he tried to roll over on his stomach after starting. He stopped as an adult ran toward him and remained on his back. He was noticed once coming down, resting across the slide, buttocks and back in the chute, neck and head on one edge, legs over the other.

22 months—3. Charles, Pat and Philip played together, taking turns on the indoor slide, climbing stairs and sliding. Philip held his own with the older children in speed and daring. While of course they did not follow each other in the same order each time there was considerable control shown in waiting for the child ahead to climb up, rather than trying to push in front of him.

23 months—1. Philip sliding in sitting position, landed on the mat with such force that he fell forward making almost a complete somersault. He jumped up gayly each

time and dashed back to the slide steps. He arrives at the foot with his legs so stiff and rigid that he tips up on his heels and is thrown forward.

23 months—2. Pat, older by seven months, went down the indoor slide head first on his stomach. Philip took the position, then stalled. An adult went to his assistance and he slid. He repeated. Later he took the position three times, seemingly trying to get himself into the mood but he did not accomplish it even with the encouragement of the adult. He repeated this performance at intervals during the week.

The approach to a new elaboration was shown in the record of twenty-two months and again here. At a later date there is a further record showing that it took a good many weeks for him entirely to mature this pattern.

24 months—1. Adult table was placed under the chute so that the children could climb and slide from the "half-way station." Philip was very appreciative of this arrangement which was placed for some older children. He continued after the others had left. They had pulled up an adult chair to stand in and once he stopped there to call "Bye, bye, bye" at least a dozen times. He also paused on top of the table to shout "Dah, dah." He gave every evidence of elation and joy.

24 months—2. Philip coming down the steps of the indoor slide facing out as Karl had started up, was asked to go back. He let go the left hand railing with his left hand, held himself safely with his right hand until his left hand swung round to join it as he turned his body, his left foot coming round at the same time to be planted very pigeon-toed beside the other. The step was so narrow that this was a very difficult feat but he achieved it quickly and with no faltering or false moves.

These two excerpts illustrate varied uses of the slide and Philip's ready control of his body.

Again the method of sliding head-first is recorded and his slow advance. The last notes on Philip's slide performance show much progress.

25 months—1. Saunders (22 months) went down the slide head-first. Philip followed and this time ventured down head-first. Several times before he has taken the position lying flat, head forward but on approach of an adult has hastily withdrawn and gone down the easiest way. Now, however, he responded to adult's "Push, push," and was eased down. He repeated several times but waited for adult's help. He has not yet taken the descent with the full force.

25 months—2. Philip walked up the chute of the outdoor slide which was resting upon its 15-inch support. He held the sides and got to the top, then slipped down on his stomach and slid.

During the last two weeks of the year he gained entire control of the head-first method and was seen thus going down the indoor slide with no concern and entirely without reference to adults.

Hammer

I have said that children differed in the amount of individual direction they needed. A child like Matthew required an unusual amount of supervision at first. This was probably due in part to repressive treatment at home but also to a very unstable nervous organization. He was very easily disturbed, laughed or cried readily and betrayed his affective state by poorly coördinated muscular movements. He was well developed and managed his body with automatic precision when nothing disturbed his physical or nervous equilibrium. Our policy was to give him free access to as much of the material as possible and to supervise his use of articles with which he could do harm to himself or his fellows.

I have chosen hammers to illustrate his progress and our method of recording it. As in the preceding records I have arranged the citations in chronological order.

28 months—1. First impression: Matthew is a "wayward" determined youngster of two years and four months. He is a handsome, husky child, well coördinated and large for his age. Though he has very good muscular coördination he lacks "caution"; that is, he falls a good deal and gets unnecessary though minor injuries. He slips on the pavement; he gets hit with the carts or blocks; he allows the swing to hit him as he passes. His first morning he raced from one thing to another as new children usually do. Tried the slide, kiddy kars and wagons. He resists directions, pushes at one's hands and is decidedly negative. That may be because he does not feel at home with us.

28 months—2. Within the first week he gradually became more amenable to reason. He now inquires if he may do certain things and yields to our ruling as to the use he makes of various articles, many of which he was inclined to abuse. His mother says he is very "self-willed."

29 months—1. First morning for nails. . . . Matthew seized a hammer and began laying about him. Mother had said that of course she had never let him have a hammer, referring to his generally destructive attitude. He was directed to pebble curb and shown how to crush stones. Rarely hit stone but banged away on the curb. Has much physical energy and the impulse to use it. Used first one hand—right—then both but hit blindly and the problem of breaking the pebbles did not get through to him. Was so vigorous and threatening that hammer was taken away when it was evident that he would not use it in legitimate fashion.

29 months—2. Matthew, hammering pebbles, held hammer in left hand far from head, showing poor coördination. Then grasped it with both hands and could not hit pebble. Grew so excited that hammer was removed.

29 months—3. Matthew was given a hammer and a nail was set for him. He hit all about it, occasionally but rarely striking head of nail. Used one hand, then both. Gave up before he had nail in. Handed adult the hammer and asked her to drive nail. It was turned back to him and he left the nail and began hitting floor and play materials. Hammer was taken from him and put away. Later he asked for it again and he was given one with a nail and a block of wood. The first nail was started for him and he drove it in, tapping sometimes with right hand, holding handle about half way down, sometimes grasping handle with both hands. His aim was better than yesterday but still poor. It was necessary to guard the three other children who had gathered around, from Matthew's hammer on the up stroke, and the down stroke hit the nail less often than it did the block. He drove in three nails, the last quite crooked. He then began his wild banging on the roof, and brandishing, and the hammer was taken away.

29 months—4. Matthew asked early for the hammer. Could not set nails himself and his coördination was very poor. He used right hand alone, both hands and left hand alone with equally poor results. Tapped eleven times in succession with right hand without hitting the nail. Left off twice to whack roof and was warned each time that the hammer would go away if he did so. He answered each time that he would pound the nail. Pounded his fingers slightly once and whimpered but wished to go on hammering. Finally pushed Karl over for peering at him too closely and hammer was taken away. He seems quite irresponsible with it.

29 months—5. Matthew asked early for the hammer and wished to pound pebbles. After trials in various positions

as per yesterday, he grasped the hammer in right hand, close to head and his aim seemed much more accurate. However he soon changed again, trying both hands and the left one alone, but grasping handle just below head. He then asked for nails. They were set in a hollow block with their points driven just through the wood and he then drove three in. A fair performance. Only one mild attack at banging things. He often started to pound with the claw end of the hammer instead of the head.

29 months—6. Matthew now gives a good and sufficient reason when he asks for a hammer but his real interest is that it gives him an extension of his swinging and banging powers and his use of it degenerates rather promptly. He drove three nails before losing interest during his first session. Each time he took it, however, it had to be removed for misuse.

29 months—7. Matthew asked for hammer as soon as he arrived on roof. Was allowed to take one but was kept in the shelter with a block of wood and nails. He drove nine without much waste, though he hit all about the head, especially when he tried to use one hand—the left. Drives better with both hands, stroke and aim more accurate. He was much more persistent than ever before. After finishing the ninth he handed adult the hammer saying, "I all through with hammer." Returned to it for a brief session later.

30 months—1. Matthew is much more persistent in his use of hammer. Does not yet set nails nor aim with skill. His stroke is so strong that if he hits a nail once or twice on the head it is sent in. If left to set his own nails he pokes them into cracks. He has the term and says frequently, "I can set it."

30 months—2. Matthew tried to set a nail into a long narrow cart axle which he found. He could not do it. It was set for him and he attempted to pound it in. Shifted hammer from left to right, then back to left again. Was

not able to get nail entirely in before he lost interest. Wood was fairly hard.

31 months—Matthew was later than usual in asking for the hammer. Wished to set his own nails and found old holes for them. Used hands alternately, forefingers along the handle. He was slower than I ever saw him. Struck accurately and with deliberation and when he looked at the nail he hit it on the head. Very good persistence. Nails often bent when he used old holes. Later three other children worked with him. They used finer nails, the points of which are sharper and easier to drive in but also much more liable to go crooked. Matthew and two of the children soon left them for pebble crushing.

32 months—1. Full-day Record.

When I arrived Kurt and Matthew had hammers and were pounding at the remaining pile of ice and snow against south wall. Apparently amicable when suddenly Matthew raised hammer and lunged at Kurt. Only grazed Kurt's head. Said nothing when hammer was taken away. Ran off and got a kiddy kar.

32 months—2. Matthew asked for hammer and nails. We have discouraged it since it has been so cold. He set his own nails and drove with strong strokes using both hands. When his attention wandered he banged away all over the block. When he looked at the nail he drove it in accurately. Interest short lived. He drove three nails.

33 months—Full-day Record.

He caught sight of a hammer and took it. Was led to nails and a block. He settled down asking many questions about the nails. Did not set them but stuck them down into a crack. Complained, "There are no holes." Two other children came in and were supplied with nails and hammers. He was asked to drive his own nails and did one or two.

Stages in the use of the hammer.

35 months—Seized a hammer and began swinging it. He was so near the two babies that they were in danger. Was asked, "What are you going to do with it?" Said that he was going to pound pebbles and proceeded to do so naming the colors as he crushed them. "That made white. That made brown. That made white." Crushed pebbles with a swinging stroke. Used left hand. Aimed well and quickly reduced pebbles to dust.

36 months— . . . Matthew hammers with left hand or with both hands. Holds hammer about four inches from the head. Sets his own nail. If it goes to one side he taps it gently from the other side to straighten it. When it is well set he takes hammer in both hands and gives very hard and accurate blows till it is in to the head. Usually takes hammer with left hand in crushing pebbles.

The fact that no further comments on misuse were made indicates that it no longer constituted a problem.

Matthew was given a group rating of two on the use of the hammer. This means a high average performance.

It may be asked why a tool, the use of which is so fraught with dangerous possibilities as the hammer, should be put into the hands of so young a child. We should not include hammers in our equipment if children did commonly misuse them. The fact that Matthew had to be supervised for so long was indicative of his individual lack of organization. The discipline involved in learning the legitimate use of a tool which attracted him so much was helpful, we believe, in his general integration. The opportunity for energy output and the exercise of the arm-shoulder girdle make it an admirable piece of material to say nothing of the skill that the children acquire in preparation for a more constructive use of the hammer in combination with other material.

Building Materials

In citing examples from our records of play with materials that are adapted to construction there are several points of emphasis which I hope to illustrate.

In the process of growth one of the demands made by society upon its individual members is that they learn to adjust to conditions and modify their behavior in accordance with them. A child's life is particularly beset by demands for adjustment, for the main interests of children are alien to those of the adult environment in which they are placed, and when they enter the nursery world in which their interests are supposed to be supreme, they do not decide upon the terms of their sovereignty, and the process of learning to share means subordination of their inclinations to those of the group.

On the other hand the stage in civilization reached by any race of people is estimated by the degree to which they have made the earth serve their needs,—that is, the degree to which they have modified their environment. It is not always realized that such a criterion should be kept in mind in dealing with children and schools. It is, however, an essential consideration for those responsible for nursery schools to make sure that children have the opportunity to affect their environment by their own efforts. The social environment they can and do affect, sometimes to a disastrous degree.* I believe

* See Part III, § 2, B. Other Children and Adults.

that children lack the technical equipment, in language and in the perception of social relationships, to make experimentation in this field profitable. On the other hand they will be able to gain power over the physical environment if materials are furnished them the qualities of which they can learn to know and the uses of which they can control. Caroline Pratt * has called this sort of equipment "adaptable" material, and blocks are outstanding examples of it.

My first point of emphasis is then that *power to deal effectively with his environment accrues to a child through the free use of constructive material.*

The Hill blocks or those used in the City and Country School † or other sets planned to meet the same requirements make it possible for a child to plan and execute constructions as large and as elaborate as he can devise. They are in an entirely different category from the smaller sets of blocks, restricted in actual number and having no stable unit form, with which parents have had until recent years to be content. These small collections of varisized and shaped blocks force the child continually to adapt his plans and his purposes to their limitations.

Blocks are traditionally appropriate play material for children of a wide age range. They are said to be appropriate because they serve the purposes of children. In considering them as educational equipment we shall do well to inquire what educational significance there is in children's purposes and

* *Experimental Practice in the City and Country School.* (E. P. Dutton & Co., 1924.)
† Bulletin VIII, *Catalogue of Play Equipment.* (Bureau of Educational Experiments.)

how they differ with different ages. If we watch the impulse toward constructive materials as it appears and develops in a group of nursery school children, we shall see definite patterns taking shape and becoming more and more elaborated with age.

Where do children get their impulse to construct? What sends them to the blocks in the first place? It seems to be first and in some cases for a long time the interest in manipulation and in the output of energy, and just as in the use of the crayons there is little drawing, so in the use of blocks there is little construction. The youngest babies may seek blocks because they see them in the hands of older children but "imitation" takes them no further. Real imitation, deliberately following a copy, demands a maturity that nursery children rarely show. A child can imitate an activity or process only if he already has the capacity to accomplish it, and even then he will not slavishly copy it. We have had one or two children who seemed actually to regard another child's method with the intention of acquiring it. It seemed like a very mature process in such young children as ours. One of these was attracted to the interlocking blocks, used as cars, and to the use to which another child was putting them. He squatted in front of the child and observed him for some time, then went to get more cars and attempted to get them interlocked. He did not for some time grasp the process but his method was definite and apparently intentional. Whether his learning was actually hastened by his attempt to imitate and whether in fact he "learned" by watching the other child or by his own use of the material is still a question.

The younger children shift the blocks about, carry them from place to place or stack them irregularly or in masses.

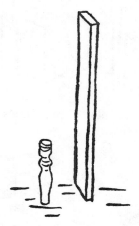

Excellent balance, achieved by a child of 23 months.

We have not found the towered pile invariably the first, though it is usual. They sometimes seem to be definitely comparing the shapes and sizes, and in their use of them to be building up some appreciation of differences.

Interlocking blocks, 24 months.

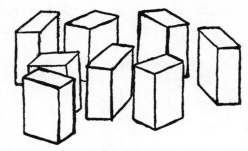

Young children place the blocks in irregular masses—25 months.

Example of a very elaborate stack of paving blocks built by Caroline at 32 months.

Very early there is seen an interest in patterns, sometimes before a child has learned the advantage of evening the edges of his blocks. The examples illustrated are taken from sketches made on the spot of the constructions of the children and represent only a few of the examples observed. There has been no attempt to reduce these drawings to a single scale; for instance, cubes and half units, unless they

are used in combination, are not exactly comparable
in scale. Diagrammatic drawings or rough sketches
were made as the children played with their materials. That there were no patterns set them it is
needless to say. There was no attempt to suggest a
form, there was no observable imitation, and no
comments were made by adults unless the child himself called attention to his product when interest
and general approval was expressed. In the case of
the serial arrangement of two blocks the child
seemed to be interested solely in the variety of possible combinations for she worked on a small table
and made no effort to get more blocks.

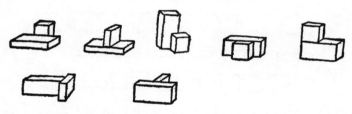

A serial arrangement of two blocks—24 months.

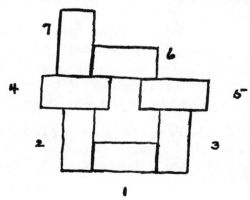

Note the alternation in placing—first on one side, then the other. Made by Karl at 31 months.

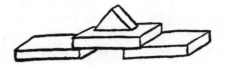

One of Caroline's patterns at 36 months. She made fewer of the evenly balanced structures than Peggy and more massive stacks.

Constructed of cubes and dominoes and named a bath tub. Dora—37 months.

There is quite evidently something in the rhythm of a balanced construction that is satisfying and it seems to be form that takes precedence of the representative structure that is named and used in a play scheme.

Materials of different sorts are often combined in making a balanced arrangement. In the illustration kiddy kars are used with paving blocks by a child of 31 months.

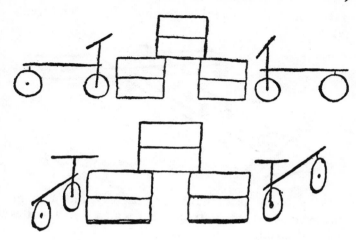

I wish then to emphasize as a second consideration the possibilities that are offered by blocks and similar materials for expressing rhythm, pattern, design, whatever we term the resulting product that has, for adults at least, an esthetic quality. Along with this and preceding the actual design goes the sensory experience that children are gaining by handling the material.

The decorative and utilitarian are not kept separate but construction is paramount when the structures are built according to a plan and are named boats, trains, houses or garages, and then with various accessories are used to play with. We shall try in the excerpts from our notes to illustrate the third consideration: *the importance of offering children material by means of which they may review, rehearse and play out their past experiences.* The value of first hand, active sharing and the waste of vicarious experience are repeatedly proved if we gather and sift the evidence given during children's play.

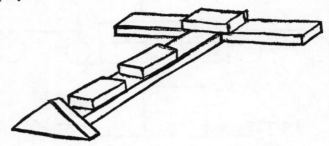

At 35 months Donald very rapidly and with no hesitation laid this arrangement which he named at once—"airplane."

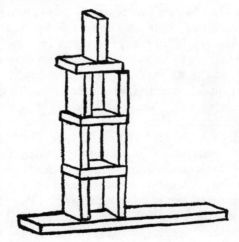

Seagoing craft may take any form. Donald at 35 months called these three constructions boats. "A 'moke 'tack up on top."

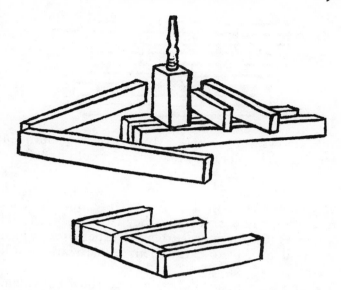

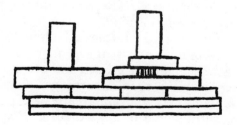

When Karl was three he began building boats
with pointed bows. The dock and boat were never
brought together, so the discrepancy in size between
them was not apparent to him.

More smoke stacks and a window, arranged for
in the construction.

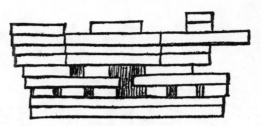

Windows appear here. Much care was shown in arranging the blocks so that spaces would be left.

Play with adaptable material gives children an opportunity to organize through use the facts, information and observations they have gathered and to get ready for more extended experiences which will enable them to carry their dramatizations still further.

At an early age children seem to show individual style in building. They have a "manner" of their own. This will vary as their ability and their content grow more adequate and especially as they become able to deal with building material imaginatively, which is another way of saying that their perception has matured. They then approach blocks with a plan already in mind.

The earliest record of Lucy's building was with cubes and dominoes at twenty-six months. She laid them in a long line and echoed the other children, "I making big train, too." Rearranged them always with nicety and care and apparently with design,—intention, but not in a patterned form. Placed fifty-two in her line. Also built a tower six cubes high. Took it down and laid cubes flat in what promised to be an octagonal figure. It did not eventually take that form however. Very exact in the way she placed them, used her hands well.

It is rather interesting that at thirty-seven months she laid cubes in a roughly hexagonal figure, two tiers high. Filled the center in and built a tower of five. Did not knock it down. Agreed with adult who admired it. Began another by arranging five cubes in a ring, then made a tower of nine inside. Knocked them both down and rebuilt tower which fell as she placed the tenth block. Laid a double track, nine in pairs, then a single line extending at right angles from the center of the double line.

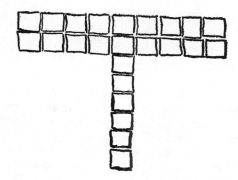

She used up her entire store of cubes. When Alec asked what it was Lucy said, "That's a design. Don't break it." Needless to say the expression is one she brought from home.

She showed a keen feeling for balance and form and also nearly always used her buildings in play after they were finished. Her ability to balance with a steady hand is shown in a construction she made at thirty-nine months. She placed two green cubes

fairly near together and balanced on this foundation twelve more, four tiers, three in each tier.

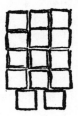

At the same age she was hauling and building
with paving blocks. She laid two tiers four blocks
long. Left a space midway in one tier, which suggested a window to adult but which she called a
"bridge."

Lucy often planned beforehand without the ability
to carry through her intention.

38 months—Lucy ran into the west room. "See what I'm
building. I'm going to make a great big bridge and I'm
going to put a smokestack on. This is the door so the
people can't get out." As she added more to it, "It's a
building. I didn't make a bridge. And here's the smokestack." Her fluency took her beyond her power of execu-
tion. She ran back and forth to the supply of blocks,
Ansel playing with smaller blocks. She was silent while
she laid her blocks. "It's going to be over to that." (The
wall.) She has the usual bridge unit with the space
closed on both ends and a chimney of three. She added
one to each "door," then built out at one side, a line
first, then a stack. Ceased to plan apparently. This is
her building type now, some sort of a tower with a flat
extension out from one end. The extension is six blocks
laid flat. Two tiers ran all the way out and now she
has separated two of the blocks at the end, roofed the

space and added to it calling it a smokestack. She and Ansel are both silent. The supply stacks are in high piles so that she had to climb in order to reach the top blocks. She stood on a chair and pushed one of the blocks out from the pile so that she could get a grip on it, then got down and reached up for it. It was a very "thoughtful" and well planned performance. Stopped for a word with Ansel. She has now started another wing out from the middle of the two-towered stack. This one also has a space left like a window. It is two blocks high and seven long. More extensions added. There seems to be no plan except that of leaving an occasional space between blocks which she roofs. After working for thirty-four minutes she laid her last block. Extended her right arm out in a wide gesture, showing house to adult. Ran out and brought adult in to see it. She was asked who was going to live in her house and answered, "Nobody's not going to live in it."

39 months—1. Ansel was asked if he wished to go into the block room and play by himself. Lucy at once ran in

and began to build. Other children joined her. Built the bridge unit and roofed it with six paving blocks topped by one on end. Lucy exultant. "It's too high for me to climb up." Went back and forth with her tongue out of her month, adding her extension, blocks laid flat, on which she stood calling, "Ding, dong." Something called her away for a moment but she returned and resumed her seat on the tail of her train. Kurt had made a boat and was pretending to rock it with extravagant gestures, shouting loudly and saying, "Too, too, goes the boat." Lucy laughed loudly and also "Too, tooed." She continued building on her extension till she had used all the blocks about her. "Blocks are all used up." She was shown more and agreed, "I want some more." Matthew warned her off and then said, "Yes, you may." Lucy, "I need one more." Placed, then repeated the remark, running back and forth. "One more, one more, one more, one more." Matthew took up the refrain. Yvonne repeated and Kurt also echoed. Lucy and Matthew began discussing the latter's building. Lucy, "Make it big like mine." Matthew, "All right." There was such a drive on the block supply that adult persuaded the other children to leave the few remaining for Matthew whose building did not progress as rapidly as that of the other children. Lucy agreed and wrestled with Yvonne who did not get the point. Lucy now has four tiers in her extension. She picked up a ball and saying that she wanted her ball to go too placed it on the building and seated herself. In the process a block fell out. "Oh, dear, oh, dear, I didn't mean to do that."

Ansel and Yvonne retired from the building trade and their piles were thus available. Lucy, calling, "I need some more," added to her extension till she had used her share of the extra blocks.

"Someone wants to get on my boat. I bet Matthew does." Conversation seems to begin as actual construction ceases. No response from Matthew who is still busy. Kurt back from play room with cubes which he called wheels. Lucy, "I need some wheels for my boat." Kurt allowed her to take some. She placed one cube on either side of the construction, then got on again. "There, now I guess it will go." Off after about two minutes saying, "I need some more, one here and one here. There, now I guess I'll get on my boat." Off again and over to the corner of the room where she grasped an imaginary something in her hands. Thrust it down into her pockets and returned, placing her treasure on her boat. "There," she said. Hearing Matthew say, "A red one and a pink one," she ran to the box of cubes echoing his remark. There are no pink ones and as she looked into the box she changed and said, "I want a red one and a yellow one." Chose them and placed one on each side so that she now has three. Matthew up saying, "I haven't got a pretty boat like yours, Lucy. You'd better make one for me 'cause I don't know how to make one." Kurt, "Make it like Lucy's,—a bridge, then a big boat." "Yes," from Lucy, "make it just like mine." Seated herself again. Was called off for fruit. Had spent three-quarters of an hour at one construction.

40 months—1. The sketch below shows a variation of her special pattern. She and Matthew were building together with paving blocks and they made very different models.

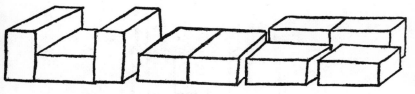

40 months—2. A charming pattern made with City and Country School blocks is shown below. She made it

more uniform finally by removing all the triangles and replacing them with half units so that both ends were alike.

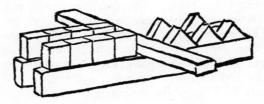

40 months—3. A pleasing use of triangles is illustrated by the next sketch. The inclination to arrange in a balanced form, spoken of many times, is also illustrated where Lucy's use of five of the Montessori blocks forming the Broad Stair is shown. The blocks are graduated so there are no two just alike. The balance of her pairs is perfect.

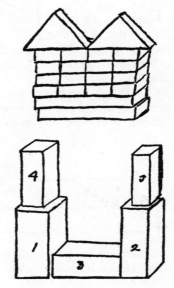

41 months—1. She made an unusually solid stack of paving blocks, leaving a pillar formation out at the front
and topping the mass by two, one laid flat, and another
set on it upright. She named it a church and repeated,
"Here's the church and here's the steeple and here's the
people," a version of the finger play rime. Later she
added two more piles at the front spoiling her effect in
the opinion of the adults. "Church" was evidently only
a name to Lucy.

41 months—2. Below is illustrated another combination of
paving bricks and City and Country School unit and
double unit blocks. She sat on it as if it were a chair but
called it a boat. After a while she changed it to a "shoe

shine place," following Kurt's example and built the sides up higher.

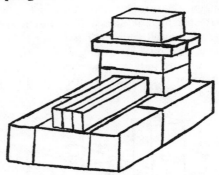

41 months—3. Another patterned building made at this time combined various materials. She alternated pairs of paving blocks, laying one pair upright, end on end and

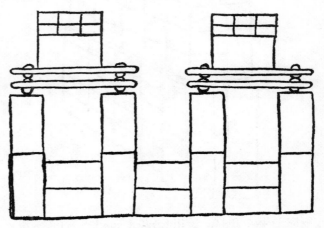

the next piled flat. She then asked for something for roofs. She was given the covers of our wooden boxes. (See list of equipment, p. 79.) She tried double unit

City and Country School blocks but removed them again and used the box covers, two to each roof. Paving blocks atop and half units on those. She was very definite in her planning. Alternated in placing the half units, first on the right side, second on the left, third on the right side, fourth on the left, etc.

Peggy's tendency to make patterned forms was shown on page 187, where she played with two blocks for some moments, placing them in many different positions.

33 months—1. Walked to a pile of yard blocks and said, "I want to play with these." Had help in pulling the top layer blocks out of the stack, then with no hesitation made the illustrated pattern. When it was done she went off to another pursuit.

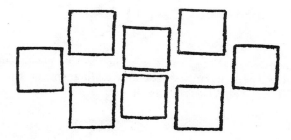

A diagram of Peggy's construction with yard blocks looking down on it. Blocks are drawn to small scale.

33 months—2. Placed four yard blocks as a base, correcting unevenness and carefully arranging for the space between A and B, showing that there was nothing accidental about it.

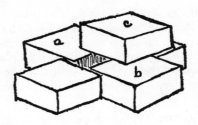

34 months—Peggy seemed to be starting to make a simple
      enclosure but before getting far changed it to the bal-
      anced pattern shown. Left it without naming it. This
      general design appears repeatedly. The yard block pat-
      tern above suggests it though it is more extended. This
      one is made of unit City and Country School blocks.

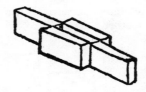

35 months—1. Peggy made a bridge unit of paving blocks,
      closing it in at the back and adding one at the side.
      Then said, "Look at my house."

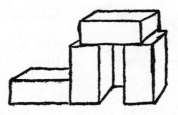

Children seem to give names to their constructions as they sometimes do to their drawings with

little reference to resemblances or to use. The next citation also illustrates this point.

35 months—2. Peggy, who was rather desultory, took the suggestion of adult to build in the shelter and built as shown below, calling it a "big truck" and showing considerable elation. Said, "I'm going to make another one," and did so, an exact replica. Then started a third, but this time began with her upright at the other end of the flat ones. She looked at it a moment, then changed it and continued till she had a third figure constructed exactly like the others, the first two side by side about five inches apart, the third parallel with them but a little out of line behind them. Changed the name to "my train," possibly because a child near her had called them trains.

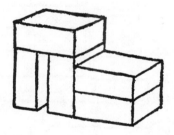

35 months—3. Late in the morning Philip (34 months) joined Peggy who was building the structure shown below. He stood watching her with an interested look. Someone mentioned a train. Peggy: "No, that's a t'ain t'ack"; Philip tried to repeat. Saunders contributed "big truck" as a name. It went through many changes and finally "tuck t'ain" emerged as a fairly satisfactory compromise. When the structure reached the height marked X Philip became inspired to great activity, and while Peggy did practically nothing more except to watch he swiftly and with squeals and chortles added

block after block flat across the top of the building until he could reach no higher. It was twelve blocks high at the left and about the same height all the way across the top. Before reaching that height it had shown signs of wavering and as each block was added swiftly but carefully Philip and Peggy became more and more excited. Finally Philip turned to adult and with dancing eyes said, "Goin' fall dow', gayess (guess)." Peggy repeated substantially his remark, adding as she warned Jim from near the building, "Might fa' dow' on oo head, Dimsie." Philip added, "Might hurt, Dimmie."

At last the expected crash came. No one touched it and no harm was done. Great joy was registered by laughter and shouts.

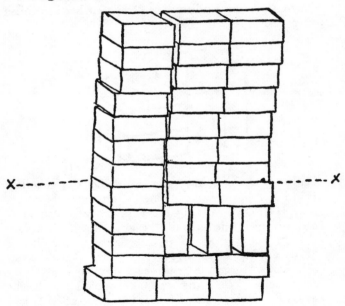

36 months—Peggy built as shown and said, "It's a cow what's in there. You can't see him. He's all covered up.

I tell you why I covered him up. He's all mud. Yep,
all mud."

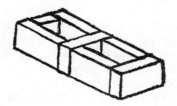

39 months—1. Peggy asked for a flat wooden wheel and
was given two. Placed one on adult table and began to
bring Broad Stair blocks and pile them on a wheel. Put
two large ones on, laid flat, then her other wheel on
top of those. Built another pile of Broad Stair blocks
beside this, no order in size. She then put all the blocks
on the floor, and began piling. She stood a large one
upright, held a smaller one on it, and pounded it with
another block. Then built an irregular mass with one
of her wheels at the bottom and the other stuck in
further up. Apparently did not select sizes but placed
the blocks as they came and added them to the mass.
She was distracted briefly but returned to the blocks
and rearranged them, finally leaving them as sketched
in a sort of stair.

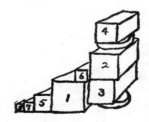

She then took up a doll and stood it on the top block
which she straightened. She held it by its head. She got

a notched (interlocking) block, and walked it up to the third step, left it there, then walked it down. Took up the doll again. Saunders sat beside her. Peggy: "Now the man's going up." Saunders: "Now the man's coming down," though Peggy was making him go up. Once she said, suiting the action to the word, "Now a man's going up, up, up, up, up. Now turn around, now down, down, down, down." Continued for some time playing with the doll and adding to the structure occasionally.

39 months—2. Peggy who had been playing for a long time stacking cubes evenly in a cube box, began building with paving blocks upon her box. Below is represented her structure at one stage.

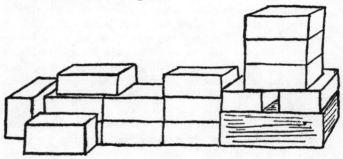

39 months—3. All the older children had been building very large structures the day before. Again to-day they built

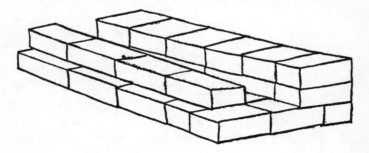

in much the same style. Peggy's structure was lower
than Saunders' or Caroline's.

40 months—1. Philip built a Greek cross structure and
roofed it, using five paving blocks in all. He and Peggy
played on and over it, then Peggy added more at the
corners, doing most of the work involved in erecting
the structure below. Between them the boards were
added and both children climbed on. Each took a small
red car and set it on top.

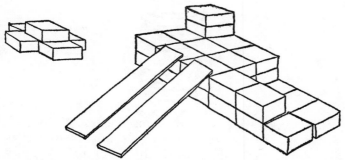

40 months—2. Peggy made an interesting arrangement
with the cubes and wooden wheels. The wheels are
4¾ inches across. She placed cubes in these figures on
the wheels:

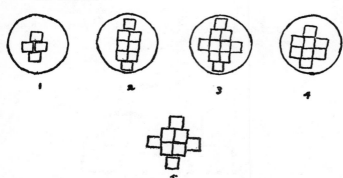

Finally she made a tower form consisting of four wheels on each of which were eight cubes in the arrangement shown in No. 5.

The cubes seem to lend themselves especially well to design. In the section on color other examples are given. In Peggy's work the color of the cubes seems not to have been a part of her planning. As far as could be observed she made no selection of cubes but took them as they came.

40 months—3. Indoors one morning the children made "houses" for their hats. Peggy's took a form which she had used before.

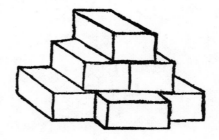

40 months—4. Peggy arranged yard blocks as illustrated,
extending them out from the wall and called it a boat.

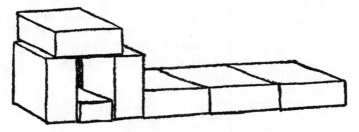

40 months—5. Peggy built another "house" of yard blocks
into which she put a pail and shovels. The blocks were
accurately placed and the plan made with no hesitation. Again she followed her favorite model.

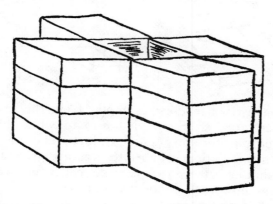

40 months—6. Peggy working alone in the block room
built a little double enclosure of City and Country
School units and half units. Then she added a few
triangles to her store and began laying flat patterns on
the floor. It will be seen that she made square figures
from triangles. After building the central balanced pattern in figure 2, a large square flanked on each side by

a unit, she fitted a small triangle across one corner (see filled in space). Then she tried to add another triangle of the same kind but could not turn it in the right direction. Took both out and tried various positions like the diamond illustrated. After three or four trials on the floor she lifted both triangles in her hands, made the desired square figure of them, then laid them down in the corner.

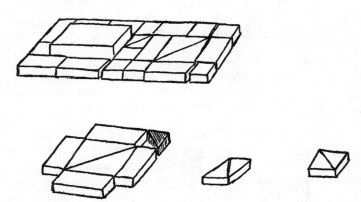

I have tried in these examples from the records to illustrate first the varied uses to which blocks may be put for very small children and the way mere manipulation grows into accurate placing and a rhythm or balance that is really beautiful; second, to show how early individual differences are found in method and manner.

If we could add to these records observations of three-, four- and five-year-old children, we should see boats more nearly resembling boats and trains suggesting trains, and we should see more planning beforehand and more play with constructions after they are built. We should see the decorative and patternful arrangements still much in evidence. And we should have convincing proof that blocks are appropriate and profitable play material for children of a wide age range.

Color

I have advanced the opinion that color often becomes a part of a child's equipment, manifested by an interest in selection and discrimination before it is manifested by an interest or ability to name. As language progresses children begin asking the names of things, colors among them. There are of course very marked individual differences. At thirty months Yvonne's attention was readily called to the names of the colored cubes she was handling (Milton Bradley inch square beads in primary colors), but she almost never seemed to select her colors or to use them in patterned forms. Lucy, at thirty-six months, knew the names of all the colors and was also interested in arrangements of the cubes to form patterns of a sort.

Lucy, 36 months, sang to herself in a high sweet voice as she selected crayons and arranged them on her paper, "Orange, yellow, black, red, green." Lucy knows all the colors and never hesitates in discrimination of shades.

Yvonne, 30 months, was playing with cubes, handling them but not building. Another child picked up one and said, "See, that's an orange one." Yvonne chose a domino and said, "That's brown." Adult tried her on several other colors. She also named red and green and orange correctly but called yellow orange. She did not know purple and blue. Lucy told her the ones she did not know.

Matthew, 35 months, had on a scarlet sweater which

Yvonne, 32 months, saw for the first time. She commented, "Oh, Matthew has a nice new sweater,—red." Matthew, severely, "It's not a red sweater, it's blue,—yellow,—orange." Yvonne: "It's *red*." Matthew: "This is blue!" Adult pointed to a blue stripe in his socks and asked, "Is it like this?" when he at once found the scarlet stripe and said, "No, like this."

Yvonne, 33 months—A visitor was present who was inquiring about our method of "teaching" colors. I explained that we exposed the children to colored materials, their cubes, crayons, squares of cloth for doll covers and other such things, and that we used the term in referring to them. I cited the refrain we sometimes chant as we dress the children, and as we sat near Yvonne's table where she was eating her dinner, I quoted, "Have you seen Yvonne's sweater, Yvonne's sweater? Have you seen Yvonne's sweater? It is yellow." Yvonne looked up at once saying, "My sweater is yellow." "Yes," said I, "yellow like your carrots?" She paused a moment to look at the carrots in her plate, then back at me and replied, "Carrots not yellow. Carrots orange,' giving the example of discrimination that I desired.

Here are illustrated Yvonne's progress in language discrimination and, in Matthew's case, an example of interest in colors before the names are used correctly. As it happens, in both families color is a part of the environment to an unusual extent.

It is of course important that children should learn to associate the names with their equivalent colors but it need not be stressed early. If colored objects are a part of their environment and are freely used and named and if the children are allowed to get affective satisfaction from the use of colors they also will name them as soon as they need to do so. Recognition of colors by their names has little relationship to sensitivity to color gradations and combinations. Satisfaction from the use of color is more closely akin to art than satisfaction in naming color symbols correctly. It may sound pretentious to speak of art in connection with the work of little children, whatever form it takes. I think of it in those terms when it is a spontaneous expression in language, in color, in arrangement of material, with a definite play element and when it seems to bring some sort of emotional, affective satisfaction to the child.

Children of nursery school age seem to get satisfaction largely in sense and motor terms. As has been said they use crayons because of muscular pleasure and only gradually come to realize that they can produce effects in color with them by their own efforts and that their scrawlings can be made to resemble objects in their environment.*

They undoubtedly receive stimulation from the drawings of other children. If adults try to amuse them by drawing for them or setting them copies it seems to act as an obstruction to their own creative effort rather than as an inspiration. They learn to say, "I can't do it," or "You make one for me." This is not the case if the drawings they observe are those of other children. It is probably because the children's work does not set a standard so impossible for them to approach. From the point of view of development human beings need and too rarely get opportunity for the exercise of an expressive art. Very young children spontaneously employ material in this way if it is made available and if they are allowed to keep within their own standards.

Another important factor in this play with

* Part III, § 2, Crayons and Paper.

colored objects seems to me to be the opportunity
that is offered for experimentation, since out of it
appears to grow an appreciation of design possibilities in the material. As we have observed our
children, satisfaction in a balanced arrangement, not
only of blocks and cubes but also of any sort of material with which they are playing, is a consistent
characteristic. Terry was twenty-eight months old.
His mother told us that he opened the laundry bag
one afternoon after he got home from the nursery.
He found his father's socks and settled down with
them. First he matched a pair of gay green golf
stockings and laid them out on the floor. On either
side he placed a pair of brown socks, matched correctly though the shades were only slightly different and the color was dull. Then he took the remaining pair of black socks and laid one at the left and
one at the right of his arrangement, making a balanced pattern. Under block building examples of
balanced construction are illustrated.

When they are working with colored blocks in the
nursery or with beads in the older groups, they are
dealing with two very different processes. In the one
instance they are learning to manipulate and the
method observable in the case of one baby of attempting to press his cubes into a tower or to pile
a handful at one time shows how much ground must
be covered before an exact structure with all edges
laid even can be made. In the second example, that
of stringing beads, they have to master an unlearned
process, involving a fine visual-motor coördination
before the interest in pure design comes to the fore-
front of their attention. This is the reason why they
sometimes seem uninterested in a balanced arrange-

ment of materials which to adults suggest design in
and of themselves.

Again it is a case of an immature perceptual pattern and the question is raised once more whether
growth is better served by instruction or by the
longer process of experimentation. I am entirely convinced that self-initiated dealing with materials, if
satisfaction results, cultivates an attitude of readiness to attack a new situation which is a dynamic
characteristic. I believe also that interest in design
and ability to make patterns which have real esthetic
value are more likely to result from this method
than from instruction.

Ansel was about three weeks older than Yvonne.
There is on record no instance of his interest in
naming colors. He left the school at thirty-three
months. There are repeated notes of his making an
apparent selection of colors in his use of the cubes,

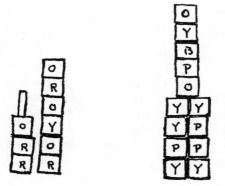

and his interest in his very vari-colored crayon pro-
ductions was marked. There were hints of pattern

emerging in his arrangements of cubes which can be traced in the following extracts:

Lucy, 35 months, lined up six yellow cubes, holes up. When adult commented upon it she began picking up more and gave them to Ansel, 27 months, who was also making a line of them on the floor. He used the yellow ones alternately with single or double ones of other colors, but it could not be said whether his pattern was designed for he had more yellow in his store than any other color. Later he made another long line with orange alternating four times and red twice almost as if he had confused the two colors. In view of the slowness of Ansel's development along certain lines, it is interesting to see emerging a patterned use of cubes at 28 months. Last week a sequence of colors repeated more than once was noted. At above age Ansel made a line of fourteen cubes with the following color patterns: Red, red, orange, red, red. Yellow, orange, yellow, orange, yellow. Purple, purple, purple. Rearranged last and laid purple, yellow, purple, yellow. A line of seven at right angles to a longer line alternated green and red; then two purples broke the scheme.

Probably the reason for the break in the pattern is that a child's perception of colors is not yet mature. He sees differentiations accurately but his attention is divided between the handling and arranging, setting in even lines or in towers which is still not an automatic performance, and the visual appearance of the color pattern.

There was always a definiteness about Alec's work and a nicety in his use of his hands. He was slow in language and was inclined to take his impulse to an activity from other children. His color arrangement, illustrated below, was his own. He was thirty-six months old at the time.

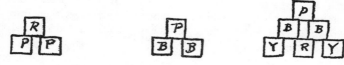

Such color combinations show unmistakable intention and discrimination but in his case they were not accompanied by an equal language maturity.

Lucy's interest in selecting and using one color at a time has been illustrated already. It is interesting, and characteristic of any behavior pattern in process of development, that it is not consistently maintained. After beginning a figure with definitely balanced colors the plan will be discarded or forgotten and an entirely haphazard and indiscriminate arrangement made. (See Ansel above.) After acquiring the ability to walk upstairs there will be noticed repeated reversions to the infantile pattern of creeping.

Lucy, 39 months, made a long row of arches, with one little tower of four at the end. After she began it she picked out all the green ones and used those first, then all the blue. After that she seemed not to discriminate.

Lucy began laying cubes in a rough diamond design. Matthew was very persistent in calling her off and she finally left before she had completed it. She began with yellow, placed two side by side for the point of the diamond and then worked from side to side balancing her colors. She used five yellow on each side but once she placed two side by side instead of zigzagging them evenly. She bore out on each side spreading her figure and placing each cube under and about half its width beyond the one above it till she had laid seven. Then she began to bear inward but stopped after she had placed three so the figure was not finished. Her mistake with the two yellows made her miss the balance but she used five yellows and one orange on each side, then four greens on the left to three on the right and a red on each side at the last.

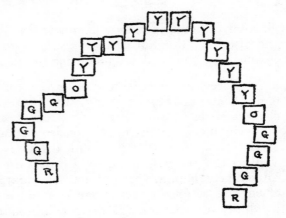

After she was distracted by Matthew's conversation she laid a flat construction, first all of green and yellow, then of various colors but matched from side to side. She placed eight in a line, then extended lines down in a rectangular figure, not quite enclosed and with one side longer than the other.

Called to Matthew and said, "See my doorway, Matthew? It's an open one." Later she renamed it a train and sat upon it.

No comment was made upon the diamond design and it was never repeated by Lucy. Another child in a previous group spontaneously made the same pattern, arranging her colors differently.

Dora, 36 months, first built a tower which she called a chimney. Then she began a very lovely pattern. She laid the

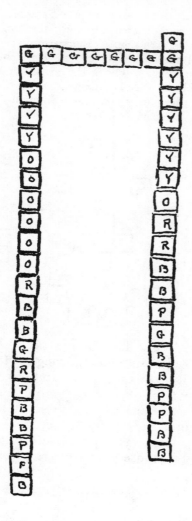

blocks from one side to the other in a diamond. That is, she alternated sides as she placed the cubes, spreading it till there were six blocks on each side. As she began making the lower half she mixed the colors but she made a complete figure except for a final cube to match the one at the upper point. Three purple blocks were laid first.

Notes state that she makes many different "designs" in cubes. (See Building Materials.)

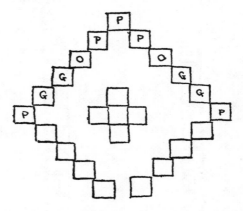

There was muscular rhythm in the way these children placed their blocks, swinging from left to right, as well as in the color selections and the resulting "design."

These illustrations and those in Building Materials show that the ability to see and execute the form of a pattern takes precedence of the interest and ability to choose and arrange colors in a balanced form.

Crayons and Paper

There have been several studies made of the beginnings of drawing. It has seemed to me that most of them omitted a factor which would account for the frequent lapse from representative drawing to scribbling noted among children whose work with crayons and paper is mature enough to be called drawing. This factor, which seems to me almost entirely a motor impulse, accounts for so much of the very little child's product that an analysis of it may throw some light on the later interest in this kind of material.

Since our records in this instance are the drawings themselves, this section is presented in a somewhat different form from the preceding one.

From the first, crayons and paper are given to our children for the sake of the motor experience gained through the swing of the arm, and for the sensory experience in the use of color.

In the preceding section will be found illustrations from the records of color discrimination, but here we are concerned primarily with the general reaction of children from about eighteen months to about forty months, to the drawing materials.

Crayons and paper are kept on high shelves to which the children are not given access. They are presented by adults when a child asks for them or when a need or a mood in an individual or the group seems to demand them. If a child seems inclined to be desultory or if the group is disturbed for some reason, we are likely to seat them at tables with drawing materials. After this has happened once or twice the children ask for crayons often enough so that we are assured of their getting experience with the materials and of our getting material for study.

We give no direction for their use and we try not to suggest a name for the process; that is, we do not call it drawing. Some children call the crayons by their name, in asking for them; sometimes they say they wish to mark or write or less frequently that they wish to draw. In presenting the drawing materials we usually speak of them as crayons and paper.

We do not tell the children what to do as we present the materials but we always seat them at tables, and if a child shows no inclination to make marks on the paper we remove crayon and paper as soon as we can do so without disturbing him.

There is a tendency to take crayons about and to play with them in various ways and though this is not absolutely prohibited, we make an effort to keep them to the use for which they are intended and substitute for them other small objects so that the impulse to shake in boxes or to stow away in pockets, for example, can be satisfied.

From the first use of the materials individual differences are shown in the strength and vigor of handling, the quality of the line and the effect attained, the amount of surface covered and the predominating movement, whether it is the circular— the round and round movement of the arm, or the angular—the back and forth movement. It is interesting to note the recurrence of an individual pattern. In a nursery group of eight, drawings of those children who draw regularly can usually be identified without the names.

In studies made with adult students there have been efforts to differentiate the feeling tone of the angular and the circular line.* Our children, as might be expected, give no evidence that the process

* Lundholm, Helge. "The Affective Tone of Lines." *Psychological Review,* 1921.

of making one sort of line is more pleasurable than another. Circular lines are more frequently made in the early months. There seems to be enjoyment from varied muscular exercise, and the circular and the angular appear repeatedly on the same sheet.

Varying the arm movement and the resulting direction of the line so that the sheet of paper will be more or less thoroughly covered, or so that finer scrawls will be placed in the corners is a step that usually follows the first scrawling which covers a more restricted area—appearing usually in the middle of the year.

We present a varied assortment of colors and have as yet made no fine distinctions regarding the children's choice. We generally give four at a time but these four may be drawn in any way from our collection which includes red, blue, green, yellow, orange, purple and brown.

Rubbing a crayon on its side to make a broad smudge is usually tried by someone in the group but there is little persistence in this method. Pounding with them upon the paper appears invariably among a group at one time or another, and is very contagious. Little attention is given to the product but the sound and movement seem to catch the attention.

For a long time there seems to be no attention paid to the colors used. One crayon after another is taken and used so that the result shows a mass of overlaid colors. The children show interest and often positive pleasure in their performance. There may be something beyond the muscle satisfaction but there seems to be little discrimination in actual colors used, and little attempt to keep them separate. The strength and boldness of the lines seem sometimes to bear a relationship to the individual's energy, but sometimes change as the child becomes more familiar with the material.

The first evidence of the affective influence of color appears in color massing. Even here there is often no sign that there is selective choice. A crayon will be picked up, perhaps without a glance, but instead of making the circular design and overlaying color, the one crayon will be used and rubbed over the paper till a mass of clean color results. Then various other colors may be treated in the same way.

Without doubt the fact of rhythm continues to act, and the adult's pleasure in the resulting product cannot be taken as an accurate measure of a child's satisfaction or intention. This pattern of color massing appears and persists in the work of most nursery children, and seems to mark a definite stage in development.

I recall only one child who made a comment upon his work as he selected his colors. He had made the usual circular scrawl and selected some of the loops on the outside to fill in with color. He made a solid patch of red and a smaller one of blue, then said, "Now I must make a green one," chose his color and filled in a loop near the middle of his pattern in solid green.

After the scrawling there comes a time when there seems to be more intentional use of the crayons, the children seem more able to control their material and they draw lines, running in an intended direction, or place the shapes they form separately upon their paper. A child who has reached this stage will frequently revert to the former infantile manner of scrawling and will overlay his "picture" so that it is hardly distinguishable.

These deliberate attempts to construct a circle, a line or lines enclosing a space and to imitate writing begin to show the development of the pattern toward representation or design. If children are not given a standard by older children or adults they begin after a while spontaneously to name the lines or shapes which they make. At first the names may seem to bear little or no relationship to the drawing, but occasionally a line will quite obviously suggest an object and with cries of satisfaction the child will declare that he has made a tree, a bird or a beast.

Frequently if adults have asked him what his picture is, or if he has come to associate the crayons with a pencil, with pictures or writing made by adults, he will announce his intention of making some object, a portrait of one of the children, a beast or what not and proceed to his usual scratching. In the records on Language an example is given under children's conversation in which each "drawing" is named but bears not the slightest resemblance to the object said to be presented. Another follows:

April 27—Peggy drew with both hands alternately and taking colors as they came from her box. At first she did angular and circular scrawls. Then turned the sheet and drew various lines and shapes carefully made and placed. Made a circular mark. Said, "I make ole man— funny ole man." "I make funny ole woman." Made another, said, "There funny ole woman." Made more small circles, with left hand, very intent. "I make funny ole boy."

We do not ask the children what they have drawn, because we have found that the inquiry at once sets a pattern for them. Left alone they show no interest in naming their products though they do show elation in the process.

Most children who are exposed to the studio use of crayons, pencils and paints because older members of their families use them, may begin at an earlier age to name their products, to make color selections and to attempt representative drawings. This depends of course upon the attitude which adults take toward them. If instead of placing pencil or paint before the children, pictures are made for them or copies are set, then their reaction to drawing material is an immediate appeal to adults, or the reproduction of a fixed pattern approved at home, or a negative attitude and refusal to use it, often with the explanation, "I don't know how" or "I can't."

When Maisie was thirty-eight months old she suddenly began making A's whenever paper and crayons were given her. This was a parent-inspired idea, as we learned, and it absorbed her for the remaining months of school. We desperately suggested things for her to draw and she made straight lines across the tops of the A's and said, "There's his hat and his hat," etc. Finally she achieved a figure which she named a chicken and which it did resemble. It had what looked like a head with an eye and two lines down from its body which made legs. Her sister remarked that "Daddy had tried to teach Maisie to draw a chicken," so we doubted the spontaneity of her inspiration. She was then just thirty-nine months and we have no subsequent drawings. Her early drawings had an entirely different character. She was using massed colors quite effectively and her interest seemed developing normally.

After observing our children for several years and studying their drawings I am convinced that in its earliest stages the interest of children in drawing material is the muscular satisfaction of the swinging arm movement, a rhythmical quality. The fact that lines and color result enhances the satisfaction, without doubt.

At thirty-five months, after Donald had made and named a drawing which remotely suggested the object designated, an automobile, he took another sheet and made a very vigorous circular scrawl all over it and said, "This is what I do to make my autobile go," illustrating the motor features of drawing.

We have been trying to make a study of the drawings accumulated over a period of several years. Taking those occurring during six-month periods, eighteen to twenty-four months, and thirty-six to forty months, the upper point in our age range, we have attempted a classification which will include the kind of lines, the treatment of color and the appearance of an inclination to name products.

The study is still in progress but there is evidently quite an age progression. The circular scrawls are the most frequent in the younger group; the angular and circular are nearly even in the last three groups. The intentional placing of lines or forms shows a steady increase from the youngest to the oldest group.

The practice of massing colors hardly appears in the youngest group and also shows a gradual increase in the three older groups. Naming the product does not begin to appear until thirty months and doubles in the last age group. Children of these ages almost never name their drawings in advance and their products can practically never be called representative.

It is obvious that personalities differ and that they differ consistently but it is interesting to see personality traits defined so clearly in relation to drawing material, and at such an early age, as is evidenced in the following brief analysis: Yvonne's drawings from the first show a differentiation from what we expect of children of her age. Her earliest sheet is dated at seventeen months. There was a difference of only thirteen days in age between Ansel and Yvonne. We have no drawings from Ansel during the first nursery school year. As we usually present crayons to the entire group, the lack of product means that the possibilities of the material and the technique of holding his paper still with one hand and drawing with the other did not become his during this time from fourteen to twenty-two months.

This is again characteristic of the two children, Yvonne more responsive to sensory stimuli than Ansel, especially if the social element played a part. Her attitude was probably also a reflection of her environment, for drawing and painting went on at home as a serious undertaking.

All Yvonne's drawings during the period observed, from seventeen to twenty-nine months, show a more definite and discriminating use of the material than do those of Ansel. He used circular and angular scrawls, in broad heavy strokes, covered his paper fairly well and overlaid his colors. She made lighter marks, also circular and angular, but the colors, even when somewhat overlaid, were kept more distinct and were more delicately placed, as if there were intention of separating them.

When she was twenty-seven months old she was observed massing colors, and a month later she made delicate scribbles with several colors in the lower corner of her sheet and called it her name. This was taken over from the adults' habit of writing the names of the children on their papers. We had to explain or they would be offended at our making marks on their sheets.

Ansel did not show the usual age progression in placing or directing his lines. After he began to draw, in the first month of his second nursery year, twenty-six months old, he was much more prolific than Yvonne, and our observations note evidences of absorption and pleasure. They also state his daily demand for "mark" over quite a period, and his varied use of crayons for purposes other than drawing, stuffing in his pockets and arranging in rows, for example.

The feeling element observable by their behavior was much keener in Ansel's case than in that of Yvonne. Our impression was that his pleasure, which was quite evident, lay in the muscle play, the expenditure of energy and the rhythmic swing of his arms, though the results were distinctly pleasing to adults and may have become so to him. The process, if not the product, was unmistakably a source of keen satisfaction to him.

Yvonne was never especially eager for crayons, and her performance seemed perfunctory. That observation was based upon the comparative number of sheets for each child and the fact that she rarely made use of all of her paper. Some such analysis could be made for each child in a group.

We have used material which is commonly presented for drawing and are expecting no product in the form of pictures. The advantages of presenting it to our children are, it has seemed to us, that muscularly it provides for release of energy in the free arm movement, that the sensory experience gained by the use of colors is valuable and that it gathers the children into the kind of social group that is suitable to their development. We have, therefore, felt justified in including it in our equipment, and in giving it to children in the informal way indicated especially as we find that age progression can be traced and that individual differences are clearly shown. That is, the material seems to meet the needs of the growth stage in which our children are found. We believe that it is appropriate material only if there is no attempt to interest the children in making representative drawings or designs.

B.   OTHER CHILDREN AND ADULTS

In Part II, the social environment was described and the opinion was advanced that the acceptance of genuine social responsibilities by children must wait upon growth. By social responsibility I mean awareness of the place that one's mates hold in a scheme and the ability to maintain one's own part without encroaching upon another's. My definition sounds elaborate but if even the simplest coöperative play situation is analyzed it will be recognized that success depends upon these factors. It is manifestly impossible for our youngest babies. In the following records, though we see children carrying on social play and finally coöperative schemes without friction and with successful adjustment to each other, the ability to sustain social relationships at a level of success is still in the process of becoming mature, and to my mind stands a better chance of maintaining itself if our demands upon the children in regard to it are kept at a minimum.

The test of any situation, social or otherwise, is the response of the group to it. We are not concerned with the immediate reaction but with what it implies in terms of development which of course takes us back again to our study of the behavior of children. What are the social activities observed in a group of young children which they seem able spontaneously to carry on with a maximum of satisfaction and at a minimum expense of emotional stability?

The early contacts that children make with each other are social in what might be called a physical fashion; that is, children seem to approach and touch each other more because they are moving objects in the field of vision than because they are fellow creatures. Often the encounters are accidental, not sought, again like their contacts with materials.

Lawton and Hal, each 14 months old, stood side by side at shelter shelves, pushing at kiddy kar and pulling pails and pans down. Lawton beat at Hal and pulled at his cap. Stopped when adult called to him and asked him to stop. Later Hal returned to shelves and Lawton regarding him gravely made passes at his face with a pan. Hal seemed quite unmoved. No change in expression.

Lawton and Hal alone downstairs while olders were on roof seemed constantly to gravitate toward each other though real contacts were few. Twice as they stood near each other, Lawton beat out at Hal with one hand, then leaned toward him with mouth open, tongue out, with exactly his "tasting" expression of face. Later in the day he made the same tasting gesture toward an older child.

Lawton, 15 months, does not creep about the play room or the roof nearly as much as Hoyt or Hal. He stays in one spot and handles small materials a good deal. Often he remains entirely alone in the shelter or in one corner of the play room playing without reference to any of the other children, and sometimes with his back to them. If one of the smaller children comes near him, however, he often reaches up and pulls at their clothing or pats at their faces. He is very serene and busy except when adults interrupt him for routine performances. Then he resists and shows his annoyance in a very generalized reaction, slumping to the floor, kicking, thrashing his arms about and slapping at the objectionable adult.

Hoyt and Lawton, each 15 months, were seated beside the box of cubes. Hoyt took out two, held one in each hand and tapped them together. Lawton reached out for them and wrested one from Hoyt who tried to stretch his hands out of reach but who made no demonstration of annoyance. He held on to the one he had and soon picked up another and continued his play. Lawton pulled at the supply box, took two cubes himself and beat them together as Hoyt had been doing. During this "companionate" play the two children were sitting near but not even facing each other. They behaved like two puppies. Occasionally Hoyt would pull at Lawton or Lawton would lean against Hoyt but usually as they changed their positions, they dragged themselves over each other's legs or pushed at each other as they might at any inanimate obstruction. Later with an entirely impassive face Lawton clutched a handful of Hoyt's hair and pulled him forward till his head was almost down to the floor. He looked about at adult as he did it. Hoyt made no outcry and no change in the expression of either child was observable. The adult asked Lawton to let go but she made no move toward him and it is impossible to say that the request affected him although he did actually release his grip shortly after. A bit later he pulled at Hoyt's sleeve. Once as he was crawling about he thrust his arm into the box of cubes and it was caught under Hoyt's knee. He grunted then in a fussing tone and seemed somewhat disturbed until he succeeded in drawing it out. Hoyt seemed entirely unconcerned.

This phase of entire objectivity toward one's mates does not last long but there is quite a period when advances are not understood and are either positively unwelcome or seem to miss fire. The evanescence of moods in which there seems to be an awareness of the social situation is also shown in some of our records.

Ansel, 26 months, sat down in front of Karl, 18 months, and hugged him. Pushed him gently from side to side. Karl put out his arms to Ansel and tried to hug him. Ansel got a cart and tried to put Karl in it, seizing him around the waist and tugging him sideways. He was discouraged by adult because Karl cannot yet take care of himself in play of this sort. Later Karl pursued Ansel as if wishing to revive the game but Ansel pushed him over twice with scowls.

Karl, 26 months, followed Saunders, 18 months, about, officiously offering him a second train while he was carrying one. Saunders became so oppressed by this attention that he began to cry and sought adult. The same performance was repeated in a few moments. Karl's intentions were entirely friendly but Saunders had not been in the Nursery School long and he was much disturbed.

Philip, 21 months, seemed to be making advances to Caroline, 22 months, in the pebbles. She was playing at the foot of the slide and he cavorted about chuckling as Caroline gazed at him. When he attempted to sit upon her as an additional pleasantry she did not resent it but continued to show interest in his performance.

Karl, 26 months, solicitously took Caroline's hand on going down to music (Caroline, 22 months). She apparently did not understand and tried to pull away from him at first. He insisted however, making explanatory remarks and taking her hand again each time she pulled away. With adult reassurance they started down stairs together, under close supervision as they were so absorbed in their attention to each other's hands that they were oblivious to their method of making the descent.

Matthew, Ansel, Kurt, 35 months, and Yvonne, 27 months, were about to go down stairs with adult for dinner. Kurt seized Yvonne's hand. She resented it at once and tried to jerk herself away from him. Kurt was asked to let her hand go and adult took it. Instantly she snatched it away and in a shrill voice and with an angry look at adult, she said, "Don't touch my Kurt," took his hand and they proceeded down stairs. Lucy, 34 months, took Yvonne's other hand. Kurt smiled delightedly. With this arrangement, somewhat more precarious than blind leading blind, adult had to remain near to act as a buffer if anyone lost his balance. Yvonne scolded if she was touched by adult.

For some time this behavior remained characteristic of Yvonne but gradually we were able to make her pause long enough to listen to an explanation of our actions or those of another child, and when she understood she was always reasonable.

Another early social interest leads children to seek materials which they see in the hands of others and to play in their immediate neighborhood. Sometimes it seems to be the play material that lures them and though they gather together for its use there is little reference to each other.

Sand box opened. Entire silence when Karl, Caroline, Ralph and Philip first got into it. Ralph filled and emptied a pail but lost interest before the others. Caroline also filled a pail, sitting in a relaxed position in the sunshine. Karl chose the perforated shovel, and spent a long time sifting sand, then filled his pail. Philip had a small shovel, a pan and a pail. He and Caroline hardly varied their activity for thirty minutes. Then Caroline got out and went to the larger sand pen but shortly returned to the smaller one. Philip continued after Caroline left. Ralph was, as usual, restless and tried to use other children's material. He played in and out of the box but we thought that he showed less tendency to spill sand out on the tiles than he had on previous days.

The same thing is also true of such materials as pebbles, hammers and nails, dolls and covers, and crayons and paper. The stimulus to the activity seems to be the other children but the play that results is often quite independent.

At fifteen months the sight of other children using material does not usually send the child to a similar toy, but the activity itself, that is, the children-in-action, often catches his attention.

Gretchen, 34 months, and Tom, 31 months, were creeping in pebbles about the large sand box with much merriment and evident reference to each other. Hoyt, 15 months, much diverted, dropped or fell to knees and chuckled loudly. Peered about box to "find" them as they appeared from behind it and laughed aloud each time they came within his range of vision. Crept a few inches after them. The two older children left pebble pit and continued their creeping down the plank. Hoyt followed them, walking, and continued down the entire length of the board without losing his balance, still watching.

Lucy, 35 months; Matthew, 29 months; Alec, 29 months; Yvonne, 26 months, and Kurt, 37 months, all scrambled about on the skylight seat trying to walk in opposite directions. They were turned by adult so that they went in the same direction, and they walked round and round, Lucy singing, "Way around, Way! Way! Way!" over and over. They climbed down one by one, and Lucy, Yvonne and Alec got kiddy kars and putting them up on the seat rode around. Kurt joined them later and Matthew tried one short ride but he could not make the corners and got down himself.

There has been much group play, carried on independently as far as the individuals are concerned but with increased enjoyment because of the group quite evident. This is shown by calls to each other, by laughter and by restraint in crowding and in taking turns. Kurt and Matthew are the most likely to grow excited and push. They have both had to be taken from the slide indoors because of pushing. Yvonne also pushes and does not at all get cause and effect when she is removed. She glowers and screams, "Mine," and cries if forcibly restrained. The group play continued longest has been on the seesaw plank, Matthew, Alec, Kurt, Lucy and Yvonne joining. On the wider double planks which are more springy Matthew, Alec, Yvonne and Kurt played. Lucy, Kurt, Yvonne and Alec composed a group playing with kiddy kars alone, or with express carts or trailers attached. Alec returned to this occupation after nap, but did not persist because the group did not join him.

In these citations it can be seen how awareness of the other children and their activities varies, and how possible it is in this kind of "processional" play for any child to enter or drop out at will.

A loosely organized sort of dramatic play and

brief periods of incipient game playing appear in all groups. Adults could stimulate children to elaborate these performances but they involve so much adult supervision that we usually do not attempt to prolong their short span. As the records stand they indicate an outstanding and characteristic social play of little children which makes no demands beyond their individual capacity and which gives each member of the group opportunity for as much initiative as he has to use. Individual dramatization, that is, playing out their own past experiences, goes on all the time in a group, but the part one child plays is not necessarily related to that of another and does not run counter to it. For example, one child will begin throwing blocks and boards into a big packing box, call "Here goes the big boat," and make noises of whistle and bells. He will attract the entire group, several of whom will enter into the play realistically, adding details from their own experience. The next younger will probably climb in and join in making boat noises and in calling "Good-by," but will not seem to carry the scheme in mind. They will not wait for the boat to reach the dock but will plunge into the waves and back again on board. The sixteen and eighteen months old children will swarm about, getting satisfaction from the presence and the sound of other children and stimulated by them to increased physical activity.

Brief and sketchy dramatizations such as these go on continually. Dolls are given bottles, put to bed, spanked and dressed. The doctor is summoned, temperatures are taken, and dolls are entered in the nursery school. It is obvious that all this is rehearsal of experiences that a child has had.

Donald, 34 months, announced, "We going in motor boat," trotted off into the packing box, set open side up, when Maisie, 33 months, and Rab, 27 months, at once entered into his plan. They put their kiddy kars in, Rab having to use some ingenuity as well as force to get his through a space between the 3-steps and the edge of the box.

Charles, 26 months, and Karl, 30 months, placed four chairs in a row and sat facing each other holding the back of the chair in front. They both called, "Bye," and waved their hands. Charles said, "I in car." Peggy, 20 months, joined them, sitting in a chair a little apart, murmuring to herself. After many good-bys Charles and Karl sat in chairs directly opposite each other, and bent over sidewise as far as they could looking into each other's faces chuckling. The chairs were arranged and rearranged many times. Peggy continued to watch with interest though they paid no attention to her.

As this type of social play develops it is concerned chiefly with materials which are used in a naïve way to reconstruct and rehearse situations which the child has met. It helps a child to organize his experience and, as other children are called in as real coöperators, it helps him establish himself in relation to his mates.

It differs from the earlier types of play together in that it is more dependent upon actual reference to each other. The scheme as it is set up reproduces a pretend situation and there must be some sort of appropriate responses to it on the part of the children who come into it or it does not work. If Mary announces that she is going to bed and Frank or Sara joins her and makes train noises, the issue is confused and Mary is likely to feel frustrated and to object in a petulant fashion since she is not mature enough to analyze the situation and to point it out clearly to the others.

Another element in this stage of rehearsal play is that there often is some brief planning beforehand. The stage is set, however simply, and in the cases cited below children were called into the drama and assigned parts in it.

Double planks put across the two seesaw horses. (See diagram.) Kurt was inclined to interfere with the activities of the other children so his attention was called to the arrangement and he was asked if he would like that place for a boat. He set to work at once, piling twelve boards on, large and small ones, including a broken platform. On the top of his load he placed seven yard blocks which he arranged as seats for the passengers. He was very abrupt with the other children who crowded about to help or to climb on, telling them that he was just going to take that board or warning them off because it wasn't yet time to go or because they were not sitting in the right places. When he finally got everything arranged to his satisfaction he invited them all on and called lustily, "All a bore! All a bore!" He was given a wheel to see if its possibility as a steering arrangement would occur to him but it did not. After the stage was thus set there was little actual playing but there were short dramatic "moments" with little sequence. "How can I get out of this water," "Boat's going now," and boat sounds were given.

Edward's social interest woke up during the last weeks of the year and instead of driving off the other children as he had often done he began to try to join them in their play. One morning we placed the two large packing boxes out on the tiles with a plank leading up to the lower box and 3-steps against the side of the larger one. After brief boat play, Edward named it a "tea place." He dragged out the long bench, two small ones and two blocks from the shelter. Asked if he might have his fruit there and invited three other children to bring their fruit out too. Edward had arranged the seats inside the packing cases so that they got the feeling of an enclosure. The long bench was the table and was placed outside the packing box.

The following is interesting because of its recall of an experience in which the adults would say there was little of the play element.

Charles, 31 months, brought three paving blocks out of the shelter, one at a time, and set them on three sides of a small table. He then called loudly, "Come and eat dinner,—get all cold." He did not attempt to get the attention of the children any further when no one responded. When Karl, 36 months, came up later and began to use the blocks and table in his own way, Charles remarked, "Don't take dinner off," but did not continue his protest. Charles did no more than set the stage. It was an incipient drama, but he had not matured enough to organize his own ideas or to get other children into his scheme.

Karl arranged the blocks in a pile on the floor, set two pails of pebbles on them and drew up a little stool in front. He then proceeded to seat himself on the stool and thrust a hand down into each pail. After he had taken his turn he called two other children into his play. By this time the adults had recognized the game as a rehearsal of the electrocardiogram experience the three children concerned had been through several weeks before. Karl had now elaborated his scheme by adding a "sheen" off at one side. It consisted of another block set on a table at some distance away. When he had his patient's hands well immersed he would retire to the machine and scrape and scratch on the side of the block to make "sheen go." It was interesting to see that Charles, five months younger, fell in with the idea almost at once. He took his turn at the machine when it was Karl's turn at the pail, and when they both took pebbles out of the pails and put them back, it was Charles who said, "More hot water."

Ralph, 34 months, though he had been with the others to the doctor, showed no evidence that the play recalled an experience of his own. He was inclined to do more with the pails than to put his hands in and incurred Karl's displeasure by tipping them over, or by introducing other irrelevant material. Here are three stages illustrated. Charles dramatized, but his impulse was not sharply enough defined and elaborated so that he felt the need of active coöperation from other children. He could, however, follow Karl's lead and make his own contribution to the dramatic content. Ralph on the other hand, though older than Charles, seemed to be in a less mature stage. The performance showed rather an elaborate recall of detail, and ability to carry on coöperative play unusual in a group as young as ours.

The child who can organize this kind of dramatic play and include his mates in it shows real power and gets from it an affective satisfaction that is genuine and developing.

Another bit of drama referred to in the section on language is given in the following record:

Boat play in the settle was popular all the week. The drama became more sustained and realistic. Donald, 39 months, announced that the boat was going to Florida. He and Maisie, 37 months, hurled in stacks of luggage, he started the motor or mended the engine, then they got on board waving good-bys to us. In a second or two Donald announced, "This is Florida," and out they tumbled. He ran to adult with enthusiasm and shouted, "Hello, grandmother," and then went off saying, "Now we will pick the oranges." All of which Maisie followed though she had not his content.

Block buildings do not play an important part in the social play of children as young as those in our nursery group, but as we observe the activities of the next years they are increasingly a vehicle for elaborate drama and rehearsal. Our babies use them in a sketchy fashion.

Caroline and Philip, at about three years, laid a long line of paving blocks flat and sitting astride the line announced that they were riding on the train. One of them suddenly said, "I have to have a seat," and added a block here and there along the row. Caroline bethought her of the sleeping car and said, "I must go to bed now." Philip took up the suggestion at once and stretched himself forward on the narrow edge of his line of blocks and closed his eyes. The play consisted largely of the language recall and the postural activity. The blocks were accessory but the actual structure was not representative.

The reason for this may be that handling and placing the blocks demands so much muscular adjustment at this age that it exhausts the resources of children. Building *per se* goes on elaborately enough as our records on blocks show, but detailed play with constructions that are planned and completed for the purpose is rare. On the contrary the same building may be a boat, a garage, a church and a train without the change of a detail of its structure.

The types of play so far cited seem to be spontaneous and universal methods and favorable for social growth. I shall in the following pages discuss certain tendencies which we have observed which seem to be immature attempts to reach ahead to a pattern of behavior which the individual is not sufficiently integrated to carry on successfully.

The early nursery experience of little children finds them unprepared for dealing with each other, but at the same time strongly attracted to each other and growing increasingly aware of each other's activities. Their impulse to make contacts is active and their method is very amateurish so that their behavior is what is commonly called anti-social. It often is anti-pleasurable to the child approached and would be a questionable general method. It was illustrated by the citations in the beginning of the chapter and occurs so commonly that it could almost be listed as a definite stage in social growth. With babies of fourteen or fifteen months it is so casual that it does not constitute a problem.

It took Tom a long time to get into the group, and his first reactions toward individuals were quite devastating and had to be countered in some way. Excluding him from the group followed his attacks quite systematically, and friendly play with his peers in age was made as easy for him as possible so that he would get the contrast himself in cause and effect.

The following list of his offenses during part of one forenoon appeared in the weekly summary early in the year:

On his car rode violently against one of the younger babies, backed and started for him again. Whacked Mary twice as he passed her. Pushed against Lawton with a chair. Tried to take a chair from Mary. Rode into Harriet twice. Was restrained by adult but renewed his attack later. Threw a block at Lawton. Slapped Mary, ran into Harriet's car with his and rode at Lawton, knocking him down. Of course he was not allowed to keep a toy that he was using as a weapon of offense. He also pushed children over and pulled their hair.

The following account from records some weeks later shows him better established in the group and able to take rough handling in a manner that was finely sporting.

Gretchen tried to drape a cover she had over the head of one of the smaller children who was somewhat disturbed. She was told by adult to put it on Tom who was more nearly her own age and more able to defend himself. She ran eagerly to Tom and when he rolled on the floor and shook it off she rolled over and over with him laughing. She kept replacing the cover as fast as he could shake it off. Once she lay across him in the attempt to keep it on. He suffered this treatment for two or three minutes while they rolled about like puppies. Then he jumped up and ran into the bathroom. Gretchen dashed after him and put the cover over his head as he passed. He got it off, evaded her, went to the low table and climbed on it, she in pursuit. As adults suggested that the play room was a better place for rough-housing he ran out and she went after him laughing. He dashed across to the wagon shelves and lay down on the lower one on his stomach. She leaned over him and laid the cover on him. He was in perfectly good humor, brushed the cover off, slid out and ran to the middle window, Gretchen in pursuit with the cover. She knelt by him and he tried to roll off the sill. A wrestling match followed wherein Gretchen crushed Tom more or less to the earth. He was wedged in between Gretchen and the window sill so she had him at a disadvantage. They struggled and thrashed about a few moments, then Tom got to a sitting position, pulled away, rose and ran off. He did not seem fussed though he was decidedly getting a taste of his own medicine. The play continued until in their wanderings they brought up near the doll's bed and were drawn off their wrestling and running interest by it. They came out together, Gretchen pulling, Tom pushing the bed. They halted near a window and Tom tried to pull it away. Gretchen squawked, "No, no," pulling at her end. A tug of war followed. Tom lay back and pulled in jerks and Gretchen did the same. They seemed quite evenly matched in strength. Neither got it away from the other. They laughed and continued for some minutes, finally dragging and pulling the bed off into the north room. There seemed nothing but good humor and plenty of it between them, though the play amounted to nothing except rough and tumble.

We allow a certain amount of this puppy play as an experimental venture when children are evenly matched so that neither feels overwhelmed. Tom especially needed it at this point in his career, for he had been inclined to resent attacks on himself though he lost few opportunities to assail the weak. With this increase in control he was also establishing himself in the group of children about his own age and the attacks upon smaller babies showed a marked decrease until they ceased to be a cause of concern.

The most devastating and dangerous kind of social play is the sort we call "supervisory," the traditional older child attitude toward a younger one. We believe that it is often due to an attempt to compensate for a lack of power in some other direction, or because it has been possible by means of it to win adult approval or attention. The following record will illustrate this kind of play and its effect as we have observed it in the group.

Dora, handicapped in physical strength by an early and long continued malnutrition, showed precocity in her social development which was fostered by her home environment. Her interest tended to center about the other children and she developed a very definite and successful method of concentrating their attention about her activities.

January—Several characteristic instances of Dora's taking responsibility are given below. Age 36 months. Directed Lucy, 25 months, where to sit on her kiddy kar, assured her she wouldn't fall. Told Winifred, 26 months, all the cars were in use and later when Lucy went to the seesaw and Winifred took her kar, Dora told Lucy of it, adding as if in argument or persuasion: "You on the seesaw. You on the seesaw." Then offered her kar to Lucy. Assured Lucy when she fell, "That didn't hurt," in adult's tones. Rebuked Winifred for climbing on table, "We don't get on tables." Winifred was asked where her kiddy kar was; Dora pointed it out. Took responsibility for turns in the swings, assuring adult that Winifred had had hers.

January 24—In the afternoon Dora placed a chair near the linen closet under the table. Anna, 32 months, and Lucy joined her. She gave directions to the others and insisted that Anna should sit apart near the window. Anna, very irate, fussed and pressed up near the others, saying, "I put chairs here so John can't get out." (Name given adult who was taking record near by.) Dora, "Anna's putting chairs up so you can't get out." Anna brought up more chairs, Lucy brought another. Dora, smiling, threatened adult, "You can't get out. You all locked in. You all locked in." Anna echoed and they climbed up on the adult table shouting, "You couldn't get out. You couldn't get out. Cry hard." As attention was concentrating upon adult, she stepped out of the magic circle over the chairs. Dora at once transferred her attention to Anna, who was still on the table, and pulled out the chair by which Anna had climbed up. Anna, marooned there, cried till adult showed her how she could get down by another chair. As she was just about to get to the floor, Dora ran about the table and seized the second chair. Anna kept her balance, but cried hard in excitement, seized the chair and shook it, then dragged it back to the table though she had no further use for it. We lured her then to other independent pursuits. Dora did not seem as much affected by the

Indoor playroom.

play as Anna did, though she pulled at the chair when Anna tried to drag it back.

February 4-11—Dora, 37 months, has discovered that she can control and also tease the children by enclosing them in a space fenced in with blocks or chairs or by keeping them out of an enclosure where she has immured herself, as the case may be. She hastily constructs a barrier, says, "You can't get out," and her victim is paralyzed. The beginning of this play is described in the notes of a previous record when Dora and Anna blocked adult in with chairs. That was fun, but Anna, 33 months, is immediately dissolved in tears and reduced to a state of panic at the thought of being shut in herself. On the roof one day Dora made a circle of yard blocks and ensnared several children. As they knocked down blocks she repaired the breaches, rushing about from side to side, keeping up the excitement and carrying on the game as long as she could get a response. We are trying to give the children a technique for meeting the situation by suggesting that there is always a door which can be opened and closed. Lucy, 26 months, was on a kar and Dora was playing with blocks, which are in a box near the slide steps, and under the balcony. (See illustration, p. 246.) Lucy rode under the balcony, through the passage between the shelves and cupboards and the chest and steps. Dora hastily began her spider tactics and wove her web from the slide steps to the piano so that Lucy found her exit barred on her next round. She accepted Dora's verdict that she could not get out. Before Lucy could turn and get out of the alley at the other end, Dora had scuttled back and set up a barrier there. Lucy looked concerned. Adult broke the spell by suggesting that Lucy could ride through the wall. As soon as Lucy was free, Dora started a wall across the doorway into the small north room and soon trapped Winifred, who wailed till released by adult.

February 11-18—We are gradually giving the children a technique for getting out of Dora's toils. Also she is taking them with less excitement as far as their attacks upon her building are concerned. If she builds herself in and they throw down a portion of the wall, she rebuilds with less agitation, and the notion of thrusting aside a block and stepping out when she has caught one of them is becoming a habit with them. We have tried to interject humor into the situation, and now Anna will sometimes entrench herself, say, "Can't get out," but smilingly, and as soon as we ask, "Where's the door," she will move a block, come out and close the door behind her.

February 18-25—There is now no more strain between Dora and the other children over building enclosures. They have firmly the technique of going and coming through "doors." Dora has, however, a determined drive to absorb the attention of children with whom she is playing. If several of them are building, she is very likely to keep up a running conversation almost like a story, calling the children by name to see what she is making, and adding irrelevant or imaginary details in order, as it seems, to hold their attention. Walter, 36 months, breaks away, but Anna is much excited by it and is growing very dependent upon Dora. She asks for her on arrival, and if Dora is present is content only when she is playing with her.

Our method of interrupting the progress of this absorbing interest in each other was a drastic one. We sent Dora to another group of older children for her morning play time. This gave Anna a chance to get herself established in her own play situation.

March 3-10—Anna and Dora with kiddy kars in shelter. Raining. Dora suggested that they go "on the station." She talked a good deal about the engine, the tracks and the station. Anna, much confused, could not follow her. She called to adult, "We're going on the station." Dora corrected her, "No, we're going on the train." To relieve Anna, adult said that Anna was on her train and that Dora could get on hers. Anna withstood Dora's invitation for some time, and really kept more or less on her own line. Dora had to change her line of attack to suit Anna's activities. Anna broke away several times, and seemed less affected than often. Finally they asked for blocks, and all of them were brought in. Anna built in one place, and Dora in another. They did the usual house building, and visited each other with amiable understanding. Anna successfully resisted Dora's insistence that she make a door to her house, and on the contrary Dora accepted the suggestion that she make a doorless house.

Dora's absence has reduced the emotional tenseness as far as Anna is concerned. She has ceased to do more than inquire for Dora on arrival, and is making a satisfactory relationship with Walter and good play contacts also with Lucy and Winifred. She has been much more independent in her play with Walter than she was with Dora. She takes the initiative occasionally in planning play, and often in directing her own activities without reference to his or in spite of his suggestion. March 10-17—Dora's second week out of our group has gone well both there and here. She and Anna are overjoyed to see each other, but it is no longer difficult to keep them apart.

The two children continued to be interested in playing together, but they did so with advantage to both of them, and at the expense of neither.

Sometimes this sort of dictatorial play takes the form of extreme "mothering," affection and would-be helpfulness. Maisie was another child whose physical weakness seemed to throw her back upon other resources and she showed a tendency to use the other children to establish herself as a force in the group. For a time Frieda Mac was her willing dependent. As Frieda's interest in the play materials matured she grew intolerant of Maisie's interference and as both children were high strung the teacher's ingenuity was taxed to maintain any approach to serenity in their relationship. Separation seemed to be the only successful method and after it had been carried on consistently for most of the day over quite a long period, it was found that each child had developed interests that were absorbing enough to hold her. Maisie's attitude reflected, sometimes with mirrorlike clearness, the treatment she received at home, from an older sister to whom she was a doll, and from a father who alternately indulged and disciplined her.

In all problems of development, we find that we have to reckon with an irreducible kernel of native tendencies which seems to be little affected by our efforts at modifying it or by environmental conditions. However, we must remember that a child's use of his native endowment is surely modified by educational procedure. Dora and Maisie will always be more dependent upon the social environment than some of the other children, more responsive to it, probably more able to affect it; but the fact that they both gradually acquired an interest in activities which demanded muscular control like driving nails or climbing about on planks and into packing boxes, activities that also required wholehearted physical and nervous organization in the performance will, I believe, make them more integrated persons than they would otherwise have been. "Occupational therapy" proved its worth many times before the term was invented.

Another disadvantageous kind of social play is that in which language is the be-all and end-all. Language in the form of communication or a rhythmic accompaniment seems to serve the play scheme. Through it children gain in power to make verbal their plans, their social interests are quickened, and their feeling of pleasure or elation regarding their association together is heightened. The children mentioned in the chapter on Language as inclined to substitute talking for working with the materials or with their bodies, are pursuing a sort of play from which we quite definitely try to divert them.

Communication of a simple kind, such as is involved in the play of a little child is quite within their powers. "This is the boat," "That is the water; you'll get wet if you don't get on the boat," and such details are announced and comprehended. *Conversation,* the interchange of thoughts, is too mature a process for our children, and when they attempt *talk* that is not related to the immediate matter in hand, words alone are the result as far as language is concerned and uneasiness and distraction from constructive occupations follow.

Maisie frequently used this method of attracting Donald's attention to herself. She employed various devices; sometimes calling him to give him some treasure, or offering to do for him something which he was already doing quite well for himself; sometimes whispering to him and laughing loudly as if the secret were very amusing and sometimes calling him a bad boy and threatening punishment. She rarely got further in her conversation than these disjunctive remarks, but the effect was to involve both children in disorganized behavior.

In stressing the negative side of social play, the deviations from the general pattern of social development that appears to be most profitable to a child, I am again trying to present the evidence upon which we have based our conclusions. I am sorry to end upon a repressive note but it would have been equally misleading to use these illustrations as an introduction to the chapter.

Both kinds of records illustrate fairly well the point which we wish to emphasize: that a child pursues with security and with advantage to himself a social life in which his responsibilities are concerned only with himself and his own activities, and that a more sophisticated sort of relationship is not favorable to development. They raise many other questions however, especially regarding the individual children, the underlying causes for their tendencies and their subsequent development, and they show how inadequate any presentation must be that does not trace the factors of heredity and environment, and the possibilities of physical or nervous disbalance as explanations of personality. The thoroughgoing study that such an interpretation would require does not lie within the scope or intention of this discussion. Our research staff is concerned with the work of finding the relationship between the different kinds of data gathered about each child and now available in our files, and a later publication will deal with this type of study.

The "whys" that lie outside the Nursery School are being discussed here only as they are known and used in current practice by the Nursery staff, and even then not exhaustively. The notes cited are submitted as fairly objective records of behavior and as illustrations which may help to present the point of view held by the Nursery staff more clearly than a statement alone could do.

C. LANGUAGE AND MUSIC

Language

In this section I am hoping to show fuller evidence for the conclusions that were drawn in the discussion of language development in Part II.

The use of vocal or verbal activity when a child is vigorously engaged in an occupation hardly needs to be illustrated. There are very individual and characteristic variations in the kinds of speech activity noted. Geordie at twenty-four months had a very fair vocabulary though he had the tendency commented upon of echoing adult expressions. However, he had the habit of accompanying his full-body activities with a very varied syllabication. These syllables were not attempts at words except when so indicated. They did not accompany definite horse or boat or train play but were chanted or shouted as he capered about the playroom or up the slide steps.

"Giddy, giddy, giddy"—repeated seven or more times back and forth, from chute to slide steps.

"Dem-me, dem-me, dem-me."

Laughed over the top: "Dub-dee, dub-dee, dub-dee." Then, "Wuh, wuh, wuh." "Duh, duh, duh," a throaty sound.

Blowing the air through his lips, "Bru-wah, bru-wah."

Drank milk and ate a cracker to the accompaniment, "Oh doo doo do, Oh doo doo do."

As he ran, "Bee, bee, bee; Lee, lee, lee; Dub, dub, dub." Capering about, "Oo oo oo," then "Nyum, nyum nyum," over and over.

I have not indicated the number of times he repeated the syllables but usually there were more than the three repetitions I have given. The remark that his voice was deep and throaty was made more than once.

The record taken when he was twenty-seven months gives fewer syllables, and more frequently actual words are interspersed.

"Ee, uh, ee; uh, ee, ee."

"Too, soo, soo, soo, soo, soo."

"Lum lot, lum lot."

"Lush, lish, lish, lush." It was interesting that these syllables followed an exercise in opposites. "Just as good," he repeated after adult, then added, "Just as bad," one occasion when he appreciated the meaning.

"Sallie, Sallie, Sallie," had no connection with anything observable.

"Bruk, bruk, bruk, bruk," said in a throaty voice.

Stood at the top of the slide chute, a hand on either post swinging the left leg out and in a deep throaty voice chanted, "Ma-wee, ma-wee, ma-wee, ma-wee, A-a."

As exercises in the use of facial and throat muscles and vocal chords, these syllables cover quite a range. Geordie, however, did not adapt his syllables nor invent words to fit appropriate occasions.

Matthew's rhythmic chants were more often suited to the situations, and they more nearly approximated words than Geordie's. The records cited were taken from his twenty-seventh to his thirty-sixth month.

"Dee dee doo dee, Scrap a row, scrap a row, scrap a row, scrap a row," chanted with no apparent reference to activity.

"Boogie man, boogie man, boogie man, boogie man up here," shouted, whispered, then growled, apropos of nothing. A favorite expression with Matthew and Kurt.

Seized a wooden peg from the settle, and beating the air with it, chanted, "Wing a dong ding, wing a dong ding."

"Loh, leh, lah; loh, leh, lah; loh, leh, lah;" shouted in a deep hollow voice.

As he was being undressed he chanted, "Nolly lolly, nolly lolly, nilly lolly, sillie Billie, nolly lolly."

"Waggle wee bo, waggle wee bo, waggle wee bo."

Clapped blocks together shouting, "Ping, poing, ping, poing."

Caroline at 37 months was throwing and chasing a ball. She shouted as she ran,

> "Oh inda, nida, ginda, go,
> Da, gane, da go."

Other children simply accompany themselves with statements of what they are doing. Jean did both. At twenty-five months we find the following record:

She was spreading a cover and chanted as she did it, "La lee, la lee, la lee."

She stood at a low table with a scoop and a little pan containing a few pebbles and said "Sha-voo" (shovel) twenty-two times in succession. Tipped stones out of the pan saying, "Stones, stones, stones," etc. Picked them up and put them back saying ten times, "Put it in, put it in."

With some other children she was pushing a chair about the nursery: "*My* chair—push, *my* chair—push."

Stepped cautiously down from a stool saying, "Go down, go down, he' we go down."

Spilled some water: "Spill it. Wipe it."

Was riding on a kar: "I riding on kar, I riding on kar."

Philip, 33 months, was playing with his doll during

music. The selection being played was Turkey Buzzard. Philip took the exact key and sang, "Dee dee dee, dee dee dee," then "Cu' daly u'," (cover dolly up), then "Bee bee bee, bee bee bee," then "da—lee."

The appearance of a definite pattern or form in the phrases used is observable. Caroline's running phrase has rime as well, which is rarely met at this age. Matthew's "wing a dong ding" is a pleasing variation of "ding dong." As Donald ran about the roof he shouted, "Up a lup a dup, up a dup I go." Donald was very prolific in syllables and is recorded as showing interest in exaggerated movements of facial and throat muscles and as having used a very varied assortment of consonant sounds before he used words. As he got older he made the syllables into songs or chanted accompaniments.

I have said that babies are responsive to the rhythmical phrases which we use with them. They have in many instances set up a pattern.

Matthew at 36 months sang on B and G,

> "Here I go to my boat up town,
> Here I go to my boat up town."

As usual he was more intent on the swing of the words than upon their meaning.

Dora, 24 months, putting her doll to bed, used a phrase from the "Sleepy time" song:

> "S'eepy time ha' co' for dollie,
> C'ose eyes and go to s'eep."

Again:

> "Go—to—s'eep my dollie, dollie,
> My dollie, dollie, dollie, dollie, etc."

and

> "S'eepy time, cover dollie,
> Time to go bylow, bylow, bylow (on a high note),
> Ba-bee, ba-bee, ba-bee, ba-bee." (Chant.)

One day adult was speaking to Rab of the approaching taxi trip and said, "Soon we'll go bumpety bump to your house." Frieda Mac, at her table drinking her milk, set down her mug, and eyeing adult solemnly, delivered herself as follows:

> "Bumpety bump to *my* house,
> To *my* mama,
> To *my* daddy,
> To *my* ba—lamb,
> To *my* table,
> To *my* chair."

Demands on the children or inquiries we often make in a chanted sing-song phrase. "Who wants water," sung on the major arpeggio may be answered by "I do" on G, or an improvised tune impossible to reproduce. Going upstairs one morning the adult chanted, "Up on the roof."

A child answered on the same intervals, "Get kiddy kar."

We chant our goodnights as each child leaves the group for nap. Philip, whose vocabulary could be enumerated once across the page, was heard making curious grunts as he was lifted off the dressing table. "Mŭ nĭ, dĕ dĭ, mŭ nĭ, dĕ dĭ," he was saying over, varying the final syllables but keeping the tempo and the emphasis consistent. When he finally caught the adult's attention, she recognized the subject of his song and joined him: "Goodnight, Caroline, goodnight, Carl-o,"

Good - night Car - o - line , etc

and so on through the list. Philip continued his chant till he fell asleep. It was weeks before he got as perfected a form as "Gŭ nī, Pă" (Goodnight, Patty), but the air and rhythm were recognizable.

There is quite a difference in older and younger children in the content of their language, but it seems to us that certain features are quite consistently pleasing to them. For instance the antiphonal chanting is for the most part quite beyond a child of two and under, and yet in the following example two children of two years showed that their attention was caught by it.

While eating their fruit, Pat, 30 months, Charles, 27 months, and Karl, 32 months, started a conversational game in which Pat and Karl shouted gruffly at Charles, "Go 'way," and Charles replied emphatically, "I won't." All in great good humor, little or no attendant action except for wagging of heads, etc. Caroline, 24 months, the fourth at the table, listened and watched appreciatively without taking part, which was characteristic of her. Peggy, 24 months, having finished her fruit and left her table, came near and joined the "go 'ways." When the group and game broke up, Caroline remained at the table with some orange juice left. She then went out to the roof, mounted a kar and riding toward

Philip, 23 months, she rose and pushed out a hand at him and snarled gutturally at him over and over, "Go 'way." He moved to one side and she pursued him and repeated her growling. He soon accepted this as a game and planted himself before her kar or ran a little way off and waited for her to follow. Each time she walked her kar up to him and repeated her guttural "Go 'way." Charles, Karl and Pat near, all looked on with interest.

Peggy, 24 months, and Karl, 32 months, seated together at table with orange water held this conversation and variations of it.

Peggy: "Oh—mudder."
Karl: "No—horsie."
Peggy: "Oh, horsie?"
Karl: "Horsie. (Pause.) Tow?" (Cow, probably.)
Peggy: "No, horsie."
Karl: "Oh, horsie."
Peggy: "Ma-wy." (Mary, probably.)
Karl: "Ma-wy," etc., etc. Twice they dropped this and then started up again, each time one using a noun, in a tone of statement, the other questioning, refusing, or accepting it as fancy prompted. The inflections were varied and marked.

Children even younger respond to this sort of play and show by smiles and chuckles and by shining eyes that it is giving them some sort of satisfaction. One of our children had an unfortunate habit of saying, "Go away," to his friends. It was a source of amusement to the others, and a chorus often rose after Saunders had introduced the phrase which resulted in a good-humored chanting back and forth. One day as Harriet, 23 months, seated herself at dinner, opposite Saunders, she fixed him with a twinkling eye and roared, "Go 'way," apparently intending to start the ball rolling.

Philip and Caroline carried on a long session of

this sort of chanting, mostly nonsense syllables, after they had passed their third birthdays. They were playing in the sand box together. They used actual words and sentences as well as the nonsense.

Philip: "Ees not."
Caroline: "Ees not."
Philip: "Eh."
Caroline: "Eh."
Philip: "Go 'way."
Caroline: "Go 'way."
Philip: "Go 'way ko."
Caroline: "Go 'way ko."
Philip: "Go 'way ki."
Caroline: "Go 'way ki."
Philip: "Aw dee, de wa, di geh."
Caroline: "Aw dee, de wa, di geh."
Philip: "My o ketty."
Caroline: "My o ketty."
Philip: "Ga de."
Caroline: "Ga de."
Philip: "Oh, see wain go in!"
Caroline: "Oh, see rain go in!"
Philip: "Ees no more holes."
Caroline: "No more holes." Conversation referred to perforated shovels. Caroline does not echo Philip's pronunciation except in nonsense syllables.
Silence, then chanting rose again.

In these intervals between chanting the children subsided into silence. Once they seemed to be letting sand trickle through their fingers.

Philip holds a perforated shovel full of sand over his pail and watches it drain through. The shovel is in his right hand. As he scrapes it down into the sand there is a corresponding movement with his left hand. Sometimes the left

stirs as he sifts sand, but usually it lies on his left knee. . . .
This position shows the tenseness of the muscles. When his
pail was full he evidently relaxed. He turned over on his
knees with the pail in his hands. "Oh, see, so heavy. I going
make nice cake."

This general muscular release after strain, and
a break into language activities, are frequently
noticed.

The fact that children make motor responses to
sounds is obvious. The power of a phrase to recall
a sensory experience is a feature of most great
poetry and literature. Children differ in their sensitivity to sounds, but most of them are responsive to
language which is expressed in sensory and motor
terms. Some children have a real flair for putting
this interest of theirs into appropriate language.
Donald, whose early tendency to use a variety of
syllables together with great mobility of his facial
muscles was mentioned, was very definite and inven-
tive in his later language.

Rolling about on a kiddy kar, trailer attached, he made
loud "Too too" sounds, and said that a big engine was coming. Then made a shorter sound like "Puh, puh," and said,
"That's the smoke coming out." Later adult said "Too, too"
as he rode off. He corrected her, saying, "Doesn't say too,
too now, says choo, choo."

At 40 months the following is recorded. Donald had
been put to bed but adult returned to his room after putting
another baby into a crib on the roof. Donald: "Why did
you come down stairs so fast? I hear-ed your feet." Adult:
"What did they say?" Donald: "They said, 'Clop, clop' and
I hear-ed the door say 'bing,'" a short crisp sound.

Alec pointed to smoke puffing out of a chimney that had
a whirling ventilator on top: "Smoke—ft, ft, ft."

Maisie saw an older child swinging a jump rope: "She is rounding the rope."

Carola said, "It raining." Dennis listened, then added, "Pit patting."

Anyone who knows children can multiply examples of this treatment of language. The point I am trying to make is that it is really important to encourage a vivid, flexible, playful approach to it.

All the features which have been mentioned are illustrated in the "stories" which children tell. I am using the term not in the sense in which it is often employed in school work as meaning any complete sentence which a child can make about a given subject but in reference to the brief narrative remarks which they make spontaneously.

Maisie's first story when she was twenty-three months old was concerned with the small chairs which are always of interest to the babies, because there are so many of them, and they are allowed to use them in their play. Her statement was also a stab at enumeration.

> "Phœbe—chair,
> Caleb—chair,
> Maisie—chair."

When she was twenty-eight months her plot was more elaborate and gave a hint of experiences which she had had. The account dealt with herself and members of her family and related an incident within her own knowledge.

> "By'n bye Maisie go on boat.
> By'n bye Poh go on boat.
> By'n bye daddy go on boat."

Nearly a year later she was attempting to hold the children by reeling off words arranged with a certain attempt at form or content.

"Frieda Mac! I want to tell you something. I fell down in the street, and I cried hardly."

Children's remarks take form before they use language with the idea of relating an anecdote. Maisie was probably doing as she had been done by. "Poh" was her older sister.

At 26 months Carter chanted:

> "And I came home,
> And Daddy came home,
> And Fay came home."

Later he charmed us by this lilting refrain, apropos the nursery equipment:

> "We've got just *one* cariole at home,
>   And that's all.
> We've got just *one* waste basket at home,
>   And that's all.
> We've got just *one* kiddy kar at home,
>   And that's all.
>   And that's broke!"

This was delivered in a monotone except for the "one" which was chanted on a higher note, and emphasized each time.

It illustrates nearly all the features which we try to use in our stories: brevity, rhythmic form, and a single, well-known fact or episode.

The determination of children to be included in a story was illustrated in Part II in the case of small Robin. There was another instance of his painstaking insistence of his place in the history. The doings of a fancied kitten were being described by adult as we watched a cat from the window.

"And Maisie took the little pussy cat on her lap, and Maisie gave milk to the little pussy cat."

Each time action on the part of the child was described Robin would smite himself on his chest and say, "Me—Wobin—take—pussy cat—on—lap."

Children often refuse to answer their own names, and enjoy making a new distribution of names to the nursery group. One day Lucy announced that she was Larry, her brother, and gave her name to an adult. She was very merry over it at first; then suddenly her face grew quite troubled and she said, "No, no, I'm not Larry; I'm—Lucy—Brown." It seemed almost as if her own identity were in question.

The first impulse at social communication often takes the form of narrative. There is no expectation of give and take.

Yvonne, 32 months, telling adult what she had seen coming to school:

> "Monkey was on sidewalk.
> Man made music.
> Monkey did dance.
> I did give monkey a penny for his pocket."

She rushed through her narration, emphasizing "penny" and raising her voice in a squeak as she said it.

Matthew, 36 months, talked a good deal about his country experience:

> "We went in the train and at Chester we got off.
> No, the train stopped and let some other people off.

And then we went at Midvale,
And Grandma was at the station.
And we got in the carriage
And Grandma slapped the horses with the reins.
And we went to Grandma's house."

These two examples are unusually well organized stories. They were given in response to inquiries from adults and are recalls of past experiences. The clap of the reins was a remembered feature.

The following also from Matthew was half spoken, half chanted and addressed to no one in particular. He was carrying on boat play with blocks.

"The smoke comes right out the chimney,
And then the boat goes.
When it has a smoke stack, it goes;
But when it hasn't, then it doesn't.
Ding, dong, the bell's ringing on the boat."

Matthew came through to stories of this sort only after he had been for some months in the nursery and had realized the motor experiences which our environment offers.

Conversation is another matter.

Pat, 30 months, and Karl, 32 months, played a long time in the small green packing box. They had several of the painted box covers stacked in it and the game seemed to consist of arranging and rearranging them. The language accompaniment played an important part in their plan. Karl would hold up a cover and say "More?" whereupon Pat would say "More," take it and place it. Then Karl would say "No more?" and Pat would reply or Pat would ask the question and Karl would reply, the rising inflection with the question and the falling of the reply making an antiphonal chant.

During the following week they repeated the language play. Pat and Karl had interlocking blocks. Pat held one up: "More?" No response from Karl. "More," from Pat with a slight bob of the head, eyebrows raised. Instead of repeating the word, Karl said, "That one go in here?"

Kurt, 36 months, drawing on Yvonne's paper:
"See, here' big boogie man."
Yvonne: "I want see big boogie man."
Kurt: "Here's boogie baby. See boogie baby?"
Yvonne: "Lemme see boogie baby."
Kurt: "Here's big Teddy bear. See big Teddy bear?"
Yvonne: "Lemme see big Teddy bear." Etc., etc.

Donald, 36 months, and Maisie, 38 months, were playing with cubes and trains together and carrying on a desultory conversation, only a little more elaborate than that of the younger children given above.
Donald: "This is a lovely big ferry boat."
Maisie: "This is a train coming. Oh, it fell over!"
Donald: "Oh, it fell over! Oh, my—engine—fell—over." (Chanted.) "My big engine coming. Is yours a ferry boat?"
Maisie: "No, this is an engine."
Donald: "My boat's going back."
Maisie's building of cubes fell off her train.
Donald: "Now make it this way." A long low line instead of several tiers.
Maisie objecting vociferously to his suggestions, Donald withdrew to his own building.
Donald: "Begin — sing,   begin — sing,   begin — sing." (Sung.)
Maisie: "Donald, I'm going to make a big long boat."
Donald: "Are you? Going in the water?"
Maisie: "The water's under the floor. In country little

spiders up under roof,—white stuff, don't you know, and he goes up your arm, don't you know?"

Donald: "Yes, I have two spiders and he walks up my arm."

Maisie: "I have two spiders, one big one and one little one. See, I have a long boat." (Had placed cubes as Donald advised.)

Donald: "Too too, going run into you." (Intoned.)

Maisie: "My boat's going back again 'cause he left his clothes."

Donald: *"My* boat left *his* clothes."

Contrast with this the following when Donald had a very definite request to make:

Donald: "Maisie, are you through with those funny trains?"

Maisie: "No."

Donald: "Well; will you let me have it when you get through?"

Maisie: "Not to-day but to-morrow I shall get through."

This incipient conversation is hardly more than a social extension of syllable chanting. The impulse here is to share however, while the earlier experience demands no audience and no response.

When more elaborate conversation which aims at an interchange of ideas is attempted, the inadequacies of understanding are revealed.

Walter at 38 months was much less attentive to word meanings than Dora at the same age. He deferred to her and asked her questions. He had declared that he was going to take the nursery safety pins home with him. Dora told him that he could not and followed it up with argument. "You can't take 'em home, 'cause these are the school's. This is the school we're in. See the top wall and the white wall? Here, this is the school, see it's painted." Walter, quite unconvinced, "It isn't." Dora, "Look how white it is, it's painted." Walter was quite unequal to the conversation. Repeated after Dora "top oil" in place of her "top wall" (ceiling) and became very vehement. Her information was definite though her logic was weak.

Walter and Dora, 38 months, looking out at a wire from laboratory across yard, threaded through an insulator. Walter: "Is that a ball?" Dora: "No, it's a screw, a long screw." Walter: "What that screw for?" Dora: "To hold the line up." Walter: "No clothes on that." Dora: "No clothes—a li-en." Walter: "Where's the lion? There's no lion." Dora: "Not a lion—a li-en." Walter to adult: "No lion there." Adult explained. Subject was dropped.

Maisie, 37 months: "Donald, was you ever in a subway? I was."
Donald, 39 months: "Did you break yourself?"
Maisie: "No."
Donald: "Did you like it?"
Maisie: "Yes."
Donald: "Nice soft wheels?"

Matthew, 32 months: "Have you got a bad cold, Lucy?"
Lucy: "No, I *haven't.*"
Matthew: "What have you got?"
Lucy: "A monkey and a trolley car. It broke."
Matthew: "Mine didn't."
Lucy: "But you haven't a trolley car and a monkey."
Matthew: "Yes, I have a trolley car and a monkey."

When we gave clay to Kurt, 38 months, and Lucy, 37 months, for the first time, he did not know what it was, and finally called it "claster" (plaster). Lucy knew the name. They were very talkative as they worked. Kurt commented upon a ball made by Lucy. "Your mother see that ball?"

Lucy: "No." Kurt: "Why?" Lucy: "She doesn't want to play with that clay, because she might get her hands *all* dirty, and then she'd have to wash them." Kurt: "Why?" Lucy: "The reason is because." Kurt: "You would get the floor all dirty with that claster at home and then your mother have to wash it and then you have to go to bed. Ha, ha, ha." Lucy, with vehemence and indignation: "I don't *want* to go home. I don't *want* to go to bed."

Kurt, 42 months, and Lucy, 41 months, were farther ahead than any children cited here in the ability to carry on conversation with each other. Kurt's thinking sometimes got ahead of his speech, but Lucy rarely let an inaccuracy get by, if it had to do with her own remarks or another's. Kurt had displeased her in some way, and she said, "You'll have to go into the other room." Kurt: "No, I not go in other room. Why should I go in other room, when I'm good? You're a funny li'l' girl!"

In these conversations there is a genuine give and take, with a distinct personal flavor quite different from the disjointed remarks of Donald and Maisie and much less often observed.

The child's conversation with adults does not reveal such inconsequential babblings because the responsibility for clarity remains with the adult. When we are talking with a child, we rarely misunderstand his references, and we see at once if our meaning is clear to him.

Shades of meaning, inexact pronunciation, references to time—past or future—may make remarks entirely unintelligible to a child, and a misunderstanding switches the entire conversation to another track, as illustrated by Dora and Walter and also by the following, when the adult was guilty of malice aforethought.

Craig arrived in the nursery with a new expression which had spread consternation in his own family. Shortly after his arrival he ejaculated in a loud voice and with a joyous gleam in his eyes, "Good God!" We did our best to ignore him but not so the children. Two others about his age took up the refrain and finally we heard Maisie, then just beginning to talk, murmur "Goo gah!" We let it pass till there was another outbreak and then one of us said, "A good dog? Where did you see him?" Craig looked startled, shook himself and blinked as he did when surprised, then said, "Yes, I saw him when I was with mother." There was no return to the former expression. We should not recommend this vicious and deliberate method of confusing a child but are confessing this example as an illustration of the immaturity of babies in the complicated technique of sustained social communication.

The children work very hard on the mechanics of language, the meaning, and especially the use of such words as "because," "to-day" and "yesterday," and pronunciation and arrangement absorb them. They play with words and expressions indicating causal and temporal relationships before they have a thorough understanding of them.

Yvonne, 29 months, tried to tell an adult that Matthew had picked up her cup for her: "Matthew picked me up my cup." Quite evidently not satisfied with her version she tried over and over, transposing or leaving out words till she finally said the sentence correctly.

In another record of the same date we find: To-day the same thing occurred again. She seemed now to have begun working at original language. She has been up to this time a veritable echo. She uses all her facial and throat muscles in her struggle to come through to the sentence she is trying for. To-day she reversed a word, "Fore-be," in her effort to make a long remark which unfortunately we had no chance to record at the moment.

One day some new perforated shovels were put in the sandbox. Someone asked, "Where did you get these new shovels?" Adult replied, "In the Ten Cent Store." Yvonne repeated. "Cen Tense Sore." Stopped, assumed a more rigid posture, eyes looking fixed and tried again: "Sten cen 'tore." Not satisfied she stiffened and raising her voice a little said still louder, "Ten—Cent—Store," and subsided. Kurt, eight months older, had watched her, smiling, and now added softly, "Five and Ten Cent Store." Yvonne however, seemed incapable of further effort, and made no attempt to elaborate her remark.

Lucy, 36 months, was very definite about language. After taking off her rubbers in the morning she said, "But I didn't take my shoes off 'cause it's not bedtime."

However, she was not always equal to clearing up inaccurate statements. One morning Matthew arrived some time before any other child and was taken up on the roof. He asked repeatedly why Lucy was not there. Adult said that it was not time for her, and that he had come very, very early. When Lucy finally arrived Matthew greeted her with enthusiasm and said earnestly, "You were not here when I came 'cause I came very late, Lucy." Lucy assented without comment.

One very pleasant day Anna, 34 months, remarked, "The sun came out. Now we don't have to go to bed, because the sun came out."

Donald, 36 months: "I have a boat at home that I'm going to bring to school to go under the bridge. Will that be good?" Adult agreed. "Then I bring it now,—next now."

Caroline, 40 months: "I going give some marbles to Philip. After I eat my dinner, and have my soup and I go home, to-morrow I going give some to Philip." The enumeration of events leading up to to-morrow seemed necessary to establish the lapse of time.

Kurt, 39 months: "I lost my scissors because I went for

a shoe shine." There may have been some sort of relationship, but questioning did not reveal it.

Edward had been absent a week. On Monday morning adult asked, "Edward, why didn't you come to school last week?" Edward: " 'Cause it was Sunday." Further questioning revealed no awareness of the lapse of time. Sunday stood out because of its recency and also probably because of the special program carried out on that day.

It has been most interesting to find that entire awareness of the difference in time meanings and ability to express them in words did not come until Edward was four. "Mamma," he said, "last week goes this way, doesn't it?" pointing back over his shoulder. "And next week goes this way," his finger stretched out in front of him.

In the struggles of little children for verbal expression, their remarks take a cryptic form quite beyond the comprehension of their peers. Sometimes they are as picturesque as Donald's "I don't mash my carrots, I eat 'em long," or "I almost swallowed my throat," when he choked. Charles entered the nursery at fourteen months toward the end of the year. He was very babylike at first and made few contacts with the other children. Within a few weeks he developed fast, took his place in the group, and was much more conspicuous than he had been at first. Kurt, forty-one months, was absent a few days. On his return he was seen regarding Charles closely and he remarked to adult, "Is Charles getting big?" Adult: "Do you think so?" Kurt: "Yes, he's getting *so* big!" It seemed to be Kurt's way of recognizing that Charles had changed.

Don, 37 months, appeared at school in a suit which had quite obviously descended to him from his older brother.

He was much pleased with it and tried to give us an explanation. He began, "Kenneth use' to have these,—when he was me." That was not quite satisfactory to him and he tried again: "Kenneth used to have these, when I was him," then as an aid to clarity, "with broken teeth!" Kenneth's mouth presented the jagged tooth line of six years. We supposed Don was trying to say that when Kenneth was about his age he had the suit.

I believe that until we study the actual language of little children we shall not realize by what gradual degrees they acquire proficiency in language and an understanding that enables them to undertake the subtleties and the complications of social intercourse.

I have said that there seems to be a tendency for vocal activity to subside when children become absorbed in the technique of a motor pattern. An illustration is given on a previous page where the record of a long antiphonal chant between Philip and Caroline is recorded. Throughout our records there are other evidences that when children are absorbed in postural activity, language response subsides.

With some of the children the reverse is equally true, and having been apparently stimulated to speech by a play interest, the vocal interest supersedes and overwhelms the play impulse. This is of course especially observable with the very verbal children.

Over and over the records show this to be true in Matthew's case. He seemed almost to be intoxicated by the sound of his own voice. It is probably closely associated with the early habit of not looking for meaning in what was said to him.

Matthew placed eight kegs in a line and called it a boat. Stood on the kegs chanting, "Toot toot," *which was the extent of his play.*

Matthew, building, chanted, "Now it must be higher," "Now I must take one off, that's too much, that's too much. Ding dong. Here goes the boat, here goes the boat to the gymnasium." *His play activity subsided as his vocal performance increased.*

Further examples can be found wherever Matthew appears in the records.

To illustrate the effect upon Matthew of a real interest, I quote from the records again:

On the 16th Matthew, 33 months, tried coasting in the rubber-tired cart. His interest was not sustained and he went only a few feet. Was offered a cart with iron-rimmed wheels since it would move more easily. He refused, however, and soon gave up the effort. The next day he coasted with left knee in wagon, holding the handle in his left hand and steering, gripping the edge of the wagon with his right hand. At first he seemed to be experimenting with the steering, but soon "got the hang of it," although he still had the rubber-tired wagon. He tried once or twice to use both hands for steering but went back each time to his first method. Lucy climbed into the back of his cart but it made too heavy a load and she was lured away. Twice she and Yvonne at different times tried to pull his wagon away from him and each time he held on bravely with loud remonstrances, and continued to coast. He finally got good speed and a long stride with his right leg. It is noteworthy that the sociable Matthew can play alone now that he has found material which really engages his interest.

Matthew, 36 months, stood in wagon, shouting loudly and monotonously, "Big man—see big man, big man going." Began pushing cart by lying down in it and revolving back wheel. *Volubility subsided as interest developed.*

In Part II, § 3, the appropriate part that language can play is illustrated. It must be, of course, the most effective tool in social technique.

I have connected irrelevance in language with the method adults use in stimulating language activities. All the children whose verbal facility and language understanding seemed most divorced, came from home environments in which the language stimuli were marked. The parents of one child were in the habit of dictating his responses, of another were verbal folk, and talked to him as they did to their friends, also using adult songs as a means of entertaining him, and the third child was kept under the influence of talk as if it were a convenient opiate.

I do not believe that the same treatment affects every child in the same way. As has been said Matthew was easily caught by the rhythm and pattern in words and tones. It was probably a peculiar combination of circumstances in his environment which brought about his habit of listening to the beat and rhythm of language, his own or that of other people, rather than to the words.

Morris would sing to himself, quite intricate and essentially adult songs and would come out of a reverie with expressions which had no bearing upon immediate concerns but which we could sometimes trace by what we knew of his past. Geordie, of whom it is recorded that he danced when eggs were being beaten, echoed whatever he heard whether or not it meant anything to him. One of the children said, "I'm shining my shoes." Geordie: "Shinny go shoo." When Dora remarked, "I'm going to fold this cap," Geordie echoed what he thought he heard and said, "I' going frow dis . . . all wound," repeating it over and over in a singsong. Adult spoke of a child on the center of the seesaw as a balance wheel which came through Geordie's dictaphone as "Winifred some bounce." On one occasion when he startled the adults by volunteering the remark, "This is Millie's room," as he entered the kitchen, someone commented, "That's a perfectly original remark," only to have it given back, "Per'fly'rig'nal 'mark." He used such phrases as, "Cute little Lucy" —"Cunning little Yvonne"—"Cute little shoes"— as he spoke to the other children. He often referred to himself with a chuckle as, "I bad boy!" or "Funny little boy." Ran calling over and over, "Don't be crazy, Don't be heady," or "Six o'clock," or "Ticks of New York."

Very little language was recorded during his first period in the nursery, from seventeen to nineteen months. He showed then none of this tendency to echo that was in evidence later. It was during the second year from twenty-three to twenty-nine months, when he left the school, that the echoing habit developed.

Matthew's records are taken from his twenty-seventh to his thirty-sixth month. He showed a similar tendency to use language without reference to its meaning. He was heard tramping about the roof shouting, "What about the reason, what about the reason," and when asked by adult, "Reason for what?" he replied, "Strawberries."

He showed a specious form of argument which we thought indicated that he did not follow the meaning of reasons given him. When being tucked into bed: "Don't you know I have to have my hands out so when the butcher comes, 'cause the butcher boy comes, don't you know," and so on and on.

One day when rain sent us in from the roof, he heard the adults talking about it and said, "It isn't going rain to-day, 'cause it's Sunday day and it can't rain to-day. It can't rain to-day 'cause it's Sunday day." This in the face of a downpour. He may have confused sunny and Sunday, but it is evident, nevertheless, that he did not have clearly in mind the meaning of the words he was using.

He had been given many nursery rimes and he was much concerned with them and his imperfect recall of them. "Don't you 'member," he would ask, " 'bout dat Simpy Simey. He fish whale in mummie's pail."

He adopted the "story" form frequently with much smacking of his lips and exaggerated inflection, smiling and wagging his head. "An' den, an' den dey sit down an' den dey climb in de water, an' den dey sit down, an' den, den"—interminably. These illustrations show our reasons for believing that language used with babies should be relevant. Humor or even nonsense finds a place on occasion, but there should be meaning within the grasp of a child's powers and related to his mental content. Late in the year, Matthew's accounts of a visit to the country, p. 265, showed much more direct and definite thinking and he gained in power to work and play without the stimulus of adult conversation.

Children know at an early age that they are the subject of adults' remarks, they take simple directions or appear to understand simple remarks and so we ascribe to them an interest and ability that they do not possess.

On the other hand they have quite a surprising amount of knowledge—of information, and we see them using it in their play and can trace it by the language which accompanies the activity. The dramatic forms which they devise reveal a good deal. The buildings they construct show a power of putting content into representative form. Dolls are dressed and undressed, given bottles, put to bed and covered, and age differences can be noted in the way the clothes are arranged, for the more immature children do not provide for air but cover the faces of their babies. Some children wish windows open when their dolls are in bed. The domestic processes are carried on: the market man, the ice man, the coal man, hawk their wares and deliver them, putting them appropriately into the ice box or down the coal chute. Cooking and eating are played interminably in sand and pebbles. Sometimes a stove is added, a fire is built and adults are warned that the food is hot. Recipes are given occasionally which, though far from accurate, show that the children realize that cake for instance has many ingredients. Shoe shining was a favorite game one year, and the stand for feet, the dressing box and dauber were represented in detail, and the process most realistically carried out. In this case pantomime held sway. Motors, and engines, filling stations and gasoline, and repair operations of various sorts appear in some children's play. Others are obviously less experienced like the child who fixed her car "with salt and pepper and gasoline."

The details of Donald's observations about travel are noted elsewhere. Getting luggage on, the differentiation in train noises and the haste of departure and arrival made a part of this picture, which was quite detailed and elaborate.

Boats play a large part in our dramatic activity, but whistle and bell sounds seem to be about all that are necessary. Kurt's elaborate boat loading * was an unusually mature performance in some ways. Even so the wheel as a steering device did not occur to him.

When constructions are made and named we get details which are not necessary in drama. Buildings have chimneys, and sometimes—though less commonly—doors and windows. Blocks of a different color are sometimes lights set atop of a tower. Caleb made lighthouses frequently, and they were quite suggestive in form. His boats too were fairly elaborate. Smoke stacks appear early on boats and trains but other details are generally lacking. Rarely wheels are spoken of. In the section on Building Material it is noted that the children used the colored cubes as wheels and set them on the floor alongside their constructions. It is noteworthy that they matched them from side to side, in number and in position. The pointed bow always appears rather late, and docks and wharves and stations, though mentioned, rarely materialize in any form that is suggestive. Karl's docks which looked as if he had seen the shore from an airplane, so accurate a representation they were, were noted only once (see p. 191). Alec used a triangle in front of his trains but he did not use the word "cow-catcher." "Newts live in the water and you mustn't squeeze them 'cause you might hurt them if you squeeze them," was a bit of natural history brought back from the country

* See Part III, § 2, B.

by one child. "Big beetles that lived under the rocks" were discussed by another child, but these city children—during their early years—not over forty-one months, have little to say about animals. I am sure if we saw them in the country environment their information about cows and dogs and cats would be more in evidence.

The airplane is a commonplace with these children. Donald built forms with his blocks that he named but which were unmistakable.* He also nailed two bits of wood together and then called it an airplane. When he and Maisie were talking about riding in one which we watched sailing overhead, it was interesting to hear Donald planning to use a ladder to climb up into it.

Reference to a building near us as a factory and an inquiry from a child about forty months old whether trucks were made there was very unusually mature.

Everything that comes to a child's mill is grist if it is not mixed with so much chaff of adult interference that he cannot grasp details. He sees what he looks at with photographic clearness and retains the memory of it. He will rehearse certain parts of it with his own person; he will incorporate other features in block play and if the method is established, later years will find him using crayons and paints, tools, wood and clay and language itself to recapture an experience which is still a poignant reality to him. He will do this only if the thing he sees, the experience that is before him, is relevant to him and if he is having a real—an actual—share

* See Part III, § 2, A.

in it. Again—he must be the artist, not merely the spectator.

Music

In Part II, in which is described the place of language in our planning, I have shown how closely our language and music are linked and, with a degree of temerity which I hope will not be misunderstood, I have given examples of our invention of rhythmic or melodic phrases which we use as accompaniments to the children's activities. Changes in the staff have interrupted our music program, affecting its continuity and development more than has been the case with our other activities. We have so far attempted no controlled studies but have limited ourselves to observations of the spontaneous responses of children during the music program, hoping that further study may reveal to us their meaning and significance.

In the period of piano music given as a regular part of the day's program we have had in mind rhythmic rather then melodic response and have chosen as our selections those that have marked and simple rhythmic patterns. We have tended to simplify our situations more and more, to use shorter phrases and fewer changes, but we are unprepared to say how this has affected the children.

At first we did not at all restrict the activities chosen by the children. Later, thinking that if they busied themselves with such things as cubes or dolls and covers even the most responsive of them responded less, we made the attempt to put in their way instead materials which more readily lent themselves to rhythmic use,—the kegs, the slide, carts or kiddy kars. It seems to have made less difference than some other factors which are more difficult to analyze.

We are inclined to believe, however, that the attempt to restrict activities is a mistake. It is contrary to our usual procedure so necessitates a different policy. The children are accustomed to choose materials and carry on activities without reference to adults except as assistance or supervision is required. Limiting their choice throws them back unduly upon adults and calls for still more adult interference.

We find the groups from year to year quite different in their response, in amount and in kind. We believe that the age of the children is one factor which is outstanding. If our average age is low, the response is so uneven, expressed in so individual a manner, and perhaps so largely implicit, that as a group the children seem unresponsive. In the years when we have a nucleus of three-year-olds we believe we are more likely to have responses which are definite, which show incipient dance forms and which include many of the individuals in the group. Another question at once arises, and that is the individual differences within each of the groups. If in the less mature group there are individuals who are outstanding in rhythmic interest or who are quick in reproducing tones or phrases which they hear, may that not bring the group as a whole up to one that averages older?

At the present time we are prepared only to raise questions, not to answer them, and as is indicated the questions are such that only further experimentation and observation will answer them.

The situation in regard to music resembles that of drawing. We are exposing the children to experiences which usually call for fairly definite responses. Because we have such young children we are unwilling to make a formal presentation of the material or to limit the responses elicited by a change in our usual method. This makes the study of cause and effect, of the impulse to respond and the form it takes, and of the factors that increase or decrease responses, much more difficult.

We do not ask the children to listen or to "do what the music says." We set no patterns in rhythmic responses, we make no attempt to teach the children words or tunes. We announce that music is to be given. If we are out of doors, music is announced by a phrase, "Down for Music."

Down for mu-sic

If we are indoors someone will usually suggest it by singing, "Music for Saunders," etc., mentioning each of the children in turn.

If the activities of the children are of such a sort that the sound of the piano is drowned, their attention is called to the fact. They are asked if they can hear it, or they may be reminded that it is music time. This is also done if they retreat from the room where the piano is. Sometimes there is an exodus of the entire group, in which case music is announced again and the children herded back. If an individual is certain enough of his inclination to ask to remain out of doors or to go into another room, he is allowed to do so.

We have tried to keep to a program that was regular and limited enough so that we could trace the responses of the children. We have used three selections for the fifteen-minute period. One of these is usually a dance or skip—another is a lullaby or a quiet composed number, and the third is broader, like a march in character.*

We have also used several very simple songs, most of them arranged by Harriette Hubbell in her work with the lower groups of the City and Country School. When these songs are played they are often sung as well and as the children become familiar with the words they ask for them. "Play the horsie song," Walter would ask. "Now play an'or horsie song," he would demand after the first. This seems to imply a degree of recognition which is surprising in a child of three or less who does not otherwise show an unusual musical endowment, who is having no training and who is not asked to name the selections. We found, however, that he did not notice whether or not his request was granted, made no remonstrance if instead of "Galloping" "Sleepytime" was played, and often having requested an encore, sometimes of a selection to which he had just given a delightful response, would give no evidence of listening at all. This applies not only to the particular child cited here but to any one of our group who made requests for special selections. Here is given further evidence of an immature pattern of awareness of melodic and rhythmic structure.

* Music Section, Maude Stewart, Bulletin XI, *A Nursery School Experiment.* Also p. 309, *List of Music Selections.*

That the children are affected by the music there is no doubt. It has a tendency to increase motor activity, to heighten general responsiveness. Their response to a specific selection is often, perhaps usually, delayed. If for instance a very loud, rapid, heavily rhythmic selection is played first, they may gradually show excitement which increases till there is much noise and confusion. If the musician then drops into a subdued lullaby the noise may persist nearly and sometimes entirely through the selection and into the third number even if that is also composed. We decided last year to begin the music period with a quiet number. The children usually come in from out-of-door play for the music, which is given just before dinner. Coming down stairs and into a different environment serves as a stimulus to renewed activity which the sound and beat of the music seem to increase.

Again there is a wide individual variation. Some children stop and look toward the piano whenever one selection is finished and another is begun. Others are able to abstract their attention entirely away from the music and go on with activities that seem unallied with the music or opposed in rhythm to it. Kurt seemed to us to hold himself from responding until the latter half of the year. He would withdraw often to a corner and crouch or sit there apparently unable to concern himself with toys or the other children, but quite aware of all that was going on about him. Anna was able to play with apparently entire absorption in her own pursuits and no evident attention to the music. At times no overt response to the music was made. Dora sometimes chose to play with materials which restricted her large muscle activities but her attention was always divided and she made frequent incidental responses.

For the past two years we have not had the advice of a special teacher, and our records have been much less satisfactory. In taking excerpts from them I have not attempted to follow any one group or any one child, but have given only examples which distinctly indicated that a child "heard" the rhythm and had an impulse to make an appropriate motor response. In the first group of citations the selections were taken from two books of French songs, "Les Aventures du Petit Jean" and Debussy's "La Boîte à Joujoux." "Le Soldat Anglais" from the latter was a march, beginning with a repeated note in the bass supposed to represent the drum. I have given the age of each child on the date at which he was first mentioned.

November 30—*Le Soldat Anglais.*

Karl, 30 months, at my side. "Too too—too too" on one note. Philip, 22 months, at piano watching and smiling. Pat, 29 months, backed up against door through which mother had just disappeared. He moved feet, did a heel and toe step with one leg in time. Swung—shifted weight but remained almost in the same place. Philip picked up scuffers and clapped several beats in exact time. After music had stopped, Pat began quite rhythmic swaying and stepping. Ralph went to piano after music. Got on stool and at bass end struck one note repeatedly in almost exact imitation of "Soldier" music which has a prolonged "drum beat." Did not look at piano as he thumped key.

December 3—*Marche Funèbre* (Les Aventures du Petit Jean).

Pat did a lively dancing step after his ball! Philip laughed loudly.

Il A le Bonnet d'Ane (Skipping).

Caroline, 23 months, showed fixed attention with one foot wagging. Charles, 26 months, sat on table and swung legs rhythmically. Philip up slide laughing loudly.

Pat began a very lovely step—half march, half skip, in which he brought down foot in emphasized beat. Later walked in a circle dragging feet and walking a bit pigeon-toed. Both kept up for only a few moments. Caroline and Ralph, 29 months, played together at table, Caroline pushing Ralph's hands off, then Caroline sat down and swung legs, tapping feet in time. Philip swung arms as he walked—in time. Pat made frequent overt responses.

December 14—*Voyez Comme Il S'Elance.*

Very gay. Karl entered from block room and began prancing about room in a circle very heavy and sober making effort to skip. Charles began rather self-consciously to step and as he did so he pushed out with his hands. Philip bounced or danced again. Charles almost at once joined Karl who was collecting chairs overturned in a row. Two children sat, one behind the other and at Charles' instigation began tickling each other. They were very merry. Laughed and squealed a good deal. Quite a bit of rhythm, especially in Charles' movements. He had kept his feet swinging, toes tapping on floor. Charles suddenly rose and ran about the room. Changed his gait, accommodating though not exactly to music. Karl joined him, again attempting a skip. His cheeks shook and he put so much effort into the management of his body that he did not last more than around the room twice. Returned to chairs again. Philip climbed and screamed, smiling broadly and again made a half-squatting, half-jumping movement.

December 17—*Le Pauvre Enfant* (composed).

Wheels given Charles and Philip and rolled for them. Philip ran after his with a very rhythmic and

full body movement, twisting and rotating trunk, bobbing head and arms which were flexed at elbow.
Il A le Bonnet d'Ane.

Philip began jumping with a squat as he has done before. Laughed and stopped. Had dropped the ball and wheel before. Went to cupboard which Charles had opened and chose cars. Took one at a time and interlocked. Quite absorbed. Jumped and squatted once briefly, laughing and adding an extra stamp. No overt and direct response to music except as noted.

January 18—*Le Pauvre Enfant.*

Caroline knelt on chair by piano and jerked her body vigorously up and down in a slow emphasized rhythm which sometimes fitted the music.

Philip rolled from side to side astride a keg. Then got down on floor and slewed himself around on hands and knees quite rhythmically and several times.

Ralph took a keg and rolled it ahead of him.

Philip sat astride a keg and rolled from foot to foot intoning. Ralph did the same. Philip, sliding off his keg, walked backward rolling it toward him with both his hands, then got behind it and pushed it with hands. Astride again briefly. Others all quiet.

Philip also jumped hard on floor with both feet, then made circles in one place fast on hands and knees, probably eight complete revolutions.

Karl rolled on two kegs.

"En Roulant Ma Boule"—French Canadian Folk Song—is one of the songs used occasionally, and is played first, then usually sung.

"Galloping" is a very excellent imitation of horses' feet in its tempo and rhythm. Voice often used with it. It is the second movement of a hunting song.

January 25—*En Roulant Ma Boule.*

Saunders, 21 months, went out to the middle of the
floor and solemnly revolved. Not a twirl but a pretty
narrowly prescribed circle. Quite a different pattern
from his swaying. Charles walked—a sort of walking
gallop—or syncopated walk exactly appropriate to the
music, six-eight time, fourth especially accented; first
also accented. Later he crept entirely across the floor
emphasizing same beat. Ralph walked briefly, bobbing.
Philip went up slide and hoo-hoo'ed loudly from balcony. Was unable to keep it up or to draw in the other
children and soon gave it up.

Galloping

Saunders first revolved, then walked in a wider circle.
Adult singing to get children's attention. Charles looked
up as adult sang Karl's name, then set off, walking in
a measured march, very even. Saunders joined him in
march but dropped out. Karl interested in mention of
his name but not moved to action.

Philip pursued his ball with his curious little
squatting bounce. He followed after ball, squatting and
jumping as ball bounced—a delightful figure if he develops it.

January 27—*Lullaby* (Brahms).

Karl walked slowly for several feet, lifting foot
rather high and placing each one deliberately almost as
if he were holding back for beat. Went up slide and on
top he trod up and down waving his arms.

En Roulant Ma Boule.

Karl again did many rhythmic movements. He and
Charles got chairs which they put on a small table.
Their impulse was to scream. They were asked to listen
to the music and adult began beating time. They trotted
their legs up and down and made various arm movements. Karl shut his fists and shot out his arms
alternately and very rhythmically, legs going at same

time. Karl inquired "Nish fight?" as he worked laughing.

Saunders revolved. Philip ran tossing ball before him and chasing it. Saunders tried to lead adult off. When not noticed he revolved again till he got groggy and tipped over. Peggy, 24 months, skipped bringing down right foot in a sort of stamp almost exactly with music. Charles had scuffers but did not use them. They were given to Karl who scuffed and made some slight efforts to skip as he used them.

February 24—*En Roulant Ma Boule.*

Peggy danced a *pas seul* in one spot, using feet—heels and toes bouncing body up—and keeping very good time with music. She did not proceed at all but did this curious jig—knees bent. At one point she did almost a shuffle. Was attracted to adult and then went up slide. Philip after her. Caroline did nothing rhythmic. Charles stood for a second, twice bending body and bobbing—taking a step bobbing and bowing. Karl and Charles also up slide.

Lullaby.

Peggy did her *pas seul* again briefly.

Galloping.

Adult left the room. On return found Philip running back and forth. He dashed up on the window sill, then sprang up into the air as he jumped off low sill, both feet. Went much higher than sill.

March 15—*En Roulant Ma Boule.*

Much vocalizing, not much activity. Children walking around rather subduedly.

Lullaby.

Karl sitting on sill beside piano hummed very softly. Caroline and Peggy used slide; Saunders tried to play piano. Charles idle.

Galloping.

Sudden increase in activity. Charles ran, feet kicking high behind him three times across room. Saunders

strode rhythmically across room and back. Caroline
went round and round on balcony bending body, looking at feet as she skipped. Peggy lay on mattress and
kicked both feet vigorously up over her head so her
toes must have almost touched over her shoulders. Repeated twice, then rose and kicked and stamped on
mattress; not rhythmic but very vigorous.

March 22.

Little apparent response during first two selections,
"En Roulant Ma Boule" and Brahms' "Lullaby," but
activity sped up at once when "Galloping" was started.
Philip and Charles slid down slide once or twice in a
hurried fashion, then Charles began to run around the
room with heels kicking well up behind, free knee-
bending, and continued many times around tables, under
slide, etc., Philip and Ralph joining him finally, all
three keeping it up for many circuits of the room. The
music was continued until there were signs of the interest flagging, the running becoming slower with occasional driftings or stoppings. The three showed slightly
different attitudes toward the game: Charles, the initia-
tor, had an air of concentration; Philip showed his
usual zest in activity, while Ralph got carried away
with excitement and giggled and laughed at adults as
he stumbled around the room.

March 26—*Il A le Bonnet d'Ane.*

Philip, Ralph and Charles up slide. Charles had
skipped across floor. Ralph made one or two skips.
Philip jumped with both feet. Charles skipped again in
exact time. Gretchen, 14 months, crept. Throughout
two selections she has made about two feet.

Le Pauvre Petit (minor—sad).

More activity! Saunders, who had been investigating
a keg, went up slide. Gretchen quickened pace. At
about end she tipped up and sat, legs out almost straight
from hips, at right angles from body. Brought left one
round from the back. Hip joints entirely flexible.

Marchons Au Pas.

Throughout Charles trotted with very rhythmic step half skip, half gallop—back and forth from kitchen to playroom. Was carrying on some sort of dramatic play for he brought an imaginary something in his hand; deposited it before Gretchen or on the table repeatedly.

In Part II, § 3, we spoke of the informal use by adults of singing phrases as accompaniments of certain of the children's activities, and sometimes as a way of asking a question or making a request or announcement. Some of the phrases we use and the situations in which they are appropriate are given there.

The children are very responsive to this sort of "music," and we note their phrases when we can verify them and in some cases use them again.

I have taken the notes on "Incidental Music" and have made a selection from them as they came chronologically. Again, the age of the child is stated on his first appearance.

October 1-5.

Sand box opened. "Oh, sand," said Charles, 24 months. Patted it, then said over and over, "Oh, nice sand," in a very varied tone—sweet, high, a wave-like sound, four notes. Varied remarks also—"Look at the sand." "I doing nat—sand." Swung arm from shoulder, back and forth. A rhythmic motion sweeping the surface of sand as he followed hand over it.

Charles seated self in at side of swing and began to sway as the "swing" phrase was sung. Pat, 26 months, ran to other swing and echoing the word, swung. He sang in same rhythm but did not pronounce word correctly and pitched his phrase lower than adult had done.

Ralph, 26 months, off on roof some distance, echoed exactly and later in shelter chanted exact intervals, "Swing swing." Children all returned to phrase again and again. Charles swayed his body as we sang and set the swing in motion.

Pat's voice was very flexible and varied and his improvisations were quite unusual and charming.

Pat (after children had been ringing the bells and adults had been singing "Ding dong" on the different intervals):

Ralph

Ralph—"Push—push—push—push—push—push—push—push—push"—chanted as he pushed small packing box with doll in it.

Pat sat on window sill singing "Na na na" on various pitches, the following phrase and many other tones, growing gradually louder until he was almost shouting. Ralph chimed in on the key once. Pat has very wide range—will attack a very high note and come down to low note in same phrase.

Much screaming during indoor play—short, sharp yelps for most part. I think the echo in these high rooms interests them. Pat and Ralph are more likely to initiate shouting than Charles. Pat sings quite long phrases also in rather good tone. Then again he is not as accurate in reproducing as Ralph. Pat—"Day day dah day dee dah"—recitatif.

October 12-19.

Ralph has the technique of the slide at last. Sings at the top.

in reproducing as Ralph. Pat—"Day day dah day dee dah"—recitatif.

Ralph, "Fing—fing,"—swing phrase, not absolutely true.

Ralph, on another day, swaying a swing in shelter for several moments and singing. No one had sung "Swing Song" before on that morning.

Ralph walked up 3-steps, then with adult's hand walked down. Sang "Walk" as he extended his foot, then as it went on the step with a stamp, "Down" but on G *above* C.

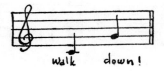

October 19-26.

Pat and Charles stood on the balcony calling in loud tones, "Hello, hello." Part of the time they used a singing quality of tone and although it occasionally grew shrill or raucous it seemed a musical response. (Music going on.) They kept it up at some length, adult singing back to them using different intervals and pitches.

Adult singing "Sleepy Time" to Caroline. Karl, 30 months, joined in with a sweet crooning quite in the spirit of the song.

Pat stepped about on the sand box top singing at length in strong voice,—"Ba ha ne" and others. He often used the 5-3 interval but it was a long singing discourse with various inflections, slurs and changes of tonal quality so that notation could not be exact.

Karl sat in swing in shelter on his first day back during second nursery year, and swung himself adult-fashion. Sang phrase—

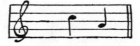

Was this song carried over from last year? Our interval is:

October 26-November 2.

Pat

The pitch is accurate—was verified.

Ralph sang the following in response to adult's spoken suggestion that he wipe up some water.

I wipe it up.

Ralph dragging two wheelbarrows from shelter sang the following in descending half tones—sang two or three similar phrases approximately following in same rhythm, an even two-four rhythm.

November 9-16.

Caroline, 22 months, sang just once as she swung in the shelter. This is the first full phrase from Caroline.

Wing, wong

Saunders, standing near block chest, made a soft wave-like sound.

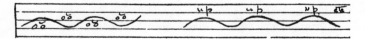

He was 18 months old and had very few words to his credit at the time.

November 16-23.

Peggy, 22 months, sings "Fwing—fwing" on about the right pitch.

Adults were jumping to keep warm and to inspire children to activity, and started Old Dan.

Old Dan can walk, walk. Old Dan can walk walk walk

Old Dan can run, run, run, run. Run, run, run run,

Ma-ny, ma-ny, ma-ny, ma-ny miles, Can run, run, run run,

Run, run, run, run, Ma-ny, ma-ny, ma-ny, ma-ny miles.

Karl joined in at once, going around the skylight in a steady trot, chanting "O' Dan" over and over—no change of step with change of rhythm. Charles thought the whole thing a performance for his edification. Sat by the skylight watching delightedly and burst into laughter each time adults executed "Run run run." Afterwards he got up and did running steps, also turning about once or twice, evidently playing the game. Caroline, after others had finished, began to take steps turning as she did so and looking at adult expectantly as if desiring the song. Adult went through it once and Caroline stepped, stamped and twice gave three double quick steps up and down in same place when "Run, run, run" came.

When we start downstairs some one of the children always begins to chant "down, down." One morning after adult had sung the customary phrase, Peggy sang, "Down, down," clearly and strongly on the top note of the octave, then dropped a minor third. We have not used this interval much.

November 23-30.

Charles on waking from nap, in a loud clear voice, over and over:

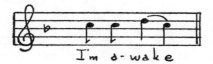

Charles' voice pitch was verified as going up to A above high C.

November 30-December 6.

Ralph—"Go t' s'eep, dollie"—crooning to his doll as he laid it in the doll's bed. Over and over. Pitch verified —phrase ended on F-sharp (middle). Tones ranged from here down to C-sharp (middle). He lay over the bed himself singing in higher tones—"Dee dee dee."

After music period, Caroline stood at the end of the piano. For a moment sang softly to herself in her upper register. Very sweet tones.

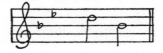

Then dropped over the "break" in her voice to her low register, and kept chanting in a low monotone.

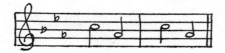

December 7-25.

Caroline accompanied activities with vocalization "Weh—lul—lul—lul," pitched very low—monotone. Charles heard and imitated. She is usually very silent. I had never heard as loud a tone from her.

Philip riding astride a long City and Country School block, said "Ah oo, Ah oo" in a deep voice. Dropped it—cooed a little, then returned to hobby and chanted same syllable. Repeated on another day. We can see no significant relationship between activity and syllables. His pitch and intensity are quite different from those he usually employs.

January 18-25.

Philip sang a long phrase with beautiful quality of tone as he rode his kiddy kar. It started at about A and progressed downward regularly to about D. It was not taken down. Just after he sang

starting at same pitch but not descending.

Later while riding he sang

Philip sang to his doll as he wrapped it in cover. "Mŭ'n ni. Kă kă kă kă kă (same quality and pitch). "Mŭ'n ni" over and over, very sweet tones,

While being undressed for nap he intoned "Mŭ'n ni"
in different ways combining sometimes with "Kah" for
Karl. "Mŭ'n-ni-eh" (could not determine what "eh"
meant, possibly "bed"). Also added "boy" to his refrain.
We sing:

Good-night Philip Boy

January 25-February 1.

Philip sang following in joyful tones as he stood in
the packing case:

Trying the goodnight song again he went into a
minor, giving us this:

m-m-nī dah boh

Ralph on the same date sang:

Oh where is Phil-ip's oth-er sock

When adult sang to tune of dressing-song, "Karl-o
picks up his blocks," Ralph, leaning against the mirror,
said at once "Criss cross criss."

Karl-o puts on his stockings, Karl-o puts on his

shoes, Karl-o laces, criss-cross criss-cross Karl-o laces his shoes.

February 1-8.

Caroline in loud voice at top of slide.

Dŏ - dŏ

Next time up, after interval of over a minute sang same phrase on same pitch. Third time dropped only a half tone.

Dŏ - dŏ

February 15-23.

We have noticed lately that Caroline is talking in higher, lighter and sweeter tones. However, when she stands on the balcony and looks over she shouts in chesty, unmusical tones over and over

Dŏ - dĕ

This morning Peggy imitated but in more pleasing
tones. Philip had done this, as noted before Caroline
took it up, but his is a gay and loud shout with more of
an "ah" vowel—"Dah dah."

February 22-March.

"Poor dy, poor dy, poor dy, poor dy," chanted by
Philip as he pushed doll's bed.

Ralph—light, sweet tones,

Charles, a few moments later after Ralph's song,
dropping a third and repeating Ralph's phrase in sweet,
singing tones not like his raucous calls of "I wan' my
apple."

March 1-8.

Philip for some time has been singing "Goo ni boyee,"
while being dressed for nap. He has begun several times
as soon as adult laid him on the dressing table. Yesterday he sang two phrases together. "Goo ni boyee. Go
see" (Go to sleep). Adult began enumerating the other
children, singing their names to the same musical phrase
and Philip repeated, "Goo ni, Peh" (Peggy), "Goo ni,
Pa" (Pat), "Goo ni, Ja" (Jane). Also, "Goo ni,
Meeah" (Millie), "Bahss" (Bessie), "John" (John).
Later in the week adult sang through the four phrases
(Good Night, Ladies) on "Good Night, Philip," paus-
ing after each. Philip came in with the promptness of a
response each time, "Goo ni, Pa."

March 8-15.

Peggy played a game of swinging the swings and the knotted rope all by herself on roof; sang charmingly using "Here see goes," and similar phrases, not repeating the same musical phrase but using similar ones something like this, usually descending.

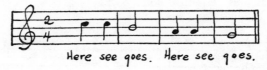

Here see goes. Here see goes.

Not as definite as this.

"Dee a dumb—a dee." She looked often at adult; impossible to tell whether she wished to be noticed or unnoticed, but adult carefully avoided catching her eye as any attention bestowed on Peggy tends to distract her from activities. She sang to herself often through the week. Hard to record phrases as she did not repeat them definitely.

March 15-22.

Adult to Ralph while trying to take off his overall, "Shake a leg out." Ralph, laughing, "Lik a lek ow. Lik a lek ow. Lik a lek ow."

Peggy having asked whose a certain seat was, adult said, "Oh, maybe it'll be Philip's. Maybe it'll be Peggy's." Peggy fell at once into a very musical little chant—"An' maybe da Peg-gee, an' maybe da Peg-gee."

Peggy has burst into song. She sings sometimes during activities, especially to her dolly but often seems to sing just for the sake of singing—long, unpatterned phrases, not many words distinguishable. (See May 3-10, for other record.)

Saunders, humming to himself.

Sang a great deal on Friday before nap—low, sweet tones (compare with Philip's high tones). We verified one note at G-flat below middle C.

March 22-29.

Philip—verified—

April 6-13.

Philip answering adult's call to orange water,

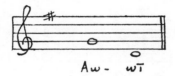

April 12-19.

Peggy—"If want wash hands, I show how"—murmured musically as she sat on dressing table waiting to be washed.

Washing up song:

April 26-May 3.

Caroline lined six pails on the window ledge, then carried them one by one and relined them on shelf chanting all the time to herself very rhythmically:

This was not chanted in a singing voice but her speaking voice rose almost every time a full octave as she said "Ne—uh." As one of the other children brought in another pail she rose from her swing to which she had retired and placed that one in her line on the shelf. Resumed her swinging.

May 3-10.

Peggy

Verified. Repeated three times.

Twice verified.

Other phrases definitely sung; notes unable to verify at the time.

May 10-17.

Children were calling in loud tones from the slide balcony. Philip began it and two younger children joined. Tones loud and joyful, not raucous. Adult used their syllables and tried their ability to follow pitch.

Adult: "Da da"—on sol mi.

Philip: "Da da"—on exact pitch.

Adult: "Da da"—on mi do.

Philip: "Da da"—on mi re.

Adult: "Da da"—on sol mi—much lower.

Philip echoed exactly.

Adult, higher: "Hoo hoo."

Philip did not get this. He seated himself and called "Too too" on a lower pitch.

Adult: "Da da"—on do sol.

Philip: "Da da da da da da"—do la do do la sol.

Adult: "Da da"—on do sol.

Saunders repeated exactly.

We have no positive and formulated musical theory about these responses of children. We encourage them because they seem to be a natural spontaneous manifestation of growth. The formulation of varied syllables certainly must give flexibility and strength to the vocal apparatus. The tone and pitch variations help on the motor and sensory experience. In this process we believe that the children's phrases represent in terms of enjoyment what any method of expression does to the artist. They are not permanent forms and it is not the form that gives pleasure, but the process. We have suggested that their early play with language and their early decorative and balanced constructions are what may later be called literature and design. Their play with tone and phrasing may be placed in the same category, not because the product as we can record it is noteworthy, but because the child is dealing with his material in the expressive way of the artist. Besides this we are trying to make sure that our environment brings forth from each child a maximum response; that he is functioning here as fully and as satisfyingly as possible; that there is a minimum of undischarged energy which has to seek other channels to give the individual a feeling of content, of satisfaction.

All teachers will recognize at once the impression given by some children always, that school is only a passing concern, that the activities and associates waiting at the end of the school day are the important interests and that energy, especially affective energy, is reserved for them. This may be due to the fact that the home environment is distinctly favorable or the contrary. It may be that in some way the nursery school is failing to supply emotional needs as it should or that the social situation at home has given the child habits which can not and should not be perpetuated. However it may be, we believe that this full outgoing, rhythmic combination of voice with larger muscle activities and with social responses is a help to children in finding themselves in the group and to the individual in the process of maintaining a satisfactory balance between his impulses and his powers.

LIST OF MUSIC SELECTIONS

1926-1927

1. Skipping Rhythm.
   En Roulant Ma Boule—Canadian French Folk Song.
   Tremp Ton Pain, Marie—French Folk Song.
   There's Nothing That a Cat Requires.
   Il A le Bonnet d'Ane. Les Aventures du Petit Jean—
   Marchesi.
   Skipping.
   Il Etait une Bergère—French Folk Song.
2. March Rhythm.
   Soldier March—Schumann.
   Le Soldat Anglais. La Bôite à Joujoux—Debussy.
   When the Sun, Bright Red—from Haydn.
   Marchons Au Pas! Les Aventures du Petit Jean—
   Marchesi.
   Le Pont d'Avignon—French Folk Song.
3. Galloping Rhythm.
   Hunting Song—Gurlitt.
   * Galloping, Galloping—Horses' Feet.
4. Broader.
   Turkey Buzzard.
   Flemish Song—German Folk Song.
5. Lyric.
   Lavendar's Blue—Old English.
   † Birdies—German Folk Song.
   Oats, Peas, Beans and Barley—Old English.
6. Composed.
   Lullaby—Brahms.
   * Sleepy Time.

* Most of these songs were adapted by Miss Harriette G. Hubbell, formerly musical advisor of the Nursery School, or by the Nursery Staff.
† The children's name given to this folk song.

Minuet—Mozart.

Largo—Handel.

Ah! Pauvre Enfant. Les Aventures du Petit Jean—
Marchesi.

Curious Lands and People. Child Music—Schumann.

7. * Songs.

On My Pony Big and Strong.

Old Dan.

Choo, Choo, Choo, Goes the Big Engine.

Rolling and Rolling and Rolling We Go.

Roll the Ball Along.

New York Horses.

---

* Most of these songs were adapted by Miss Harriette G. Hubbell, formerly musical advisor of the Nursery School, or by the Nursery Staff.

PART IV
CONCLUSION

CONCLUSION

I HAVE tried in the foregoing pages to give a picture of the lives of children in the Nursery School, and to tell how far and specifically along what lines we who have been watching them have come through to a policy and a philosophy regarding early childhood education.

In formulating our opinion we have referred back constantly to our recorded observations. They are our source material,—the evidence on which we rely to test out and check up our statements regarding individual children and also regarding facts about growth.

The facts of growth with which this study is concerned are those which are most affected by the children's own activities in their own environment,— their responses to the stimuli offered them. That is, I have left for another time a discussion of the details of the health program or the problems of nutrition, and how we have met them, because these are measures for which the adults are entirely responsible and in which adult patterns of action are the significant ones. Provision for them is, as I have said elsewhere, in the nature of minimum essentials. The least one can do for the children in a school is to give them adequate food and safeguard them from infectious disease. However I do not mean to minimize their importance in growth but to make sure that the other concerns of education are not obscured by the prominence that is given to learning to eat spinach and to wash one's face and hands. It may be true that many a man has been wrecked by his appetite—or lack of it, but surely there are more who are living meagerly because of a lack of developed powers and a paucity of interests.

If I could offer evidence in the form of test scores or teachers' ratings or physical growth charts or behavior records, which would prove that nursery school children excelled when they reached the upper groups, it might serve as a convincing argument in support of the theses put forth here. At this particular stage of the game I am more eager to show children living in a rich and satisfying present than being prepared for a life to come, however excellent. Of course this does not mean that their future does not concern me. In the course of time it will be profitable to follow the histories of our babies and of children in other similar experiments, through elementary and high school. Just now it is most important for us to ask ourselves what the children are getting out of the nursery school experience for their own Here and Now. It is that question that has confronted me in the presentation I have made here. My conclusion is that they are leading productive lives. They are learning to live happily away from intimate contact with the family whose concerns are most emotionally bound up with theirs; they are establishing control over their own bodies so that they approach the physical environment with readiness and confidence; they are learning to route themselves through a day with the least possible amount of direction and dictation; they are establishing interests which they can explore independently and they are learning to share the life of a social group, to modify their demands upon the world in relation to their fellows, and to appreciate the compensations as well as the restrictions that social living implies with the result that their emotional lives are functioning on a normal level.

These—it seems to me—are the features that make nursery schools important in education and that need to have more thought and more experimental observation brought to bear upon them.

The question of behavior problems arises wherever there are children. The seriousness of personality defects indicated by fears, attacks of temper and other emotional disturbances is shown by the number of clinics which have been established for their treatment. Our group probably presents its quota of problems, which we endeavor to understand and for which with the help of the parents we try to institute remedial proceedings.

These problems in personality must be regarded from the standpoint of their biological significance. Fear or temper, when it constitutes a deviation from the normal, hinders the development of the individual. It is an unuseful tendency. As with other tendencies which are not biologically useful, we do not try to deal with them by a direct method. If a child is persistently antagonistic or aggressive toward his fellows, we try to bring about the substitution of a socially profitable pattern for the socially adverse one through influences in the environment rather than by informing him of the error of his ways. We attack the manifestations of emotional instability in the same way. A conviction of sin may occasionally be valuable to adult offenders but is never so to babies.

We have put our stress upon what seems to us a preventive program. We look to the experiences which the nursery school world offers to a child to give him physical control, to quicken his interests and to allow him to pursue them as freely as is possible in the situation which he shares with his peers and of which he has command, to the extent of his powers, as long as he does not interfere with the common good. We believe that in so far as we actually do provide the conditions which offer experiences such as these, we are fulfilling the requirements of mental as well as physical hygiene and that abnormal behavior modes are not likely to develop. When they do arise, however, there is unusual opportunity in such an environment for suiting conditions to individual needs and for dealing with the deviation on its first appearance and in the place where it is noted.

One of the problems of nursery school planning that needs further consideration is that of age grouping. We all make certain distinctions between the child of eighteen months and the one of two years. From two and a half to three there is marked age progression. The state of being three carries with it something definitely different from what being four or five implies. Some of the differences are the result of physiological growth, but I have in mind now differences in activities and interests.

An age range as wide as ours would, I am convinced, be calamitous if the group were not so small that older and younger children could be literally separated on occasion and protected from interference by each other whenever necessary.

The criteria by which we should make a decision

regarding the size and age range chosen should be I think those mentioned in the first section. If we believe that activity and experimentation are characteristics of the young child on which education can most profitably build, then we must make sure that his impulses to be active and to explore his environment are not thwarted.

What does the child of two and under busy himself about if he is allowed to direct his own activities? If locomotion is established so that the mechanics of keeping upright are fairly well met, we shall find him experimenting with such activities as climbing, balancing, or stepping off, on and over obstructions. Most of his effort will go into these performances. He will at the same time be using a great variety of small materials but if our record of his behavior is analyzed it will be found that it is largely manipulation that engages him. He uses pans and shovels in pebbles and sand but there is little digging and filling. He handles blocks, but very little stacking or piling is observed. Occasionally toward or just after two years there come high spots in various performances. We may find a lofty tower, irregularly piled, to his credit, or dolls roughly put to bed and blanketed with creditable technique. If we are called upon to evaluate his performances in terms of maturity we find that the patterns he has developed in bouncing on inclined planks, in using the slide or kiddy kars or in going up and down stairs are far in advance of those that involve smaller muscles and finer coördination. The former have arisen more uniformly among the group, have received a greater degree of absorbed attention from the individuals at work and, once developed, have persisted and grown in elaborateness and technique to a wider extent. All the children have had access to the small materials but they have not been urged to use them, and sufficient space and protection from interference have given them opportunity for full body activities.

Our observations of the three-year-olds show that interest and elation in what we may call locomotor activities is still in evidence, though more elaborated, and is developing more in the direction of "stunts," feats of strength and of coördination, but we find an absorbed attention given the finer muscle performances, including language. Dolls are covered with meticulous care, their blankets arranged with much attention to smooth surfaces and properly tucked in corners. Blocks are piled or arranged in patterned forms with precision in placing and skill in balancing. The use of crayons is still largely motor but there is more intention in the way the lines are placed, and some representative forms begin to appear. The impulse to treat materials experimentally follows the course of the developing ability to plan beforehand and to execute; the increase in language facility provides a tool for social experimentation and the richer background of experience that the years have accumulated gives content for the rehearsal play in which groups of children join.

Similar differentiation in maturity of interest and understanding can be traced through the fourth and fifth years. These age variations are significant in education because they point the way to a differentiation in the experiences that children will find profitable at the different ages.

By the time they are four they are indeed well launched on their careers. Given an opportunity in experience and in things-to-do-with the integrative process will go on. We shall probably never learn how to educate children beyond their native equipment, but we may succeed in time in allowing the growth impulses to take the individual as far as the capacity they carry with them can go, and that after all is a goal that we have never yet reached.

AUTHORS CITED IN TEXT

ALDRICH, C. A., M.D., "The Prevention of Poor Appetite in Children." National Committee for Mental Hygiene, N. Y.

BUREAU OF EDUCATIONAL EXPERIMENTS, *Bulletins* VIII, XI.

CAMERON, HECTOR CHARLES, *The Nervous Child.*

DEWEY, JOHN, *Democracy and Education, Human Nature and Conduct, How We Think.*

FLÜGEL, J. C., *The Psycho-Analytic Study of the Family.*

FOREST, ILSE, *Preschool Education: A Historical and Critical Study.*

GODIN, PAUL, *Growth During School Age.*

GRUENBERG, SIDONIE MATSNER, "Twigs of Prejudice." *Survey Graphic,* September, 1926.

HEAD, HENRY, "Vigilance: A Psychological State of the Nervous System." *British Journal of Psychology,* October, 1923.

HERRICK, C. JUDSON, *Neurological Foundations of Animal Behavior, Brains of Rats and Men.*

KANTOR, J. R., *Principles of Psychology.*

KOFFKA, KURT, "Growth of the Mind." *Psychologies of 1925.*

KÖHLER, WOLFGANG, "Mentality of Apes." *Psychologies of 1925.*

LAY, WILFRED, *The Child's Unconscious Mind.*

LUNDHOLM, HELGE, "The Affective Tone of Lines." *Psychological Review,* January, 1921.

MITCHELL, LUCY SPRAGUE, *Here and Now Story Book.*

MURSELL, JAMES L., "The Sucking Reaction." *Psychological Review,* September, 1925.

PIAGET, JEAN, *The Language and Thought of the Child.*

PRATT, CAROLINE, "Collective Formulations in Curricula," "Before Books," "Experimental Practice in the City and Country School." *Progressive Education,* 1925, Vol. II, No. 4.

RAUP, R. B., *Complacency.*

STANTON, JESSIE, *Before Books.*

WHITE, WILLIAM A., *Mental Hygiene of Childhood.*

WOODWORTH, ROBERT SESSIONS, *Dynamic Psychology.*

SUBJECT INDEX